CUBA

CUBA

RELIGION, SOCIAL CAPITAL,

AND DEVELOPMENT

Adrian H. Hearn

DUKE UNIVERSITY PRESS

Durham and London

2008

© 2008 DUKE UNIVERSITY PRESS
All rights reserved
Printed in the United States
of America on acid-free paper ∞
Designed by Amy Ruth Buchanan
Typeset in Quadraat and Quadraat Sans
by Keystone Typesetting, Inc.
Library of Congress Cataloging-in-
Publication Data appear on the last
printed page of this book.

CONTENTS

ACKNOWLEDGMENTS

This book has resulted from the patience, encouragement, and vision of a good many people. I cannot thank them enough. I would like to mention especially Vicente Portuondo Hechavarría and Miki Alfonso for showing me the path toward profound understanding; Margaret Crahan for her mentorship and guidance; Barry Carr, Rowan Ireland, and Joel Kahn for providing me with unparalleled conceptual support; my students for their illuminating classroom discussions; Ariel Armony, Susan Eckstein, and Diane Austin-Broos for their insightful suggestions; Richard Flores for introducing me to cultural anthropology; Valerie Millholland and the team at Duke University Press for meticulously guiding the book through the editorial process; La Trobe University and the University of Technology, Sydney, for funding my research; Alex Broom and Assi Doran for being the very best of scholarly companions; Jesse Wolff, Bruce Hearn, Tom Freeman, Nicholas Lyon, Sergio Fredes, and Felipe Cornejo for creating a harmonious working environment; Karina Hearn for her sharp proofreading; Shani Hadiya Shakur for focusing my energy on the important issues; Beatriz Adriana García for seeing sun even through the rain; my family for providing me with the confidence to transcend borders of every kind; and Echú Alaguana for keeping me on track.

INTRODUCTION

STRUCTURE

AND

SPIRIT

The prospect of having to lead the Sunday *rumba* without a freshly laundered white shirt was more than Miki could tolerate. His desperation reflected the anxiety of the eight families living in the *solar* (housing complex) that they may have to pass a third consecutive scorching day without running water. Most of the solar's residents belonged to the same *rama* (branch) of the Afro-Cuban religion Santería, requiring them to prepare poultry and pork according to meticulous ceremonial guidelines that were impossible in the absence of fresh water. The blue plastic barrels inside the door of each family's unit were nearly empty, the residents periodically eyeing the small pipe in the corner of the courtyard for the unpredictable trickle to appear. The sun had already gone down when the excited voices of children playing in the courtyard announced, "Vino el agua!" ("The water has arrived!"). The neighbors emerged from their units carrying an assortment of plastic and tin buckets, which they placed in a queue next to the pipe. Since each bucket took four or five minutes to fill, they also brought stools and benches into the courtyard and set about completing sewing projects and homework assignments, or exchanging manicures and hair styles while discussing the day's events.

The municipal government of Old Havana, with support from the United Nations Development Program (UNDP), had recently begun a housing improvement initiative to combat structural collapse, gas leaks, and water shortages. Along with a number of other houses in the neighborhood, the solar's internal architecture had been reinforced and its electricity system upgraded. A hosepipe had been supplied for the plumbing system, but the solar remained on a waiting list for a water pump. His patience exhausted, Miki explained to me that with a donation of twenty-five American dollars he could acquire such a water pump himself from a mechanic up the street.[1]

The device, he said, would suck water from the pipe in the courtyard and transport it through the hosepipe directly to each of the unit's tanks, sparing residents the arduous task of carrying water-laden buckets by hand. Having lived in the solar for five months by this stage, I was easily persuaded, and within three days the new plumbing system was up and running.

The residents seemed impressed with the water pump, and were content to relegate the precarious task of connecting it to the solar's electricity grid to Miki or me. But the indisputable efficiency of the new water delivery system also made lining up with buckets unnecessary, effectively putting an end to the evening gatherings in the courtyard. Only a handful of children continued to gather, hoping, I suspect, for a repeat of the small explosion I had caused while connecting the machine one evening. Soon even they stopped coming.

One evening about a month later Miki switched on the machine to find the hosepipe spraying water from innumerable piercings along its length. The project had apparently been sabotaged, though to my surprise—and Miki's fury—nobody seemed particularly concerned, nor had they any idea who the culprit might be. A series of heated discussions in the solar did not reveal the identity of the saboteur, but did reveal general dissatisfaction about the new system's antisocial impact, and concluded that rather than replace or repair the hosepipe, the best solution would be to adopt a modified version of the old system. The machine would still be used to suck water from the pipe, but instead of delivering it directly to each unit's tank, it would spout it from a shortened hosepipe into the buckets one by one. It was never discovered who had vandalized the hosepipe, but over the following weeks and months the chairs, manicure kits, and public conversations once again became a feature of evening life in the courtyard of the solar, now to the background of the whirring water pump.

Daily life in the solar was a constant stream of visits from neighbors, plans for resolving daily problems, and unwritten social contracts. Some plans worked out and others didn't, but all drew on individual investments of time, energy, and trust in broad networks of community support. The solar's circle of collective trust was inseparable from the personal histories of local protagonists, and its wide radius had accrued over generations. Yet the solar is not unique; rather, it reflects a broad, increasingly public, expansion of local initiative and social capital in Cuba since the early 1990s. Particularly in the country's more economically dynamic zones the state has attempted to harness and assimilate this emerging human resource into official structures of governance, both to facilitate neighborhood development projects and to bridge a growing rift between official institutions and unregistered community actors.

This policy orientation has evolved in the context of the withdrawal of economic support from the Soviet Union after 1989 and the evaporation of trade with former Eastern Bloc countries, precipitating a 75 percent reduction in Cuba's import capacity and a host of apocalyptic predictions about the fate of the Castro government (e.g., Oppenheimer 1992; see Uriarte 2001:ii). Suddenly forced to buy everything from food to heavy machinery on the global market, Cuba turned desperately to tourism and foreign investment for hard currency. As Andrés Oppenheimer puts it, "The Revolution's ideological principles were bent every which way in the bid for new tourist dollars" (1992:286). Struggling to keep its economy afloat, the Cuban government asked its anxious citizens for renewed austerity, self-sacrifice, and understanding until the passing of this horrendous financial nightmare that it called the "Special Period in Time of Peace."

The trauma of relinking with the global economy during the past decade can only be compared in scale and magnitude to the profound strain of delinking from it in the 1960s. Richard Fagen's 1969 account of that transformation, with the obvious omission of Lenin, is strikingly reminiscent of the present day: "In ten years Cuba has seen the advent of Leninist politics, agrarian reform, educational reorganization, economic transformations, and international realignments—all force-drafted at a rate that leaves outsiders as well as many Cubans bewildered" (1969:1–2). Fagen went on to identify the crucial role of popular participation in the formation of early revolutionary projects: "There arises a pervasive and continuous effort to mobilize the people and enlist their energies, loyalties, and skills in creating the new Cuba. Where existing energies, loyalties, and skills are found wanting by the revolutionaries, they have taken upon themselves the job of creating new ones" (1969:2). The literacy campaign and agricultural work brigades of the 1960s and 1970s were powerful examples of the new revolutionary emphasis on mass mobilization, but equally significant were the civilian-staffed comités de defensa de la revolución (committees for the defense of the revolution), which monitored the revolutionary loyalty of the population on a block-by-block basis and organized a range of social welfare activities, from school enrollment programs to blood drives (Eckstein 1994:22).

The committees survive to the present day, though their neighborhood activities, once generously subsidized by the central state, now consist of little more than the nightly guardia (street watch) of a vigilant and ageing few. But in spite of the hardships of the Special Period, life goes on even in the most impoverished urban neighborhoods without the malnutrition, violence, gangs, and drug problems that ravage the marginal centers of so many contemporary cities. And despite the decline of the committees, ordinary residents have come together of their own accord to protect the social and physical well-being of their neighborhoods through forms of associational life based as often on religious, ethnic, and professional connections as political allegiance. In the following chapters I want to examine these emerging grassroots initiatives and the recent efforts of the Cuban state to incorporate them into official structures of governance. Studying the complications and opportunities arising from collaboration between neighborhood associations, decentralized state urban planning institutions, and international development agencies reveals that community groups have gained broader capacities for self representation over the past decade, and that understanding these capacities is critical for discerning the character and potentials of civil society in Cuba.

Social Capital: Vice or Virtue?

Since the mid-1980s development agencies, policy makers, and scholars have increasingly invested time and money in empowering and promoting the formation of voluntary civil society organizations in target communities around the world. By building cooperative relationships between individuals and groups, they reason, participation in collective projects is boosted, social delinquency is reduced, and bottom-up democratization is more easily realized (Cardoso et al. 2004:7–10, 24–25; Putnam 1993:88–90, 2000:15–19). Initiatives pursuing these goals have stressed the strategic importance of associational life at the grassroots and the value of "social capital" as a cost-effective, renewable resource that can help disadvantaged communities to generate new opportunities and help societies to become more tolerant, egalitarian, and prosperous (Cohen and Rogers 1995, Coleman 1988a, Diamond 1999, Fukuyama 1995, Inglehart 1999). Optimism about civil society and social capital has more recently been tempered by insights into their potentially detrimental influence on democratic governance when well-connected, often nonrepresentative groups, influence public opinion and policy makers to support their goals and objectives (Armony 2004, Fiorina 1999:395–403).[2] An important aspect of this critical approach has been a wider vision of civil society and the public sphere that accounts for the social and political influence not only of formally registered groups but also of informal professional ties, the media, public debate, protest movements, and informal popular networks (Armony 2004:33).

I want to try to extend the debate by framing it in a context where the efficacy and meaning of civil and economic liberties are qualitatively different from that assumed in most studies of social capital and civil society. In Cuba these differences stem not only from the intended omnipresence of the central state but also from the rapid adaptation of the state to the pressures and opportunities of a liberalizing global market. Structures of representation and authority in such cases are not only shaped by the character of the economic and political context, but also by its constant transformation and evolution.

As the central state struggles to manage this transformation in a way that conserves its authority, allegiances at the grassroots, also in flux, carry a heavy political weight. The crisis of the 1990s forced the state to more openly recognize this weight and engage with independent community initiatives, from neighborhood gardening schemes and dance troupes to religious mutual aid and welfare projects, to incorporate their productive strengths into official, legally authorized programs. In terms of maintaining authority this was more effective than oppression, which would have forced emerging community initiatives underground and potentially alienated a broad range of local actors. The strategy was largely successful, in part because initiatives at the grassroots, while harboring high levels of internal solidarity, were often flexible and trusting enough to reach outward to develop cooperative relations with the state, and to an extent, with one another. What I am interested in here is how these kinds of initiatives, critical as they are to the maintenance of civic order and stability, depend largely on the functional integration of different kinds, or "dimensions," of social capital. This process is crucial to understanding the character of civil society in Cuba and the broader role of social capital in influencing the course of rapidly changing societies.

The concept of social capital draws on a long line of sociological inquiry, whose trajectory has been effectively mapped by Nan Lin (2001), Alejandro Portes and Julia Sensenbrenner (1993), Michael Woolcock (1998), and others. Portes and Sensenbrenner trace contemporary understandings of social capital to four theoretical roots: Marx and Engels's discussion of "bounded solidarity" among social groups facing external pressure and adversity; Weber's analysis of self-imposed collective conformity or "enforceable trust" at the grassroots; Simmel's work on mutually beneficial favors or "reciprocity transactions" among friends and neighbors; and Parsons and Durkheim's "value introjection," which accounts for the influence of informal moral considerations on formal or contractual relationships. The contemporary development of social capital theory reflects this rather wide range of conceptual orientations, but as Nan Lin (2001:24) has argued, recent work on social capital also reflects a more fundamental rift between Durkheim's interest in cross-societal "organic solidarity" and Marx's emphasis on class antagonism. While the first concept evokes the biological metaphor of individual organs functioning cooperatively for the benefit of the larger organism, the second focuses on the economic inequalities that result from the domination of some sectors by others and the construction of exclusionary social boundaries between them.

This core tension finds contemporary expression in analytic distinctions between social capital's introverted and extroverted dimensions, for example, in discussions of "bonding" versus "bridging" social capital (Putnam 2000:22–23), and the fundamental contrast of "particularized trust" that "strengthens in-group relations while discouraging members to trust beyond their kin" from "generalized trust" in "those whom we don't know and who are different from us" (Uslaner 1999:124–125; Yamagishi and Yamagishi 1994; quotations in Armony 2004:21).

A practical question emerges from this distinction: is it possible, or always desirable, for particularized trust to be transformed into a more generalized form? Many studies of social capital answer in the affirmative on both counts, arguing that a broad variety of overlapping voluntary associations is a crucial building block for inclusive and participatory civil society, and that countries with active civil spheres also exhibit more democratic systems of governance (Putnam 2000:22–23, Warren 2001). As a collection of voluntary associations spanning sports clubs to religious groups to debating societies, civil society at its brightest is envisioned as a cradle for learning essential civic skills such as dispute resolution, democratic decision-making, and the formation and articulation of collective desires and needs. Attributed most famously to Robert Putman (1993, 2000), this "neo-Tocquevillian" orientation—as it has come to be known in reference to Alexis de Tocqueville's (1964 [1835]) classic study of voluntary associations in the formation of North American democracy—has been criticized by scholars who stress the influence of contextual sociopolitical conditions on the capacity of social capital to promote or erode civic democracy.

Johannes Federke et al. (1999), for instance, argue that different contexts develop different kinds of social capital, and that egalitarian strategies for incorporating local perspectives into national priorities depend on balancing the quality and quantity of relationships between community representatives and official authorities. Projects attempting to build up and harness local capacities should therefore approach social capital as a resource to be optimized rather than maximized (1999:713–717). Alejandro Portes elaborates this observation by showing that although social capital can benefit community groups by facilitating access to scarce resources through extrafamilial networks, "negative social capital" can nevertheless reproduce scenarios of social intolerance and economic inequality (1998:15–18). Strong social ties within tight-knit communities, he argues, can restrict resources and favors to group members, potentially generating enclave communities and deepening inequalities between groups. Furthermore, internal obligations, for example in immigrant communities, can discourage ambitious members from developing relations with external sources of support and resources. As a result entrepreneurial members often find that the only way to live and interact as they choose is to leave the community altogether. The cumulative effect for disadvantaged sectors is that they maintain characteristically low, "downward-spiraling" self-expectations. As Portes concisely concludes, "Sociability cuts both ways" (1998:18).

Ariel Armony (2004) has developed this line of thought by arguing that the "dark side" of civil society becomes visible when dominant—though not necessarily democratic—ideas become widely circulated and supported in the public sphere, subverting processes of bottom-up democratization. Citing such examples as the consolidation of Nazism in Weimar, Germany, in the 1930s, public support for racial segregation in the United States in the 1950s, and the inability of civil society to promote public interests in Argentina in the 1990s, he concludes that "we cannot take civil society's democratizing potential for granted. . . . [C]ivil society in general—not just formal groups—tends to potentiate dominant features in the broader sociohistorical context" (2004:212, 213). His perspective resonates with that of Cuban sociologist Rafael Hernández, who writes that "civil society is not just a realm of economic relations and of pluralism but also a realm of inequality" (2003:104).

Armony's analysis draws attention to the role of informal social networks in the consolidation of discriminatory movements and the resulting "dubious link" between civil society and democracy. In this light the public sphere is shown to be dynamic and contested, constantly responding to the conflicting influences of the formal and informal sectors (Cohen 1999:56–59, Newton 1997). Armony's study shows that these conflicts often give way to the diffusion of dominant ideas throughout society as "direct relationship[s form] between social movements and formal groups in civil society" (2004:229). In other words, informal expressions of local interest tend to evolve into more institutionalized modes of representation, but in the process often suffer an erosion of original commitments and priorities. As Cohen and Arato put it, from a "linear" perspective, "all social movements move from forms of non-institutionalized, mass protest action to institutionalized, routine interest group or party politics. . . . [F]ormal organization replaces loose networks, membership rules and leaders emerge, and representation replaces direct forms of participation" (Cohen and Arato 1992: 556, quoted in Armony 2004:229).

Armony's attention to the potentially corrosive effects of institutionalization on local interests and commitments distinguishes his analysis of social capital and civil society from the optimistic assessments of Putnam and others. Nevertheless, behind their diverging conclusions, both scholars (and most others) draw to some extent from this "linear model" of evolution from informal expression of popular interests to independent formal representation. This is understandable because studies of civic democratization have typically focused on either postsocialist or neoliberal political contexts, where formal channels for asserting popular interests and autonomy from the state are legally protected, and where the concept of civil society has come to symbolize and champion this cause.

In Cuba, collaboration between state institutions and unregistered community associations since 1990 has raised local concerns about the loss of independence and autonomy, but the Cuban political context differs in important ways from postsocialist Eastern Europe and the neoliberal West. The following chapters show that Cuban modes of popular advocacy, civil society formation, and democratization do not conform to a "linear" path toward independent institutional representation, but rather to a less formal, often more spontaneous, process of exchange and negotiation between state and nonstate actors. This has come about in response to a constrained public sphere in which politically antagonistic publishing, broadcasting, and protest are generally not permitted, weakening the ability of popular associations and movements to openly develop a civic agenda (representative or nonrepresentative) independently of the state. Under these conditions semiformal modes of communication have developed between unofficial neighborhood leaders and local state institutions, often linking together communities and organizations in a way that internal local solidarity and protectionism have impeded in other contexts (Portes 1998:15–18; also see Fiorina 1999:395–403, Heller 2001:138).

Comparative evidence suggests that unregistered associations in politically authoritarian scenarios tend to either evolve into tight circles of underground opposition to the state or devolve into loosely structured expressions of "self-protective apathy" (Foley and Edwards 1996:48). The Cuban civic landscape reflects a more subdued—though no more predictable—process of socioeconomic transformation led by a government undergoing something of an identity crisis as the forces of economic globalization render the function and legitimacy of a centralized political system uncertain. Alternative informal systems of prestige, hierarchy, and economic exchange have expanded, but the state's response, informed by events in Eastern Europe, has been to officially recognize the social influence of these emerging systems and attempt to engage them rather than force them underground. This has ceded political space to interest groups willing and able to work within the state's administrative structures, though their capacity to represent and advocate local needs depends largely on how creatively and diplomatically they use this space to generate new opportunities. Recent years have seen a deepening of this process, resulting in an increasingly "mixed" civil sphere that is neither entirely independent of, nor entirely reliant on, the state.

Prominent on the Cuban civic landscape are religious communities, which harbor high levels of internal solidarity, and in some cases significant financial resources. Indeed, the resurgence of religious practice in Cuba appears to be directly related to the economic and psychological strains of the Special Period, providing stable structures of community and identity, and financial assistance from overseas religious nongovernmental organizations (NGOs) (Clemente et al. 1995:55–57, del Rey Roa 2002). The state has prioritized engagement with religious communities for both of these reasons, but also because the fluid nature of religious allegiances in Cuba endows them with considerable practical potentials. An active member of a Christian congregation, for instance, may also belong to an Afro-Cuban religious house, and simultaneously be a loyal member of the Federación de Mujeres Cubanas (Federation of Cuban Women, or FMC) and the Unión de Jovenes Comunistas (Union of Young Communists, or UJC). Overlapping networks of this sort carry important implications for understanding the ways that social relationships are employed for acquiring resources and resolving daily problems. As early scholars of social capital argued, individuals whose ties and loyalties are fluid enough to permit them to move between groups often function as important "bridges" for the flow of information and resources between them (Burt 1992, Granovetter 1973, Lin 2001:27).

While intergroup contact is often mediated by individuals with fluid ties within their respective communities, mutual benefit at the collective level tends to be maximized through the collaboration of groups with complementary but different kinds of resources to exchange. Lin (2001:39–40) argues that models of "homophilous" interaction, which predict that groups with similar social standing and endowments of material and social resources generally "stick together," need to be more sensitive to the complementarity of different kinds of resources. He therefore sets out to "extend the homophily principle to occupants of similar positions in multiple resource structures (e.g., authority, status, or class) because, by the rules of congruence and transferability of resources, interaction may engage partners with different kinds of resources as long as the values of their resources are equivalent" (2001:39–40).

Lin's point is that intergroup exchanges are not guided so much by the organizational similarity or difference of "resource structures" as by the relative value that each group's resources hold for the other. The intensification of interaction between the Cuban state and religious communities confirms this point, but also suggests that the value that one group's resources holds for another fluctuates in step with contextual transformations. In the pre-crisis context the social and political resources held by religious communities vis-à-vis the state (and vice versa) did not carry the same exchange value, making the two unlikely collaborators.[3] But the contemporary political importance of local allegiance to the legitimacy of the state, and the simultaneous opening of opportunities for community actors to achieve official recognition, has imbued the resources held by each with a high relative value. The coming together of previously remote social sectors or "resource structures" in Cuba has therefore resulted in cooperation between some unlikely official and unofficial actors. In short, changing socioeconomic conditions have brought distinct forms of social capital into close proximity, resulting in photographs like the one on page 89 depicting Fidel Castro shaking hands with a locally respected priest of the Afro-Cuban religions Santería and Palo Monte.

From the state's perspective the goal has been to build new, broader forms of solidarity out of preexisting informal social ties. Both James Coleman (1988b, 1993) and Pierre Bourdieu (1985:248–249) have argued that the deliberate creation of official social networks out of grassroots allegiances produces a range of socioeconomic benefits for formal institutions, and in Coleman's view, for society at large. Similarly, Federke et al. (1999) write that prospects for economic development in any context are improved by the incorporation of *substantive* local rules and values into a wider system of procedural norms, a process characterized by "the gradual replacement of informal associations and networks by formal administrative structures, and the impersonal market mechanism no longer tied to individual identities. . . . Action premised on social capital with a rationalized mode of delivery is rendered more flexible, and stands a greater chance of successful adaptation to a wide range of environmental circumstance" (1999:719, 721). The tensions and conflicts that can result from this process are evident in the Cuban state's recent attempts to integrate local circles of cooperation into a framework that facilitates national development goals, commercial engagement with the global tourism market, and cooperation with international development NGOs. As in many other contexts, this has provoked local concerns about the loss of community autonomy and substantive relevance as informal systems of mutual aid are "scaled up" through a process of formal rationalization. Cooperation with the state requires community actors to weigh this loss against potential gains and opportunities resulting from formal registration.

Social capital research has shown that the terms of this calculus are not fixed. Rather, as the sources of social capital transform, for example, from personal allegiances within a well-integrated community group to official legal recognition, so do its costs and benefits (Woolcock 1998:175). On the one hand, community-state engagement can bring recognition and empowerment to previously unregistered groups, transforming them from relatively small, closed circles of mutual assistance into officially endorsed networks reaching out to and consolidating international support from NGOs and other resource providers.[4] But on the other hand, official collaboration may transform locally respected participatory associations into socially disconnected platforms for accomplishing instrumental, short-term objectives with little administrative autonomy. The case studies in this book show both results, but also that the costs and benefits of engagement can pass through phases of greater or lesser prominence over time as state and community actors learn to work with, or around, one another.

State and Civil Society: Cooperation or Conflict?

The character of contemporary relations between state and nonstate actors, particularly in the religious sphere, distinguishes the Cuban reform process from the political transitions of Eastern Europe in the 1980s. The harsh and sometimes violent treatment of Catholics and other Christians by the governing regimes in those countries was never replicated in Cuba, even when church-state relations were at their worst (Albacete 1998:37). Furthermore, the Catholic Church's prominence in the struggle against communism, especially in Poland, may have contributed to a lack of social diversity and plural representation within political opposition movements. Juan Linz and Alfred Stepan argue that this lack of diversity, conditioned by an internal emphasis on unified opposition to the state, ultimately impeded democratic transition in Poland: "In any movement of liberation, an extremely high value is attached to 'unity' within the struggle, and the ideas of *compromise* or *internal conflict* are spoken of pejoratively. . . . In fact, most of the values and language of ethical civil society that were so functional to the tasks of opposition are dysfunctional for a political society in a consolidated democracy" (1996:271–272, emphasis in original). In Linz and Stepan's analysis, mounting pressure for conformity within the Polish Solidarity movement resulted in "a virtual blockade against the articulation of different interests" (1996:273). If a healthy civil society is characterized by a diverse range of participatory and voluntary structures and a "democratic ecology of associations" (Warren 2001:12–13; see also Rosenblum and Post 2002:4), then the very cohesion of social elements that gave the Polish and other Eastern European opposition movements their strength may also have unwittingly undermined their democratic aspirations.

The gradual emergence of a wide variety of grassroots organizations in the Cuban context suggests an alternative, potentially more egalitarian process of social development. While a "democratic ecology of associations" does not in itself protect against cooption from above and the infiltration of dominant, potentially nondemocratic practices (Armony 2004:23), the political gravity of grassroots initiatives in contemporary Cuba has endowed them with a greater capacity to engage with the state on their own terms. As the decentralization and diversification of social welfare mechanisms progresses it is possible that Afro-Cuban religious networks could come to fill an expanded role in protecting the interests and rights of their constituents in a similar way to Afro-Brazilian organizations like Ilê Aiyê and Olodum (see Ireland 1999:127, 2000; Sansone 1996). Official moves toward dialogue and collaboration with Afro-Cuban religious communities strengthen this possibility, though as chapter 2 shows, this has sometimes led these communities to recast and modify their priorities.

Official anxieties about excessive local autonomy in Cuba are evident in many of the case studies presented in the following chapters, from the state's controlled empowerment of decentralized development projects in Havana to its careful mediation of contact between community groups and foreign development agencies. These concerns are driven in part by the stated intentions of U.S. foreign policy. Together with the 1996 Helms-Burton Act (which was drafted in order to strengthen the U.S. trade embargo by punishing foreign corporations that trade with Cuba), the Cuban Democracy Act, or "Track II" legislation, remains committed to "reaching around" the Cuban government to support organizations that could eventually destabilize it.[5] Inefficient implementation procedures have compromised the effectiveness of these schemes, and there is a general consensus that the Cuban "civil sphere" remains too weak to pose a serious threat to the state (USGAO 2006, Otero and O'Bryan 2002:29–30). Nevertheless, the prospect of internal dissent remains a concern for Cuban authorities, not least because senior North American analysts and advisors maintain the long-held view that "U.S. policy should continue giving highest priority to nurturing the growth of Cuba's fledgling civil society" (González and Nuccio 1999:21).

Faced with ongoing international efforts to incite change from within, it is unlikely that the Castro government or any nationally nominated successor will relax the stern treatment of dissidents and would-be-defectors, which has consistently drawn criticism from Human Rights Watch, Amnesty International, the Inter-American Commission on Human Rights, and the United Nations Human Rights Commission. The arrest of sixty-one dissidents in 2003 adversely affected Cuba's diplomatic relations with the European Union, though the damage was largely repaired when fourteen of these were subsequently released. Spain has actively encouraged greater European dialogue with Cuba since the 2004 election of José Luis Zapatero, but as in the past, crackdowns on dissidents in Cuba could compromise European investment (LARR 2003:6). In June 2006 the European Council affirmed its long-standing vision of pluralist democracy in Cuba, though it also committed itself to constructive engagement and dialogue.

Recent Cuban reforms designed to attract foreign investment and facilitate decentralized social welfare will likely strengthen rather than weaken the legitimacy of the Cuban state because, unlike in Eastern Europe, they have promoted the stable coexistence of the state and nonstate sectors rather than pitting them against each other (March-Poquet 2000:91–93). The quest to find a functional balance of state and nonstate inputs, very much at the heart of the reform process, is naturally replete with tensions and conflicts, for instance over the management of resources that have historically been delivered by the state. But the emergence of such conflicts has not seriously destabilized broader public acceptance and endorsement of state authority. This is because the consensual subordination of many Cuban neighborhood groups and organizations—in some respects a good example of Gramscian hegemony—is not based exclusively on coercion from above, although as Crahan (2000:26–27) points out this is a factor, but also on widespread popular recognition and identification with the Cuban revolution's commitment to social justice (Uriarte 2001:10, Sinclair 2000).

The degree of social influence that neighborhood organizations retain from—and are capable of exerting on—the state is difficult to discern in a context where licenses permitting greater local management seek both financial and ideological compliance. Political and economic power continues to reside with the state, though the decentralization of administrative authority has relied increasingly on the social power of community loyalty and solidarity. Incorporating this social power into official projects has become a key state objective, both because of the positive impact this has had on their development and because of the potentially negative consequences of not doing so. The failure to engage ethnic, occupational, religious, and other social groups in public initiatives can produce marginalized communities whose high levels of internal solidarity and social capital can lead to societal segregation, the consolidation of illicit exchange networks, and in extreme cases insurgency (Pritchard and Hearn 2005). It is no coincidence that opponents of socialist regimes around the world have focused their efforts on building the institutional capacities and consolidating the internal cohesion of nonstate organizations; nor is it a coincidence that Cuban authorities have gone to great lengths to monitor and mediate local-international linkages.

While state attempts to preempt the emergence of oppositional sectors in Cuba are not new, the past decade has witnessed a shift from strategies of containment to strategies of engagement, designed not so much to suppress social diversification as to address the underlying causes of disaffection at the grassroots. The legitimacy of the Cuban state has become closely entwined with the outcomes of these efforts. This is not only because of the potentially explosive combination of local social capital and illicit structures of trade and exchange (see chapter 2), but also because, when managed effectively, local solidarity and compliance can drastically enhance the outcomes of state-directed development initiatives.

Recognizing local actors as legitimate social representatives entails a shift of authority away from the central state. While economic decentralization in Cuba has been slow, and according to some researchers insufficient (Fernández Soriano 1999), the conferral of certain administrative powers to local authorities signifies a modification of the state's bureaucratic structure. Understanding how local empowerment in Cuba is related to transformations in the internal structures of the state clarifies how forms of social capital produced at different levels of society interact and adapt to each other. At the micro level, a number of studies have shown how distinct forms of social solidarity can adapt, compensate, and adjust to one another's presence or absence (Gold 1995, Hagan et al. 1996, Portes 1998:11–12). These studies show that when extrafamilial networks are lost to immigrant families, for instance, they often compensate with higher levels of internal family solidarity. Recent developments in Cuba suggest that similar processes of interaction and adjustment can occur at the macro level between distinct forms of solidarity and cohesion produced by the state and nonstate sectors. The turbulent widening of avenues for local representation since the early 1990s, for example, has not only entailed a downward shift of administrative power but also concerted efforts to reassert state authority in new ways.

A useful language for describing this process is provided by Michael Woolcock, whose four "dimensions" of social capital permit an integrated analysis of micro- and macro-level forms of cohesion. Woolcock's four dimensions are "community integration," or local solidarity within close-knit social groups; horizontal "linkage" between such groups; vertical "synergy" between community representatives and state institutions; and "organizational integrity" within the state. Applied to the Cuban case, strong preexisting solidarities between groups at neighborhood scale (community integration) and the promotion of horizontal collaboration between such groups (linkage) have proven more effective for confronting emerging local development challenges than traditional top-down mechanisms. This has resulted in diminished centralized control and a modification of the state bureaucratic structure (organizational integrity). In turn, this has provoked official efforts to establish vertical relations with nonstate actors (synergy), designed to conserve political hegemony by incorporating a diversifying social base into state-led initiatives. For the state the goal has been to harness local social capital into programs that simultaneously address local welfare needs and consolidate its political authority.

The Impact of Religion

The increasingly short-term interactions of development institutions, commercial enterprises, and community groups involve an intense degree of sociocultural interaction and exchange. Sensitivity to local modes of cooperation, exchange, and knowledge does not deny the critical importance of material realities, but rather takes closer account of the agency of subjects, their perceptions of one another, and the projects they get involved in. Tessa Morris-Suzuki writes of "the pervasive and irreversible interpenetration of the material and the symbolic. . . . [D]evelopment, no longer simply a matter of modes of production, becomes a clash between forms of life embodied in different types of food, dress, music and dance. . . . The colonization of the world by capital makes starkly clear the extent to which economic value is a function of moral and social value" (2000:73–74). Development institutions that fail to recognize this produce project analyses and progress reports that lack sensitivity to local priorities and reflexivity about institutional values, overlooking the pervasive role of culture in the implementation and break-down of projects. As Clifford Geertz (1973) might say, the professional *ethos* of contractual terms, development objectives, and economic policies is underwritten by the *worldviews* of development workers and community leaders, conditioned by spirituality, ideology, and personal conviction. By examining the interactions of project participants, this study, following John Tomlinson (1991:164) and Anthony Giddens (1977, 1990), locates cultural agency in the reflexive decisions of self-conscious actors.

In order to examine cross-cultural exchanges at the heart of collaborative alliances in post-1990 Cuba, I pay special attention to the emergence of religious communities as key players in urban neighborhood development initiatives. Since 1990 Christian congregations have augmented their community welfare activities, complementing the overburdened public service sector with welcomed overseas humanitarian donations. The injection of scarce medicine, clothes, food, and finances relies on the institutional legitimacy of Cuban Christian organizations, whose corresponding legal status distinguishes them from Afro-Cuban congregations (Pedraza 1998). In short, Christian-affiliated projects benefit from established modes of dialogue and cooperation with state authorities, while such lines of correspondence are only now tentatively beginning to open for Afro-Cuban religious communities.

Structures of popular religiosity and the strong circles of social capital they possess have not figured significantly in studies of Cuban civil society, but as Haroldo Dilla Alfonso has written, leaders of Afro-Cuban religions have risen to prominence in many neighborhoods as influential figures capable of mobilizing popular support for projects ranging from health education to housing construction (1999:33). The participation of Afro-Cuban religious groups in decentralized social welfare projects reflects the historical role of these religions in protecting the material and spiritual well-being of urban communities since the colonial era (Brandon 1993:69–73,

Domínguez 1989:46, Orozco and Bolívar 1998:152). As early as the sixteenth century, mutual aid organizations called *cabildos* were set up in conjunction with Catholic churches to evangelize, house, and provide basic services for free and enslaved black Cubans (Portuondo Zúñiga 2000:85). In many of these cabildos the religious traditions of Yoruba, Carabali, Arara, and other West African ethnolinguistic groups became integrated with Catholic practices. Catholic statues and images introduced by the ecclesiastic authorities of the day were adopted by cabildos, but were typically used as substitute representations of forbidden African deities (Ortiz 1993:61).

After Cuba's independence from Spain (1898), a series of laws drafted by the U.S.-administered regime to regulate public association resulted in the fragmentation of cabildos into private temple-houses, which served as neighborhood centers for collective Afro-Cuban worship and social support (Brown 2003:56–57, Murphy 1988:33). These temple-houses emerged as the foundational basis of the religion called Santería, devoted to the veneration of a pantheon of Yoruba deities (*orichas*) and the practice of a divination tradition called Ifá. Consolidated by prominent Afro-Cuban religious leaders such as Lorenzo Samá, Latuán, and Tata Gaytán in the early nineteenth century, Santería gradually spread from the poor neighborhoods of Havana and Matanzas to towns and cities throughout the island (Bolívar and Cepero 1995:16–20).

In the 1930s Reynerio Pérez, Aurora Lamar, and Rosa Torres brought Santería to Santiago de Cuba, setting up temple-houses and initiating the city's first line of devotees (Millet 2000:112). The religion's associated tradition of sacred *batá* drumming was introduced to the city by Milián Galis in 1962, though it was not until 1989 that Galis and Vicente Portuondo Hechavarría brought the first fully consecrated batá drums to Santiago de Cuba from Matanzas and Havana.

Batá drumming is central to the practice of Santería. As Olavo Alén, director of the Centro de Investigaciones y Desarrollo de la Música Cubana (Center for the Analysis and Development of Cuban Music, or CIDMUC) explained, "The Oro Seko is an order of rhythms meant to salute and communicate with the orichas of Santería. Consecrated batá drums are believed to be alive; that is, they form a part of religious liturgy much more than, say, a pipe organ in a Catholic mass" (interview, 26 February 2002).[6] Pedro Pérez Sarduy (1998:40) estimates that Santería and other Afro-Cuban religions are currently practiced in some capacity by approximately 70 percent of the Cuban population, particularly in poor, urban communities, while batá drummers and priests of Ifá divination command a great deal of respect: the

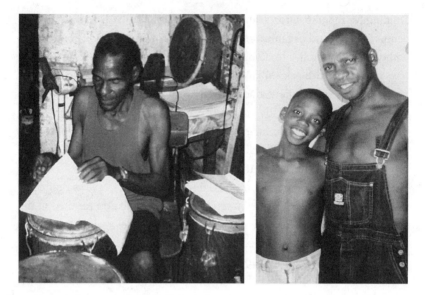

Milián Galis, pioneer of the batá drums in Santiago de Cuba (left); Vicente Portuondo Hechavarría and son, two of the most proficient batá drummers in Santiago de Cuba (right).

prior as channels of sacred communication, and the latter as neighborhood role models, advisors, and doctors of natural medicine (Amira and Cornelius 1992:18, Betancourt 1995).

Anthropological research on Afro-Cuban religions has largely followed two literary models: historical analysis of West African cultural adaptations in Cuba, and ethnographic description of firsthand experience and expertise in specific ceremonial techniques. The first of these trends, initiated by the classic works of the Cuban anthropologist Fernando Ortiz (1950, 1973 [1906], 1987 [1916], 1984 [1921], 1995 [1940]) and William Bascom (1969a, 1969b, 1980), has provided detailed ethnological data on the ethnic foundations of Afro-Cuban religious traditions such as Palo Monte, Espiritismo, Santería, Abakuá, and Arará.

Ortiz's original interest in these traditions resulted from his study of criminology. His earliest books, entitled *Los Negros Brujos* (The Black Sorcerers, first published in 1906) and *Los Negros Esclavos* (The Black Slaves, first published in 1916), sought to establish links between Afro-Cuban religions and criminal social tendencies, while the title of his 1913 article, "Los Comedores de Niños" (The Eaters of Children), speaks for itself. The Cuban sociologist of religion Jorge Ramírez Calzadilla argues that soon after the publication of these works Ortiz adopted participant observation as his primary research method, bringing him into intimate contact with religious practitioners and leading him to revise his negative perspectives and assumptions about their activities (2001:8). In 1936 Ortiz openly lamented the errors of his earlier work (in particular *The Black Sorcerers*) in a public forum entitled *Cómo Pensaba Yo Hace 30 Años* (What I Was Thinking 30 Years Ago), and in 1942 one of his closest protogés, José Luciano Franco, quoted his mentor's confession: "I began to conduct research, but soon realized that, like all my fellow Cubans, I was wrong" (quoted in Ramírez Calzadilla 2001:9).

Reflecting this existential transformation, Ortiz's numerous books and articles from the mid-1920s onward recognize and celebrate the deep presence and influence of African ethnicity in Cuban national identity. Some, like his *Contrapunteo Cubano* (Cuban Counterpoint, 1940) and the 1943 article *Por la Integración Cubana de Blancos y Negros* (For a Cuban Integration of Whites and Blacks), are clearly aimed at celebrating Cuba's multiethnic heritage, while others, including *La Africanía de la Musica Folklórica de Cuba* (The Africanity of Cuban Folkloric Music, 1950) and *Los Bailes y el Teatro de los Negros en el Folklór de Cuba* (The Dances and Theater of Blacks in the Folklore of Cuba, 1985 [1951]), take a more descriptive, ethnological approach.

Ortiz's research program, particularly its ethnological branch, continues to guide the work and literary output of Cuban institutions such as the CIDMUC, the Casa del Caribe, and the more theoretically sophisticated Fundación Fernando Ortiz; while a more narrative-based, ethnographically oriented literary stream, inspired largely by the work of Lydia Cabrera (1971 [1954]), has sought to bring a detailed understanding of Afro-Cuban ceremonial practices to both aspiring and practicing religious readers (e.g., González-Wippler 1992, Hagedorn 2001, Karade 1994, Moreno Vega 2000). Responding to growing international interest in Cuba since the expansion of foreign tourism to the island in the mid-1990s, this commercially successful literature, written by practicing Cubans and foreigners, offers its readers an opportunity to explore alternative forms of spiritual awareness. While some Santeros (practitioners of Santería) and *babalawos* (practitioners of Ifá divination) criticize this literature for revealing secret ceremonial information, others eagerly embrace it as a practical guide to their religious faith (Palmié 1995:89, 91).

A small number of writers have explored processes of Afro-Cuban religious commercialization, performance, historiography, and social engagement from a critical sociological perspective (Dilla Alfonso et al. 1999; Martínez Furé 2001; Menéndez Vázquez 1995, 2002; R. Moore 1997; Palmié 2002). This literature has identified the broad social impact of Afro-Cuban religions, the power relations that continue to shape their role in Cuban society, and the importance of appreciating the dynamics of cross-cultural exchange in the Cuban context. Before presenting a brief outline of the book's four chapters I want to dwell for a moment on these issues and how they influenced my approach to conducting research and writing.

Counterpoint, Competition, and Power

Santería continues to be practiced predominantly by the poorer, darker sectors of Cuban society, but the expanding scope of people getting involved in the religion endows it with a level of social capital that is at least as influential as the financial variety. The social ties embedded in Santería are strikingly evident in public liturgies that often bring together hundreds of devotees, guests, and friends spilling out of home sanctuaries into the street, unified by a shared system of belief and identity. Interpersonal bonds of this sort have begun to attract the attention of domestic and international development organizations, which identify here an unparalleled emerging human resource for building voluntary neighborhood health and education programs. Indeed, strong allegiances at the grassroots have become a key resource that community leaders have started bringing to the table in negotiations with state urban welfare organizations and international development agencies.

It would be naive, though, to suggest that the social capital of community associations, the legal authority of the state, and the finances of international agencies each exerts equal influence or receives the same priority in project planning and implementation. Relations of power, shaped by both historical inequalities and contemporary processes of social transformation, condition the way these resources are exchanged. The analysis of collaborative initiatives between state institutions and Afro-Cuban religious circles is therefore also a study of power and dominance, not only between distinct socioeconomic sectors of Cuban society but also between different ethnic identities and philosophies of development.

Appreciating this cultural turbulence is crucial for understanding contemporary state-society relations in Cuba. As Ortiz (1940) argued, the "counterpoint," "transculturation," and ultimately interdependence of distinct philosophical traditions have always been at the core of Cuban nationhood. Ortiz's analysis of the cultural interactions of Europeans and Africans, whom he metaphorically described as Sugar and Tobacco, respectively, clearly signals a dynamic of power, but as Antonio Benítez Rojo has argued, it also signals a process of interaction that transcends binary opposition and outright antagonism. Ortiz described this tension as "counterpoint," which as Benítez Rojo reminds us, recalls the musical form of the baroque fugue:

> Voice S (Sugar), which is the second to enter, tries to exert dominance over voice T (Tobacco), the one that began the theme. Note that if the fugue exists it is only because the second voice is present; it is this one that properly speaking generates the counterpoint and makes it possible as a polyphonic genre. It might be said the S carries a *praxis* or mechanics of a technical sort that T does not possess. But, as I have said, it would be an error to think that T and S relate to each other only in an antagonistic or exclusive way. I would say that they relate also in the complementary and diachronic sense of mutual interdependence that recalls the complexity of power relations. (1992:173)

This power relation, he goes on, is difficult to define because the elements that comprise it are qualitatively different and not, as a result, capable of reducing or overcoming each other in a zero-sum fashion:

> It's clear that Ortiz's counterpoint, which is the relationship between the narratives of tobacco and sugar, does not imply a parity, or even a synthesis derived from the contradictions of thesis/antithesis, but rather there is another kind of difference here, specifically the difference between power and prestige, between history and myth, between machine and hand, between Industrial Revolution and agricultural revolution, between mass production and artisanship, between computer and drum. It's a question of voices that come from different centers of emission, from differing moments and discourses, which coexist beside each other in a complex and critical relationship, one that is impossible to clarify entirely. (1992:174)

Benítez Rojo concludes that an ongoing undercurrent of Cuban (and Caribbean) social life is the unresolvable tension between traditional wisdom and scientific knowledge. For the purposes of this study we might identify the persistence of this dynamic tension in the turbulent interdependence of state legal authority, foreign financial capital, and grassroots social capital in emerging Cuban development initiatives. Each of these is a necessary ingredient of effective projects and exerts a *different kind of influence* on them, with the result that none is capable of dominating the others entirely.

I tried to be sensitive to this interactive power relationship, its historical foundations, and contemporary implications in the way I conducted and wrote up the research. While I draw from my experiences of life in two Santería temple-houses in Old Havana and Santiago de Cuba, where I stayed for thirteen months and eleven months respectively (2000–2002, 2005–2006), I do not attempt to describe or analyze the daily ceremonial activities that took place there. This decision was personal as much as professional. Not only is it beyond my ability to "scientifically" convey the spiritual meaning of a living religious tradition, but having been entrusted with a degree of confidence in both houses it strikes me as inappropriate to even try. Thinking back to my childhood I can recall periodic Catholic masses held in the dining room of my parents' home in London. These were not secret events, but the degree of privacy and interpersonal trust they involved would in my view preclude a public discussion of their spiritual intimacy and ceremonial procedures.

An Afro-Cuban liturgical ceremony in Havana differs in important ways from a dining-room Catholic mass in London, and yet both have in common a profound respect for collective spiritual experience and trust. I made a decision early into the research that the intimate details of religious practice, despite their potential literary appeal, would not be included in my research diaries or the manuscripts that would follow. This decision was reaffirmed following a Santería funeral service in Havana, when Miki, the priest of the Havana temple-house, warned me that to write or speak publicly about what I had seen could bring serious spiritual consequences. For me these words strengthened an ongoing philosophical perspective that spiritual health, personal integrity, and the attempts of people to understand and trust each other are not foreign pursuits. It seems to me that to dwell on the description of private spiritual events and procedures would compromise this perspective and in the process fall short of the potential contribution that ethnographic writing can make to building cross-cultural understandings of social change.

At the heart of this potential is the distinctive capacity of applied social science, anthropology in particular, to vividly amplify voices and concerns that to the outside world might otherwise remain silent, or silenced. With this in mind the book examines a process whose significance has not been widely reported in academic literature or the media: the formation of sustainable collaborative relationships between informal community actors, formal state institutions, and foreign development agencies in post-1990 Cuba. In the chapters that follow I have tried to emphasize community perspectives and priorities by drawing from interviews and ethnographic research conducted over a total of twenty-four months. While much of the existing literature on Cuban popular religions is similarly engaged with the lived experience of local subjects, analysis of Cuban political decentralization has typically focused on legislative reform at the national level. Mindful of Rafael Hernández's call for "an approach that restores the specificity and autonomy of the *social* as a factor that interacts with the *institutionally political*," I have attempted to frame religious practice in the context of political reform while drawing attention to the interpersonal exchanges and loyalties that underpin the design and implementation of specific projects (2003:30, emphasis in original).

The interdisciplinary character of the book reflects a range of personal interests developed since my youth in Europe. Some of my earliest memories are of Geneva, where my family lived for two years because of my father's work with the World Health Organization. Sunday afternoons spent building miniature castles on the living-room floor with the children of my father's colleagues, usually to the backdrop of grown-up conversations about world hunger and population growth, were in their own way my introduction to development studies. These encounters continued for ten years in London, though by this time persistent dinner guests had habitually taken to extracting my opinion in discussions spanning football to economic development.

At age fourteen I moved with my family to the United States, and at seventeen I began to study anthropology at the University of Wisconsin-Madison. It was at this time that I became interested in researching the details of my Brazilian heritage, which my maternal grandfather, from Rio de Janeiro, had recorded in an intricately annotated family tree. One aspect of this interest, which soon came to encompass all others, was percussion. Employed by the UW-Madison Dance Program by the dancer and scholar Claudia Melrose to accompany classes and performances, I had the opportunity to study with leading Brazilian, Cuban, and West African percussionists, and the good fortune to conduct a year of musicological research in Senegal (Hearn 2004b). My experience with percussion was the original stimulus for my interest in Cuba, where a primary goal was to expand my musical horizons. This goal was given concrete form through my initiation as a batá drummer (*Omo Aña*, or Son of the Drums) in Santiago de Cuba in 2002, publicly recognizing my ability to contribute musically to ceremonial celebrations of Santería. The process of musical training and apprenticeship brought me into close contact with some of the same religious communities that have become, since the early 1990s, increasingly involved in collaborative partnerships with state development agencies. This book can be read as an attempt to reconcile my interests in sacred drumming and community development at a historical moment that has brought these two spheres of activity—the religious and the political—into unprecedented proximity in Cuba.

Studying simultaneously with religious leaders and development professionals meant engaging with actors with distinct cultural backgrounds and occupational priorities, which at times generated considerable tensions. The temple-house where I stayed for the first period of research was located in an Old Havana solar that suffered frequent power outages, water shortages, and gas leaks: precisely the kinds of problems that local development projects were aiming to resolve. Living in this setting by choice rather than necessity, and with the added luxury of a plane ticket out of the country, no doubt conditioned my participation in the experiences and interactions that form the basis of this book. I have tried to draw attention to my presence in the process of investigation and interpretation by supplementing analytic observations and data from interviews with excerpts from my research diaries.

If my privileged status as a foreigner at times faded into the background, then it was thrown back into sharp focus on the increasingly frequent occasions that I left the house for the day, wearing a shirt and tie, to attend meetings with international development delegations in exclusive hotel lobbies and bars. At one point I was asked by a Cuban development institution to translate its project reports into English and given a laptop computer by a foreign delegate for this purpose. But in the temple-house the computer seemed out of place, and although I followed the suggestion of the house's priest to use it for teaching basic word-processing skills to the solar's residents, it was a constant symbol of my access to a world of distant opportunities.

My residence in the temple-house and my intensive study of batá drumming did not go unnoticed by Cuban development officials. Some expressed alarm and even admiration for the "determination" my chosen home life must require, while others maintained the opinion (in public at least) that my interests amounted to little more than a study of superstition. One project director, encouraged by the laughter of his subordinates, was fond of exclaiming, "If we can't fix the street lights, we'll get Adrian to sacrifice a goat to the gods and ask for their help!" These comments disturbed me, not because I didn't know the first thing about how to sacrifice a goat (nor would

I be permitted to do so by Santería codes of practice), but because they were usually based on trivializing the practices and traditions of the communities that these officials were employed to serve. The social distance between the government officials, religious practitioners, and foreigners discussed in the book is reflected in the way their collaborative projects matured. From the interactions of babalawos with development workers to the negotiations of foreign NGOs with the state to gain access to Cuban community groups, projects were characterized by the challenge of reconciling divergent political objectives and economic philosophies.

The scenarios discussed in the following chapters raise the issues of tourism and the commercialization of religious traditions, the consequences of political decentralization for local governments and community organizations, forms of dialogue between international NGOs and the Cuban state, and the capacity of Christian and Afro-Cuban religious believers to openly express their faith while enjoying the legal, economic, and spiritual benefits of public sphere legitimacy. These are historically contentious issues in Cuba that have long been charged with political energy, resulting in polarized and entrenched perspectives that tend to circumvent opportunities for compromise and understanding. By focusing on emerging processes of consensus building and interdependence in actual projects and encounters, the book aims to identify potential points of practical and theoretical convergence.

The Book's Four Chapters

Total economic collapse following the fall of the Soviet Union was averted in Cuba largely through the development of the tourism industry. Political collapse was averted through consequent economic recovery, and also through official attempts to "bridge the widening gap between state structures and community life" (GDIC 2001:1). Afro-Cuban religions have played an important role in both of these developments. Tourism promoters have increasingly relied on "heritage tourism," with Afro-Cuban folklore as its emblem, as an integral part of their commercial strategy. This has involved establishing official institutions that portray Afro-Cuban religious practice for the tourism market, but that also claim—not without a measure of legitimacy—to represent the interests of religious devotees in a public and visible manner. Chapter 1 looks at these developments and a range of local responses to them. While critics argue that the institutionalization and "folklorization" of Santería has damaged its spiritual integrity and eroded its networks of social allegiance, others view the emerging public and commercial dimensions of Santería as a reflection of its historically proven capacity for adaptation to changing socioeconomic conditions.

In the spotlight of this debate are the Casa del Caribe in Santiago de Cuba and the Asociación Cultural Yoruba in Havana, whose official promotion by the state as institutional representatives of Afro-Cuban religion is widely suspected to harbor political and commercial motives. Indeed, unregistered rival organizations that endeavor to resist the influence of the state and the market in their ceremonial practice generally attract broader popular support. The distinct orientations of official and unofficial forms of religious association reflect a fundamental tension between vertical modes of engagement with the state and the formation of horizontal lines of solidarity independent of it. For individual religious practitioners the resolution of this tension largely comes down to their ability to maintain relationships within close-knit religious communities while simultaneously reaching out to forge external links. The chapter concludes with an ethnographic encounter with an Old Havana priest of Santería as he forges a path between the responsibilities owed to his local religious community and opportunities arising from engagement with the state and with the tourism market.

Chapter 2 deepens the discussion of state interaction with Afro-Cuban religious communities through an analysis of decentralized community welfare initiatives in Havana. A key challenge for local initiatives is to leverage public benefits from community solidarity, and thus make local social capital work for the larger civic agenda. State urban development organizations have approached this challenge by attempting to build interdependence between informal community networks and official projects in a way that openly recognizes the legitimacy and value of grassroots loyalty and allegiance. It has become clear to Cuban development workers that working through community networks—rather than in competition with them—to design and implement programs, ranging from sexual health to literacy promotion, not only benefits disadvantaged communities but also better protects the interests of the larger public. The challenge, then, is to convert "bonding" or "particularized" social capital into a more "bridging" or "generalized" form.

In some of the most impoverished areas of Havana, state development agencies have attempted to do this by building collaborative relationships with locally influential priests of Santería, who command substantial respect and authority in their neighborhoods. The chapter examines three projects that have resulted from these efforts, looking particularly at their capacity to integrate commercial activities with community welfare needs. While the case studies show projects struggling to balance commercial and community interests, the accomplishments they eventually achieve result from a convergence of state intervention in project development and local creativity in the design and implementation of community welfare actions. The intensifying collaboration of grassroots associations with decentralized state institutions suggests their political significance in contemporary Cuba, the strength of their informal social ties, and the responsibility they increasingly share with the state for representing local interests.

Chapter 3 considers the politically controversial link between community empowerment and international NGOs in Cuba. Since the early 1990s foreign NGOs have played a crucial supporting role in Cuban social intervention programs, but their access to grassroots community groups has been closely controlled. Examining the interactions of foreign development agencies, state-affiliated partner organizations, and community groups opens a useful window into the state's claim to represent and maintain stewardship over civil society. The state's meticulous supervision of domestic-international channels of contact reflects a socialist conception of civil society in which the activities of the paternal state are integrated with community interests through legally sanctioned neighborhood projects and government-administered social welfare organizations. Most international development agencies also prioritize community interests, local knowledge, and popular participation in their vision of civil society, but many also understand the concept, by definition, to signify administrative independence and autonomy from the state. Promoting this form of democratization is what earns many international NGOs the patronage of private, philanthropic, and government donors in their home countries. Those that operate in Cuba are therefore posed with the problem of satisfying the demands of their donors for projects that strengthen civil society and democratic governance while simultaneously complying with the tight regulatory requirements and administrative authority of the Cuban state.

A second, more serious challenge to the state's claim of stewardship over civil society arises from the Castro government's attempts to reintegrate Cuba into the world economy. Economic reforms have supported market-driven growth, but as in other countries, this has tended to prioritize commercial effectiveness over social welfare needs. The problem is particularly serious in Cuba because it directly compromises the legitimacy of the state's claim to represent popular interests. The chapter presents four case studies (two from Havana and two from Santiago de Cuba) that reveal some of the political and ideological tensions that arise from foreign-financed projects in Cuba and explore some of the positive and negative consequences of market-oriented development strategies.

Chapter 4 argues that the state's ability to maintain legitimacy and authority largely depends on how effectively it draws together a diversifying social base into relationships of exchange and interdependence with its local institutions. This entails offering nonstate actors material concessions, broader administrative freedoms, and ideological flexibility in return for their political loyalty and assistance with providing social welfare services. By entering into this kind of collaboration, many community organizations have augmented their ability to protect their members' interests while tentatively expanding relations with state and non-state organizations, ultimately strengthening their position as emerging civil society actors. The first part of the chapter discusses Christian communities, which have emerged as major players in delivering social and economic relief directly to the population, typically with financial support from overseas. With a growing base of popular support, Christian organizations are realizing long-held evangelical ambitions and beginning to show potential for political action much as they did in Eastern Europe in the mid-1980s. Key to this potential is the development of horizontal relations with allies, from domestic religious (including Afro-Cuban) congregations to foreign NGOs.

The second part of the chapter discusses the historical development of a community mutual aid organization, the Cabildo Carabalí Isuama. Founded in conjunction with the Catholic Church in the early nineteenth century, the Cabildo enjoyed the legitimacy and power to represent the interests of free and enslaved black Cubans in Santiago de Cuba. After 1959 its symbolic value to the early revolutionary government as a focal point of Afro-Cuban identity and solidarity in Santiago de Cuba earned it national visibility and state financial support. But officialdom also drove the Cabildo's religious activities underground, supplanted its mutual aid functions, and visibly transformed it into a symbol of national rather than ethnic identity, complete with "The Triumph of the Revolution" as the new theme for its carnival parades. Since the early 1990s the Cabildo's relationship with the state has transformed again, the evaporation of state subsidies resulting in a revival of its mutual aid functions and increasingly public celebration of its religious and ethnic heritage. It is unlikely that the Cabildo will assume representative capacities comparable to those it once possessed, but its contemporary experience shows that a changing political context has allowed it to develop the kinds of organizational prerequisites necessary for open civic engagement.

The chapter concludes with an analysis of a neighborhood welfare organization in Santiago de Cuba, whose combination of community-building activities, capacity to develop external linkages, and willingness to work within the prevailing legal framework have made it an effective intermediary between the central state and the local population. Although it is officially managed by the state the organization has worked actively to incorporate traditionally marginalized communities, including religious believers and homosexuals, into projects ranging from job placement to popular education. This convergence of local and national loyalties at the grassroots raises questions about the interdependence of state and society in the formation of Cuban civil society.

Recognizing and incorporating the power of grassroots social solidarity into state-led initiatives has become an increasingly critical task of Cuban development programs. Among the diverse forms that local solidarity takes, social capital embedded in religious circles of cooperation and exchange has emerged as both a potential threat and a key resource for the political leadership. Studying state engagement with religious groups therefore opens a useful opportunity for understanding the factors that consolidate and inhibit the formation of cooperative links between official and unofficial sectors, and the influence of these links on the formation of civil society. A crucial task in this pursuit is to clarify the place of Afro-Cuban religious groups in this process. As a historically enduring form of protection against oppression and racism, they harbor stronger ethnic and interpersonal bonds than other associations or groups, as well as a broader social influence. As Benítez Rojo writes, any study of a contemporary Caribbean society would be incomplete if it failed to acknowledge the profound and encompassing influence of African-based religions:

> African beliefs don't limit themselves to the worshiping of a given group of deities, but rather inform an authentic body of sociocultural practices extending through a labyrinth of referents as diverse as music, dance, theater, song, dress, hair-style, crafts, oral literature, systems of divination, medical botany, magic, ancestor cults, pantomime, trance states, eating customs, agricultural practices, relations with animals, cooking, commercial activity, astronomical observation, sexual behavior, and even the shapes and colors of objects. Religion in black Africa is not something that can be separated from knowledge, politics, economics, or the social and cultural spheres; it can't even be distinguished from history, since it is, in itself, history; we're dealing here with a discourse that

permeates all human activity and interferes in all practices. In black Africa, religion is everything, and at the same time it is nothing, for it can't be isolated from the world of phenomena or even Being. Keeping this in mind, we can affirm that the influence of Africa upon the nations of the Caribbean is, in the final analysis, and in the totalizing sense that we've just spoken about, a predominantly religious one. So a scientific model applied to investigate Caribbean societies and to predict their movements and tendencies would turn out to be grossly inadequate if it were to try to do without the input of beliefs formed under the African cultural impact. (1992:159)

The chapters that follow attempt to keep this insight in focus by drawing attention to the elusive sources of popular energy and creative potential that official projects set out to harness. Their successes and failures in this objective, and their manner of going about it, provide what I hope are some useful insights into the way social loyalties at the grassroots are influencing patterns of socioeconomic development and the evolution of civic democratization in contemporary Cuba.

1

SPIRITS IN MOTION:

FOLKLORE AND

FUNCTION

In May 2002, as I was nearing the end of my first stay in Cuba, I was invited to attend a theatrical performance of popular traditions in Santiago de Cuba. As with folkloric recitals in hundreds of hotels, cabarets, cultural centers, and nightclubs throughout the island, the spotlight focused on the most exotic, visually stimulating aspects of the Afro-Cuban religion Santería. It was a night of drumming, dancing, spirit possessions, and, to the fascinated shock of the audience, an animal sacrifice. The program for the performance, printed in English and Spanish, noted the central importance of these ritual activities to the practice of Santería in Cuba. The following week I returned to the house of Miki Alfonso, a babalawo (priest of Ifá, a divination tradition related to Santería) and my teacher of batá drums in Havana, with whom I had lived for nine months. When I showed him the program from the performance he commented that its theatrical sketches of Santería deities were inconsistent with the religion's spiritual teachings, but to my surprise, he also laughed and said that to get away with this, the performance directors must be adept salespeople and true *cabrones* (literally "bastards," though used in Cuba to signify cunning).

Miki was no stranger to the folklore stage. He dealt frequently with foreigners, from percussion students and anthropologists to filmmakers and tour operators impressed with his lively explanations of Afro-Cuban religions. But he also had a substantial local religious following. He owned a set of sacred batá drums, consecrated by the renowned Pancho Quinto, and his house operated as a center of religious activity in Old Havana, drawing a wide range of relatives and friends into a network of community support. The ceremonial gatherings that took place there served the community both spiritually and materially: the pork, chicken, and goat meat used as ceremonial offerings were subsequently divided and shared among participants, and *derechos* (fees) were paid to those who helped facilitate these occasions.

The social welfare activities of Miki's religious family reflect a historical concern for community support in Afro-Cuban religious practice that dates back to the establishment of cabildos (mutual aid societies) in the sixteenth and seventeenth centuries. This tradition of grassroots social welfare has remained an important focus of Santería, and many practitioners view folkloric performance as a logical way to protect their communities' economic interests and openly celebrate their spiritual heritage (Bettelheim 1991:75; Menéndez Vázquez 1995, 2002). Other practitioners and commentators disagree, arguing that the forces of commercial "folklorization" are blurring Santería's social focus. They contend that growing opportunities for employment in hotel cabarets, not to mention the birth of a profitable informal market for teaching foreigners the ways of Santería, has undermined the internal solidarity of religious communities and the efficacy of spiritual symbols and practices (Brandon 1993, Martínez Furé 2001, C. Moore 1988a). There are even claims, discussed below, that this has been a calculated political strategy of the Ministry of Culture, which has drawn additional criticism for sponsoring (allegedly divisive) multiple readings of the *letra del año* (letter of the year) ceremony, the country's most widely followed Afro-Cuban religious practice.

The chapter analyzes these issues with two objectives: first, to provide the study with a contextual basis sensitive to the cultural dynamics underlying state engagement with Afro-Cuban religion since 1990; and second, to outline the opinions of local protagonists about the complicated task of balancing community autonomy with official collaboration. I begin with an analysis of two organizations at the heart of the issue: the Casa del Caribe in Santiago de Cuba and the Asociación Cultural Yoruba in Havana, both of which have been promoted by the state as key representatives of Afro-Cuban religion. Despite their official status, or perhaps because of it, both have attracted the suspicion of religious practitioners for their role in developing commercially oriented programs of folkloric training and performance. Their activities have been widely perceived not only as a profanization of sacred practices, but also as part of a wider attempt of external, state-sponsored "representatives" to coopt grassroots structures of religious authority. Public suspicion about contemporary structures of representation and authority in Cuban Santería has given rise to the formation of grassroots associations committed to the rediscovery of more traditional "African" modes of religious organization. Although they have been criticized for promoting a reductive, purist understanding of Santería, these groups have set out to "rescue" Afro-Cuban religious heritage from commercial erosion by carefully defining traditional spiritual and social teachings while endeavoring to stay loyal to community interests.

The extent to which religious communities exploit economic opportunities arising from the state-managed tourism industry reveals not only their degree of willingness to recast traditional practices in a commercial format but also their level of readiness to endorse the state institutions that employ them and claim to represent their interests. I conclude the chapter by arguing that religious Cubans have increasingly resolved this conflict by developing flexible ties and allegiances that permit them to maintain their loyalty to their religious communities while engaging strategically in the tourism market. Those who accomplish this not only forge a path between cultural continuity and change but also go some way toward conserving horizontal lines of community trust while developing vertical lines of cooperation with the state. Miki is a good example of such a person. His orchestration of presentations and meetings to accommodate the diverse needs of foreign filmmakers, percussion students, aspiring initiates, and local religious followers effectively combined community, commercial, and political objectives. These overlapping loyalties allowed him to work within distinct religious and professional codes of conduct while simultaneously transcending their limits.

Collaboration, Cooption, and Tourism: The Casa del Caribe of Santiago de Cuba

International interest in Afro-Cuban religious exotica has swelled and subsided over the centuries, peaking prominently between 1920 and 1940 (R. Moore 1997), but the expansion of tourism in Cuba since the early 1990s has generated unprecedented commercial appeal around Santería and other elements of Cuban "traditional" life, including prerevolutionary music as portrayed in the *Buena Vista Social Club* phenomenon (R. Moore 2001). The economic ascendancy of tourism in the Caribbean region is evident in a 100 percent growth rate in the industry between 1990 and 1999, compared to a 65 percent global average (Henthorne and Miller 2003:84). As preferential trading arrangements for traditional Caribbean exports like sugar, bananas, and bauxite are progressively dismantled, most governments in the region have identified tourism as a key instrument for national development, despite the economic enclaves and local social disparities it generally produces (McDavid and Ramajeesingh 2003:182–183).

Dependency on tourism has made it the Caribbean's largest industry, and Cuba's emergence as a popular destination has intensified regional market competition. Tourism had established itself as Cuba's largest industry by 2000, generating an estimated U.S. $1.95 billion. The island attracted 1,774,541 visitors in 2001, or 11 percent of total visitors to the Caribbean, and 1,850,410 visitors in 2004 (CTO 2002, 2005). One result of the intensifying regional competition is the growing promotion of "heritage tourism" alongside more conventional "sun and sand" packages offered by contemporary Caribbean tour agencies (Adams 1984; Brunner 1989, 1991; Henthorne and Miller 2003; Palmer 1994; Silver 1993). Industry promoters throughout the Caribbean have increasingly focused on the folkloric representation of African-based traditions, often resorting to the shock value of exotic religious practices to ensure visitors a memorable and "authentic" experience.

Cuban tourism promoters have frequently developed commercial strategies in partnership with domestic educational and research institutions. One of Cuba's primary research institutions in the field of Afro-Cuban religious traditions is the Casa del Caribe, located in the relatively affluent Santiago de Cuba suburb of Vista Alegre. In January 2002 the Casa held a public meeting in its amphitheater to outline its accomplishments for 2001 and to discuss its ambitions for the new year. It was announced that the Casa's team of researchers had completed ten projects on local popular traditions that year and published sixteen articles in foreign and Cuban academic journals. These achievements were cited as evidence of the Casa's ongoing commitment to its 1982 inaugural mandate as specified by the Ministry of Culture: to investigate, report on, and "rescue" Cuban popular traditions. Joel James, the Casa's director, expressed this mission in his own words: "Our task is to dignify our religions rather than prostitute them to commercialization. We have to support the grupos portadores [community groups that "carry" cultural traditions] because every time they perform in the streets and on a stage it's a pro-revolutionary statement." During his speech a Cubanacán tour bus pulled up, dropping off holidaymakers at the door of the amphitheater. As they filed in and took their seats the formal presentations ended and a local folklore ensemble took the stage. I recorded my impressions of the performance in my research diary:

THEATER OF THE SAINTS

Although I'm seated in the sixth row of the open-air amphitheater, I can see the stage clearly. The batá drummers are at the back of the stage, the singer (or akpón) to their left, and the dancers, all women, in front.

Dressed from head to toe in the white robes of recent Santería initiates (iyawó), the eight dancers move in a slow, graceful circle to the
rhythm of the goddess Yemayá, " . . . asesu Yemayá, Yemayá olodo, olodo
Yemayá . . ." The akpón's phrase is repeated in soothing tones by the
dancers. The rhythms gradually build tension and the phrases of the call
and response songs become shorter and more energetic: " . . . tsikini . . . a
la modanse . . ." The dancers have broken from the circle and are stepping
quickly now, the largest batá drum (iyá) filling the electrified evening air
with torrid, thunderous improvisations. One of the dancers near the front
of the stage starts to convulse, eyes rolled back, taken by the goddess
Yemayá. The other dancers catch her before she falls; she regains balance
and starts to spin faster and faster: " . . . yaale yaalu ma o . . ." The three
batá drums are locked into a controlled, very rapid polyrhythm, punctu-
ated by the calls of the iyá and responses of the second drum, itótele. The
spinning dancer collapses and hits the floor.

The show is over and the audience is on its feet applauding. The lights
come up and the air gradually fills with the sound of European conversations: "The energy was incredible! Where can I get a recording of this
music?" "Grabaste esa última parte con la cámara?" "A quelle heur vient
l'autobus de l'hotel?" Slowly the crowd disperses.

—Santiago de Cuba, January 2002

After the performance, the tourists paid the entrance fee of two U.S.
dollars for a guided tour of the Casa's "Museum of Popular Religions,"
which introduces visitors to each of the deities of Santería (orichas) and their
mythical attributes (an ax, a shell, a fan, etc.). These tours typically culminate
with a personal invitation for visitors to kneel before the altars of the orichas
to ask for their blessings and assistance in daily affairs. Local Santeros also
visit the museum to kneel before the altars, which, the guide explains, is why
Cubans prefer to use the term "temple-house" (casa-templo) rather than "museum" to describe this and similar cultural centers in Cuba, "because in fact
they are places of worship."

The guide's explanation implied that putting a religious object on display
in a museum does not detract from its sacred significance, dignity, and
power. Religious dance and music spectacles have been described similarly
by Judith Bettelheim, who notes that many artists view their performances as
genuinely spiritual experiences (1991:75, 1994). Rescued from objectification
and reductionism by spiritual authenticity, folkloric dances, she notes, are
interpreted in Cuba both as genuine religious expression and as evidence of

progressive multiculturalism: "I believe that these images, these carnaval performances, are double coded. For African Cubans they are powerful messages, reminders of an ongoing rich and powerful reality. According to official culture they are indicators of the new status, an elevated status, of the African Cuban in post-revolutionary society" (1991:75). According to the Casa's deputy director, José Millet, it is this elevated status that the Casa is responsible for maintaining and guarding:

> Our folkloric stage performances are a fundamental way to support Afro-Cuban religions, which would otherwise have no way of supporting themselves. Notice that you don't see religious groups practicing openly in public places. Do you know that the few public religious celebrations that do occur, like the procession to El Cobre on 7 September and the festivities for [the Santería deity] Changó on 4 December, are not legally supported by any institution? Except for these rare traditional occasions, it is only the Casa del Caribe that openly supports the practice of popular religions in Santiago de Cuba. (Interview, 28 January 2002)

Each July the Casa organizes the Festival del Caribe, which showcases religiously inspired folklore performances on stages around Santiago de Cuba. According to Gladys González Bueno, a historian linked to the Casa, the festival, which has started to generate considerable profits, was founded in the early 1980s to raise awareness of ethnic diversity in Cuba and the Caribbean: "The purpose of the festival is to celebrate regional cultural diversity. I was involved from the start. I studied with the descendents of Haitian immigrants in the countryside and brought them to the festival to perform their religious songs and dances. No one here had ever seen this before so it was a tremendous success" (interview, 18 October 2001). Today the festival also attracts the interest of foreign tourists and students, many of whom enroll in the Casa's annual summer school program, which features workshops on the ethnology of popular religions.

The Casa's involvement with local religious believers goes beyond the folklore stage. Throughout the year it allows practitioners of the Haitian-derived religion Vodún to conduct weekly ceremonies in the back patio of the museum. The encounters between religious practitioners and ethnologists that result from this arrangement serve as opportunities for the Casa's staff to conduct observational research, much of which appears in the Casa's academic periodical, Del Caribe. For a fee, foreign visitors can also enter to watch, take snapshots, and bring home a small piece of paper from a box in the hallway: a sort of fortune cookie, inscribed with spiritual advice. These activities allow the Casa to function as a center of both religious performance and religious practice, enabling it to realize its official mandate while attracting the interest and dollars of a growing foreign clientele.

But it is not universally accepted that religious performance and religious practice are mutually supportive. Some critics do not support the folkloric representation of religious traditions, contending not only that staged performances of Afro-Cuban religions are a clear reflection of commercial irreverence but also that there is a more sinister process of ideological manipulation operating here, driven by a political agenda: "Afro-Cuban religions received some tolerance and solicitude when the dance and music which are part and parcel of an entire religious complex were presented as 'people's folklore.' In the context of contemporary Cuban society, such folkloric performances of religious music and dance served not to promote religious practices but to desacralize them. In this guise the Afro-Cuban religions were represented by government-sponsored dance and theater companies which traveled throughout Cuba and to foreign countries" (Brandon 1993:101). Carlos Moore, a controversial and outspoken critic of the Castro government's treatment of black Cubans, takes this point a step further, alleging that state organizations like the tour agency Cubatur have intentionally endeavored to weaken the social cohesion of Afro-Cuban religions by portraying them as exotic, backward customs (1988a:420).

Concerns like these have produced a degree of suspicion of state agencies that set out, as the Casa's director put it, to "dignify" Cuba's religions, especially when the request to do so comes not from (apparently undignified) religious communities themselves but from the Ministry of Culture. But where Moore sees political foul play, others perceive a more strictly economic objective behind religious folklore. According to the renowned North American batá drummer and educator, Michael Spiro: "Fidel promotes and supports the staging of Afro-Cuban religious traditions because it makes him money. End of story. In fact, the religion has grown incredibly since its most recent commercialization. Probably 500 percent more people are becoming initiated these days than ever before" (interview, 29 May 2002). For Spiro, folkloric performances generate income for state institutions and may simultaneously be contributing to the expansion of Afro-Cuban religious practice. Nevertheless, as the Casa del Caribe's recent hosting of the Ifá ceremony known as the letra del año (letter of the year) suggests, this expansion may be undermining the potential for the larger organizational solidarity of practitioners. The ceremony, which is performed early each January, reveals foresight into the events that will take place during the new year and suggests specific actions that believers should take to improve their opportunities. Gillian Gunn reports that 75 percent of Cubans place some credence in its forecasts (1995:9).

January 2002 was the first time ever that the letra ceremony was performed in Santiago de Cuba. Previously, it had been conducted by three other groups: the Asociación Cultural Yoruba de Cuba (Yoruba Cultural Association of Cuba) in Havana, an independent group of babalawos comprising the grassroots organizations Ilé Tun Tun and Ifá Iranlowo (also in Havana), and an Ifá brotherhood in the town of Palmira, situated between Havana and Santiago de Cuba, in the province of Cienfuegos. To discuss the significance of the new Santiago de Cuba ceremony a forum was convened at the Casa del Caribe on 9 January 2002, involving the city's four chief babalawos, who had presided over the ceremony, and the city's most prominent researchers of folk traditions. The following diary excerpt describes some impressions of this unusual meeting:

ALL IN A DAY'S WORK

I was invited to today's forum by a photographer who works at the Casa. All of the researchers and their guests were there, filling every seat in the Casa's main room, waiting patiently for the arrival of the babalawos to discuss the reasons why they carried out the letra del año ceremony in Santiago de Cuba this year. When they finally arrived I was surprised to see that they were led by my friend, the babalawo Rolandito Maseda from San Pedrito. He comes to my house frequently, and was there just last night, talking with Vicente [a very well known teacher of batá drums, with whom I lived in Santiago de Cuba]. When Rolandito saw me his eyes widened and he looked me up and down before we greeted each other, laughing. He seemed to be surprised to find me, whom he has known for months as a percussion student living in the poor neighborhood of La Playita, wearing a shirt and polished shoes, mixing with the academics of the Casa del Caribe. Rolandito and his colleagues took their seats at the front of the room and addressed the crowd.

When the presentations were over, the Casa's deputy director handed out photocopies of the ceremony's outcomes and sent around an email list for any researcher who wanted an electronic copy. This surprises me because when I was living with Miki in Old Havana last year, his photocopy of the letra's outcomes [circulated by Ilé Tun Tun and Ifá Iranlowo] was guarded carefully from the eyes of anyone who wasn't a Santero or baba-lawo, myself included. Apparently some circles of academics have privileged access to this kind of information.

When I returned to La Playita this evening, the streets were filled with families chatting and children running around as they tended horses, goats, and pigs in the cool evening air. It seemed like a different world from Vista Alegre, though it's only fifteen minutes away on a mototaxi [unofficially operated motorcycle taxi]. People greeted me, now accustomed to my presence in their community, as I walked along the dirt road. I arrived home and walked into the living room, where six or seven neighbors were sitting around the TV, Rolandito included.

—Santiago de Cuba, January 2002

During the meeting Rolandito explained that the previous year the predictions made by the three other letra ceremonies rang true in their local territories but not in Santiago de Cuba. This, he said, was because of age-old geographic differences and rapidly growing industrial and economic variation between the three regions, which have now become so amplified that they require the letra del año ceremony to be performed in Santiago de Cuba as well. From this day on, he explained, the jurisdiction of the Santiago de Cuba ceremony would stretch from Guantánamo, at Cuba's eastern tip, to Las Tunas to the West, beyond which the Palmira predictions assume jurisdiction as far as Havana province. In an email to Cuban scholars and research institutions, José Millet, the deputy director of the Casa del Caribe, noted the significance of holding the ceremony in Santiago de Cuba:

We declare that this consultation, which has been performed in Havana for many years, has been performed in our city for the first time, which is historically significant not just for our locality but for Cuban culture. This act of consultation constitutes an act of great wisdom on the part of the carriers of Afro-Cuban culture because it has shown us a way to preserve these African customs and traditions, which have been jealously guarded and defended by this considerable part of our population, which now knows that it can count on the support of the students, researchers, intellectuals, and all people who are aware of the importance of rigorously promoting and strengthening their transmission.

Every year national visitors—be they religious, academic, or people interested in cultural issues—and visitors from foreign countries, go to Havana to witness the letra del año ceremony; we hope that in the future they will come to Santiago de Cuba, famous for its proverbial hospitality and considered the Cultural Capital of the Caribbean for many reasons, among which is its spirituality. (Group email message, 2002)

The email message celebrated the ceremony's confirmation of Santiago de Cuba's national cultural significance, and by extension the institutional legitimacy of the Casa del Caribe vis-à-vis older, more established research centers in Havana. But not everybody celebrated the Casa's hosting of the letra ceremony with such enthusiasm.

While researchers have attributed multiple readings of the letra to a historical process of cultural fragmentation rooted in the slave trade's destruction of cohesive social groupings (de Lahaye Guerra and Zardoya Loureda 1999:125), one local Santero suggested to me in a private conversation that by promoting this new location for the ceremony the Ministry of Culture, working through the Casa del Caribe, harbors a similarly divisive intent:

The more the solidarity within our religious community diversifies, the less we are united. Look what happened in Havana: when the Yoruba Cultural Association became legally registered with the state it was allowed to accept money from foreign organizations. It has been promoted as the one truly legitimate Santería body, and so individuals and groups that are excluded from it become subordinated and jealous as a result. I know how much resistance to unification exists in high places because when I tried to form a nation-wide Afro-Cuban religious organization they told me straight out: "You'll never accomplish it, and we at the Ministry of Culture would never support such a movement." And so instead, four different letra del año ceremonies encourage us to focus on our local communities instead of thinking about a unified movement. (Interview, 27 January 2002)

While a subsequent discussion with the babalawo Rolandito confirmed that the new letra ceremony would have gone ahead with or without formal institutional recognition, the Casa's participation as host framed it as an officially endorsed activity. For the Santero interviewed above, this official endorsement represented a tactical effort of the Ministry of Culture to contain the emergence of an alternative, grassroots initiative potentially capable of developing informal horizontal linkages across the island. As Crahan and Armony (2006:43) have observed, among the variety of protocivil society organizations tentatively beginning to occupy social and political space in Cuba, only religious groups appear to represent substantial national

{ A street block of La Playita, Vicente Portuondo Hechavarría's house left
{ of center. Photo by the author.

networks. It is reasonable to suppose, as the Santero suggested, that the
state has attempted to retain legitimacy and authority by actively engaging
with grassroots religious initiatives to influence the way emerging spaces
are filled.

Official discourse about partnership and cooperation between state and
nonstate actors reflects this process, going some way toward integrating
Christian social activism (see chapter 4) into structures of official authority.
But the prospect of growing nonstate solidarity emerging through Afro-
Cuban religions, or from what Benítez Rojo (1992:174) calls an ethnically
distinct "center of emission," poses a different kind of challenge to state
hegemony. Whereas the efforts of previous governments to contain regional
and national Afro-Cuban unification have resorted to political opposition
and outright violence (Helg 1995, Pérez 1986), the Castro government has
generally employed more subtle means such as covert infiltration (E. González 1996:58), religious folklorization (Matibag 1996:227–247), and more
recently official sponsorship of emerging grassroots initiatives. State sponsorship of Santiago de Cuba's inaugural letra del ano ceremony may reflect
this more delicate approach, effectively preempting the establishment of an
unregistered nonstate endeavor capable of attracting the allegiance of potentially tens of thousands of regional followers. Suspicion of the Casa del

Caribe, fuelled by the fact that it is staffed primarily by white intellectuals and party members of a "scientific" persuasion, centers on its alleged complicity in this ideological project.

Already beset by historical rivalries, prejudices, and differing agendas, the capacity of religious communities to consolidate what collective interests they do share appears to have been further reduced by this kind of engagement with the state. The classic challenge of protecting fragile, preexisting, horizontal ties while developing vertical patronage relationships with the state (see, e.g., Evans 1996:1122; Woolcock 1998:168, 176) is compounded in Cuba by the need to acquire official authorization for open horizontal collaboration to begin with. Perhaps it is not surprising in such a context that unregistered initiatives aiming to establish alternative structures of religious representation and authority have begun to emerge. I would now like to discuss how some initiatives have built popular legitimacy by promoting broadly appealing cultural criteria, such as a reserved stance toward folkloric performance and an uncompromising regard for religious orthodoxy, to distinguish themselves from state-affiliated institutions such as the Casa del Caribe and the Asociación Cultural Yoruba de Cuba (Yoruba Cultural Association of Cuba).

The Politics of Religious Orthodoxy

The Asociación Cultural Yoruba de Cuba is an organization that perhaps more than any other has found itself caught up in disputes about commercial objectives, religious practice, and state patronage. Now the country's largest official representative of Yoruba ethnic heritage, the Asociación was founded in 1976 by Filiberto O'Farril and Manuel Ibañez under the name Ifá Ayer, Ifá Hoy, Ifá Mañana (Ifá yesterday, Ifá today, Ifá tomorrow). At that time the organization was not recognized by the Ministry of Justice Register of Associations with a license for public operation. Ibañez worked to consolidate the support of local babalawos in Old Havana and, when O'Farril died in 1989, he presided over the organization until the 1992 election of its current president, the babalawo Antonio Castañeda Márquez. Within a year Castañeda succeeded in formally registering the organization with a license for official operation, allowing it to develop relationships with foreign NGOs and to host international conferences in 1992, 1994, and 1998.

When the group achieved legal recognition it changed its name to the Asociación Cultural Yoruba de Cuba, and in 1995 it started to take advantage of this status by developing fruitful domestic and international relation-

The Asociación Cultural
Yorubá de Cuba, Havana,
October 2005.

ships. Donations from international NGOs (particularly from Spain), and a generous loan from the central government negotiated personally between Castañeda and Fidel Castro, funded the construction of the Asociación's permanent headquarters near the Capitol building in Old Havana, which freed members from having to conduct meetings in their private homes. Every two weeks, the Asociación convenes meetings for local babalawos, Santeros, and uninitiated members, who are allowed to enroll in a variety of Yoruba dance and drumming folklore classes at reduced rates. Members are also exempted from the ten-peso (ten convertible pesos for foreigners) fee to enter and worship in the Asociación's "museum of the orichas."

The Asociación celebrates important feast days of the Yoruba pantheon of orichas with ceremonial drumming and singing events. One event that I attended in December 2000 brought together over a thousand local Santería priests and believers. At a similar occasion in March 2002 a notice board at the front entrance reminded visitors that, in line with one of the tenets of Ifá, practitioners must be diligent in keeping their sacred ceremonial objects clean. This, the notice read, involves frequently changing bowls of holy water at home altars, which should also prevent the reproduction of mosquitoes and the spread of dengue fever. The notice concluded that this would support the Ministry of Health's 2001–2002 campaign, which had enlisted young people from nearby country towns, to fumigate every building in Havana.

. While this particular overlap of religious prescription and government initiative may be relatively inconsequential, it draws attention to wider suspicions about the nature of the relationship between the Yoruba Cultural Association and the central state. The Asociación's commercial activities, for example, are not viewed favorably by many of Havana's babalawos and Santeros, who habitually refer to the institution as "estatal" (belonging to the state). Technically this is not correct because the Asociación, thanks to its license from the Ministry of Justice, differs from state-owned organizations in its capacity to manage its own finances. Nevertheless, as one of its employees explained (under condition of anonymity), the political potential that the Asociación had at its outset began to deteriorate when it became officially registered: "The situation changed when the Asociación got its license. The original founders, who worked so hard to get the organization started, wanted to call it the 'Asociación Yoruba de Cuba,' but this was not permitted. Instead, as a condition of legality, they had to call it the 'Asociación Cultural Yoruba de Cuba,' which gives it a very different orientation. It went from being a genuine black association capable of voicing the concerns of black Cubans to being a center of folklore and ethnology" (interview, 2002).

Other critics of the Asociación have questioned its role in the letra del año ceremony, which it performs early each January. In her well-known study of Cuban NGOs, Gillian Gunn notes that because of the social influence of the letra del año, Cuban authorities have long attempted to influence the babalawos that conduct the ceremonies at the Asociación to ensure that the predictions are neutral or favorable to the government (Gunn 1995:9). Among the twenty recommendations that emerged from the Association's 2002 letra del año ceremony were the following:

— We have to steer clear of problems involving civil justice.
— We must try to solve problems through our religion's system of divination.
— Mothers should encourage the formal education of their children so that they do not become socially deformed.
— Parents should make sure their children go to school so as to avoid their involvement in prostitution, corruption, and drugs.
— The use of firearms is prohibited to avoid grave consequences.
— We should not use our religion as a means of commercialization.
— We should avoid being in the streets late at night if not absolutely necessary.
— It will be a difficult year. We must be loyal workers to make sure we acquire necessary items for daily consumption. As a rule, we should be patient and not lose hope since losing hope often leads to mistakes that we later regret. (ACYC 2002)

Although the recommendations appeal to the (potentially faltering) civic loyalty of believers, the Asociación unequivocally denies that any of its activities respond to official pressure, pointing out that it refuses membership to "pliant" babalawos (Gunn 1995:9). Even so, as the interviewee noted, the Asociación's expanding folklore museum and performing arts program reflect an increasingly market-driven, ethnological orientation to Yoruba ethnic heritage that seems to have compromised its ability to voice the interests and concerns of followers of Yoruba religion in Cuba.

To learn more I spoke with the president of the Asociación, Antonio Castañeda Márquez, who emphasized its role in defending the interests of both local and foreign believers:

> We represent all lovers of Yoruba culture, not just Cuban practitioners. Many people conduct ceremonies in their houses, but this often requires them to acquire official permits. One of the things we do for our members is relieve them from this responsibility by allowing them to conduct their ceremonies here in the Asociación. Their membership card identifies them as belonging to a respected and legitimate spiritual family, which has become important because these days the foreigners who come to Cuba for religious reasons often meet dishonest babalawos in the street, who charge them too much money.
>
> One result of our work is that certain people have become upset about their loss of illegal business, and so they criticize us because we're officially registered. Some say I'm the babalawo of Fidel. I wish I was! Then maybe we'd get favors from the state! The fact is we don't have anything to do with the state. Fidel lent us money to build our center, but it wasn't a gift, and I'm still paying it back. (Interview, 9 January 2006)

According to Castañeda the Asociación protects the spiritual and economic interests of believers in an officially approved yet independent manner. The membership card held by associates in return for 250 pesos per year (ten U.S. dollars) not only allows them to use the Asociación's facilities but carries a variety of additional benefits, such as authorization to allow foreign students to stay (supposedly rent-free) in their homes during periods of religious initiation and training in folkloric dance and music. It also allows members to enter the Asociación's folkloric events at reduced rates and even authorizes them to carry a knife in public, supposedly for use in sacrificial rites, but according to some I spoke with, "for self-defense." Nonmembers, religious or not, can attract severe fines and even political problems for accommodating foreigners or carrying a knife. An additional benefit enjoyed by members is access to the Asociación's team of administrative workers, who handle applications and paperwork for associates invited to perform folkloric art overseas, including passports, permission to travel, and foreign visas. Benefits such as these suggest that the transformation of the Asociación from a small circle of informal mutual aid into an official institution has not only allowed it to develop links with external donors but to directly advocate the interests of its members by widening certain avenues of formal civic participation.

It did not surprise me to learn, then, that most babalawos in the municipalities of Old Havana and Centro Havana carry an Asociación identity card. It was somewhat more surprising—though no less logical—to meet a particularly industrious babalawo with a degree in computer science, dedicated to producing counterfeit Asociación identity cards in his home office. His success in this endeavor, evidenced by over one hundred clients, illustrates a fundamental problem faced by the Asociación: that the transformation of its previously tight, unregistered modes of authority into transparent official structures of administration has been accompanied by a transformation of meaningful, collective trust into instrumental, individual interests.

The antiquity of this problem is illustrated in the classic work of Emile Durkheim and Max Weber. Durkheim (1993 [1893]) believed that the difficult transformation from community-oriented "mechanical" to professionally ordered "organic" solidarity eroded collective societal trust in the West, producing widespread "anomie" and a consequent rise in suicide rates. Shortly after, Weber (1930 [1904], 1968 [1921]) lamented the gradual replacement of socially meaningful "substantive" codes of conduct by "rational" bureaucratic structures of governance as capitalism took hold in the West. The issue has been taken up in recent years by theorists who discuss the rationalization of locally meaningful, "substantive" social capital into an institutionalized, "procedural" form (Federke et al. 1999), the problem maintaining "community integration" while developing "synergy" with state authorities (Woolcock 1998), and the challenge of building institutions that are at once "embedded" in local concerns and "autonomous" enough to act beyond partisan interests (Evans 1995).[1]

Considering the fundamental difficulty of integrating locally meaningful, collective priorities into market-friendly structures of formal representation, it is no wonder the Asociación has attracted criticism. Many of the concessions its members enjoy—from authorization to teach foreign students to assistance with visa requirements—reward individual entrepreneurship particularly through the commercial, folkloric representation of Afro-Cuban religions. One outspoken critic of this kind of "folklorization" is the Cuban cultural critic Rogelio Martínez Furé, who writes that commerce in religious art has become an economic lifeline for both state institutions and for private individuals across Cuba. His recent articles condemn the way some Cubans have abused foreign interest in Santería for personal gain: "There are people who hardly know how to sing or play, yet they give music and dance classes to foreigners. And what they transmit is a popularized pseudo-tradition that is deformed and deforms. . . . The temptation to earn easy money has captured many opportunistic hearts. . . . [S]ince the good grain is mixed in with the dirt, they take advantage of the historical moment to prey on traditional culture for personal gain" (2001: 11–12). It is worth mentioning that Martínez Furé was one of the key founding members—and is currently the artistic director—of the state-sponsored Conjunto Folklórico Nacional (National Folklore Ensemble), which since the early 1970s has been Cuba's most celebrated dance company, specializing in staged performance of Afro-Cuban religious folklore. Criticizing the organization, Carlos Moore alleges that the Conjunto's hidden purpose has always been to undermine and weaken Afro-Cuban religions (1970:71). When I asked Martínez Furé about this he drew a distinction between representation and authenticity, and suggested that it is not folkloric interpretation, but rather the commercial aspirations of recent years, that have caused real damage to Afro-Cuban traditions:

> In the Conjunto Folklórico we acknowledged from the start that we weren't presenting rumba and Santería as they are, but making a representation; a show. And the goal wasn't just to sell our representation but also to encourage a sense of pride among the folks who, at a time when these practices were looked down on, really were practicing Santería and rumba in the solares [low-income housing complexes].
>
> Many of the people who play these forms of music today still bring a sense of pride to their communities, but they often go about it the wrong way. For there to be any real community education the music needs to be based on historical traditions. Unfortunately, most of these young players know very little about these traditions because they're focused on earning dollars. What kind of lesson does that teach to their communities?
>
> I call this the *jineterismo* [hustling/pimping] of pseudo-culture. We have a serious problem here with the commercialization of music and religion. Foreigners come to buy religious knowledge and experience, and many babalawos will do anything for dollars. (Interview, 29 May 2000)

For Martínez Furé the commercial aspirations of young religious practitioners and musicians, made possible by the growth of foreign tourism, are

causing cultural transformations.[2] His point, though, is not that the representation of cultural traditions on cabaret stages does them harm, but rather that it is their misrepresentation for unknowing foreign audiences and students eager to "buy religious knowledge and experience" that is the "deforming" offense. Cultural degradation, in Martínez Furé's view, is exacerbated by religious artists who deal privately with tourists rather than commit to the quality control mechanisms of official institutions like the Ministry of Culture and the Conjunto Folklórico.

The role of foreign expectations in the commercial presentation of Afro-Cuban religions is also noted by Michael Spiro, who describes how foreign demands have brought new pressures to bear on the way religious knowledge is transmitted in Cuba:

> When I was initially in Cuba in the early 1970s, foreigners weren't just showing up and saying, "Hey, teach me to play batá drums," even if they had money. Back then, in Cuba, no one would teach you anything unless you first got "on the team," which meant spending a good deal of time with people, building friendships and trust. Since then there's been a very clear transition toward the transaction of money, because that's the most significant thing about tourism: it has brought a lot of money into a very poor place. You'll know not to take this the wrong way, Adrian, but look at your own experience: did you have to prove yourself to become omo aña [sworn to the batá drums]? (Interview, 29 May 2002)

Whether or not the tests of character and musicianship I endured during the sixteen months of training prior to being sworn to the batá drums constitute what they did in Spiro's day, his point stands that foreigners have come to expect access to spiritual knowledge in exchange for money.[3] Indeed, as Spiro pointed out in a research seminar in 2004:

> Now that the process of commercialization has begun, where will it end? Certainly not with the music: do you know that if they want to, a person with money can now become a Santero, a babalawo and omo aña—the three pillars of Yoruba religion in Cuba—all within one month!? The tourism company Folkcuba is a typical case: all of a sudden in the mid-1990s women were arriving in Cuba demanding to be taught to play the batá drums. This was unheard of according to Yoruba tradition [which restricts this activity to men], but the customers of Folkcuba insisted that this knowledge was part of the package that had been advertised; the package they had spent a lot of hard-earned money to buy. And because of the amount of money being offered, many Cubans are willing to teach these things to foreigners, including women. (Hearn and Spiro 2004)

While foreigners in Cuba are content to pay for spiritual and musical knowledge, many show neither suspicion nor concern that what they buy is, in Martínez Furé's terms, a "popularized pseudo-tradition that is deformed and deforms" (2001:11). Their concern seems to lie, rather, in the fulfillment of personal artistic goals and religious expectations for a fair price.

If foreign expectations have brought about transformations in the way Afro-Cuban religions are practiced, it is not surprising that in recent years resistance to folkloric representation and engagement with state-affiliated "representatives" has begun to emerge. In the Havana municipality of Diez de Octubre, a group called Ilé Tun Tun consults the letra del año independently of the Asociación Cultural Yoruba. The organization is strongly committed to maintaining religious orthodoxy, an objective it shares with its sister organization, Ifá Iranlowo, located in Los Sitios, on the edge of Old Havana. The two grassroots organizations have become increasingly identified with an emerging "Africanization" movement in Santería, though neither is recognized by the state with a license for financial autonomy or public sphere activity. According to Anet del Rey Roa, a former researcher at Havana's Center for Psychological and Social Research (CIPS), both groups have gained significant popular support and respect among practitioners of Afro-Cuban religions in recent years because of their democratic organization, their thorough research of Santería orthodoxy (largely through review of ethnographic literature and oral consultation with religious elders), and their reserved stance toward folkloric performance of sacred traditions (interview, 14 May 2002). The two groups demonstrated their popular backing during Pope John Paul II's visit to Cuba in 1998, when two of their leaders, Victor Betancourt and Lázaro Cuesta, convened approximately 450 babalawos and Santeros in an attempt to lay the foundations of a unified church of Santería (Ramos 1998:21).

Having established Ifá Iranlowo in 1991, Betancourt published a book in 1995 to outline the fundamental responsibilities of the babalawo as a social role model and doctor of natural medicine. The book's introduction states that the purpose of Betancourt's work and the mission of his organization is "the restructuration of the Afro-Cuban belief system; the rescue of ancient traditions and cultural roots deformed by syncretism" (1995:4). This quest for orthodoxy, though, has come at a price. Following Yoruba custom, Betancourt recently initiated a woman as a babalawo, a vocation restricted to men in the Cuban tradition of Ifá. Shortly afterward, a committee of senior babalawos convened by the Asociación Cultural Yoruba de Cuba signed a petition declaring Betancourt and the members of Ifá Iranlowo banned from participating in the Asociación's activities and expelled from official religious practice.

The episode aggravated the already sharp differences between the two organizations stemming from their distinct letra del año ceremonies. Indeed, the tone of the Asociación's recommendations listed above make for interesting contrast with the more critical recommendations circulated in 2006 by the Organizing Committee of the Letra del Año of Havana (comprising members of Ifá Iranlowo and Ilé Tun Tun):

— Beware of rising social delinquency, violence, and robberies.
— The penal system should be reformed.
— Exercise caution if dealing with the public health system, which is in crisis.
— Families should be vigilant about how their children are being educated.
— All individuals should comply with moral law.
— Seek unity with neighbors and try not to upset or disturb them.
— Promote family unity. (COLAH 2006a)

The Organizing Committee takes what it views as a special precaution when conducting its letra ceremony. While the Asociación's letra is read by the oldest, most experienced babalawo present in the room, the Organizing

Committee follows the Yoruba custom of requiring the youngest, least experienced babalawo to conduct the ceremony since he will be incapable of duping or tricking his colleagues. Betancourt's attention to detail in such matters has become widely known, resulting in his participation as a primary speaker at a 2006 conference in Mexico sponsored by the United Nations Educational, Scientific and Cultural Organization (UNESCO) to induct the ceremonial practice of Ifá, together with forty-three other historically significant traditional customs from around the world, into its *Third Proclamation of Masterpieces of the Oral and Intangible Heritage of Humanity* (UNESCO 2005). Betancourt's speech, written collectively by the Organizing Committee, stated that: "The 'letra del año' event does not present sensationalist or polemic news; on the contrary, it is considered a primordial necessity for improving humanity and advancing societies in crisis. Furthermore, it promotes the conservation of human understanding and the improvement of interpersonal relations, which can help minimize the chaos we live in today" (COLAH 2006b). When I met Betancourt he suggested that the emphasis that Ifá Iranlowo and Ilé Tun Tun place on promoting the politically unbiased "spiritual" elements of Ifá and Santería has complicated the prospect of collaboration with the state:

When I was in the airport last week I noticed that among the thirty or so shops there, there wasn't even one black employee. The only black employee I saw in the airport was cleaning the toilet. And yet in nearly all the shops, alongside Che Guevara T-shirts, cigars, and rum, were black dolls depicting Santeras. The point is that the state wants to package up our religion and turn it into a product for sale. The Asociación Cultural Yoruba was recreated not as a spiritual organization but as a legally registered cultural institution so that interested foreigners could go there and pay dollars to see the museum and hear drums played badly.

... In 2005, together with Ilé Tun Tun, we had 1,108 members. Within our community we're very organized, just as the practice of Ifá was—and is—in Nigeria. Just because we're not officially registered doesn't mean we're not organized. We've been asking for a license for years, not because we need one to be more organized, nor because we need one to collaborate with foreign groups or people; I mean, here you are sitting in my house, and here I am working with UNESCO. It's more a question of being recognized for what we are: a representative of Yoruba religion in Cuba with a spiritual rather than cultural basis. ... No Cuban government has every truly wanted to work officially with Afro-Cuban religions. The revolution hasn't openly accepted Afro-Cuban religions either, though in the early 1990s it was forced to allow more breathing space. I call this "accepting religion" in inverted commas.

Fernando Ortiz did us a favor when he started referring to our religion as Santería rather than brujería [witchcraft], as it was known before him. But there still exists a strong official prejudice. The state tells us: we can't give you a license because the Asociación is the official representative, and it already has one! It's not that the state tells us what we can and can't do; it's more the way it reacts to us. I'll give you a recent example: we recently initiated a member of the Cuban Communist Party. After the initiation she was expelled from the party. Now, you tell me: if she'd been initiated through the Asociación would it have been the same story? (Interview, 26 January 2006)

Ifá Iranlowo's inability to become officially licensed, despite growing recognition both at the grassroots and internationally, illustrates how popular interests in Cuba do not necessarily follow a "linear model" of development from informal sector interests to public sphere representation. Neither politically apathetic nor overtly opposed to the state, Ifá Iranlowo suggests a divergence of local and official interests expressed in its commitment to protecting the integrity of Afro-Cuban religious traditions from commercial misrepresentation. A similar commitment has been adopted by some babalawos in the United States, such as the former leader of New York's Yoruba Theological Archministry, Oba Ofuntola, who views foreign elements (including Catholic influences) introduced into Santería as "cultural abominations on the free and enlightened Afro-Americans" (Ofuntola, quoted in Palmié 1995:80). The current leader of the Yoruba Theological Archministry, John Mason, points out that in recent years the integrity of African-based religions in the Americas has increasingly been challenged by commercial pressures, resulting often enough from academic projects:

I don't think one can truly respect something if they don't believe in it, and there's no question that most of the academics and curators of museums that display sacred objects don't themselves believe in the related spiritual traditions. I remember being at an exhibit of Haitian Vodún shrines here in the United States. The curator told us how proud he and the other researchers were to have bought this set of burial shrines and brought them home. Well I told the curator what I thought: that this is the height of disrespect. How can you buy someone's religion? It's ludicrous! (Interview, 8 May 2003)

Mason makes the point that attempts to "buy religion" are common among a wide range of people and professions. As I observed in the Old Havana temple-house of Miki, though, not all attempts are successful:

SPIRITUAL PRIORITIES

It has been a busy weekend in the temple-house. There were over thirty people involved in the ceremonies last night to initiate a woman to Yemayá, and many of the guests were still here this morning. After lunch seven batá drummers came to the temple-house and we prepared the drums for tonight's ceremony, which will present the Iyawó [new initiate] to the aña [spirit of the batá drums]. More drummers gradually arrived, and by 4 P.M. there were eighteen omo aña [initiated drummers] chatting in the street outside the temple-house. That's when Lázaro showed up. He said his group was hired for the night to play in the rooftop bar of the Hotel Inglaterra. He needed six drummers and could pay each of them fifteen U.S. dollars [double what a drummer typically earns in a religious ceremony]. Since only four or five drummers are needed to alternate on the three ceremonial batá drums, I expected that Lázaro would take six or more of the eighteen drummers with him. But only one went. I asked some of the others why they didn't take the opportunity. One of them replied: "We need money to survive, but we need los santos [the saints] even more."

—Havana, May 2001

This episode shows how the decisions of religious drummers to accept or reject commercial opportunities can involve more than a utilitarian calculation of profits. Such decisions are also based on community loyalties, fear of rebuke from religious elders, and a sense that the public performance of religious music is simply disrespectful to Santería's spiritual foundations. These concerns can and do lead some musicians and dancers to subordinate commercial opportunities to religious loyalties and restrict their performances to sacred contexts.

Attempts to balance economic and cultural priorities were a theme of daily life at Miki's temple-house. As the months went by some of the drummers mentioned in the diary excerpt above started a weekly public performance in the courtyard of the temple-house, initially for the enjoyment of neighborhood residents. Soon, the musician Lázaro used his links with the Hotel Inglaterra to bring holidaymakers on unofficial excursions to the weekly event, receiving from Miki a commission of half the money they spent on the entrance fee and refreshments. The resulting convergence of religious setting, folkloric art, and economic transaction was the beginning of what would become a larger transcultural project (a case study of which is presented in chapter 2) that ultimately forged a collaborative relationship with the local government of Old Havana.

The musicians of the temple-house sought to integrate economic aspirations with religious allegiances by creating a commercially viable performance in a context of sacred celebration. Given the economic pressures of the Special Period, it is perhaps inevitable that religious practitioners and artists have developed Santería's new commercial potentials; there are, after all, few avenues of escape from economic hardship in contemporary Cuba, and fewer still are opportunities that are left unexplored. But whether or not the promotion of Santería folklore for economic ends constitutes a rupture with the religion's history is debatable, for not only have Afro-Cuban religions long been a source of intrigue and fantasy for Western audiences, as Robin Moore (1997) has shown; they have also historically functioned to improve the life chances and economic opportunities of their followers. When Cuban and Yoruba cultural influences were blending in the poor neighborhoods of Havana and Matanzas in the early nineteenth century, for example, Santería operated largely as a haven for the economic and cultural survival of enslaved and free black Cubans (Brandon 1993:69–73, Murphy 1988:27–31, Stubbs 1989:72). Furthermore, Afro-Cuban religions have since maintained an active role in the material and psychological support of communities in Cuba, the United States, and elsewhere, often more so than the Catholic Church, which in Cuba has been less associated with poor, urban sectors (Cros Sandoval 1979, Domínguez 1989:46). Economic transaction between initiated healers and lay clients has always been, and continues to be, an important aspect of this solidarity (Murphy 1998:91, Moreno Vega and Shepard 2002).

Under Castro Santeros have faced new challenges, ranging from the covert infiltration of religious communities by authorities concerned about the possibility of organized dissent (E. González 1996:58) to persisting stigmatization, particularly in professional contexts, of symbolic identifiers like religious beads and clothing (Jesús Guanche, interview, 20 March 2002). Carlos Moore argues that official concerns about religiously based Afro-Cuban solidarity led the Castro government to host the 1987 visit of His Majesty Oba Okunade Sijuwade Olubuse II, the paramount spiritual leader of the Yoruba people in Nigeria. During his visit to Havana, the African dignitary reportedly urged cooperation and dialogue with the Castro government when he received twenty Cuban babalawos (C. Moore 1988b:199). The year before, during the Third Party Congress, Castro had signaled his awareness of (and commitment to rectifying) growing black discontent with the regime, though for Moore, these symbolic gestures did not address the ideological foundations of continuing discrimination: "In sum, *racism* is altogether alive and well in revolutionary Cuba, well-entrenched behind an all-encompassing *ideology-religion* which tolerates white supremacy but does not accommodate black distinctiveness" (1988b:198, emphasis in original).

For many black Cubans, religious or not, material conditions nevertheless improved greatly under Castro, particularly in rural areas. Indeed, the revolution's efforts to build unity and solidarity between social sectors with diverse ethnic, economic, and geographic backgrounds is generally recognized as one of its most enduring successes (Knight 1990:256, Pérez Sarduy and Stubbs 1993:4–8). This is not to say that the Castro government has succeeded in abolishing racism, but it has made important advances in this regard at the institutional level. During a visit to New York in 2000, Fidel Castro recognized the ongoing challenge of interethnic solidarity:

> There has never been nor will there ever be a case where the law is applied according to ethnic criteria. However, we did discover that the descendants of those slaves who had lived in the slave quarters were the poorest and continued to live, after the supposed abolition of slavery, in the poorest housing. . . . I am simply saying that we are aware that there is still marginality in our country. But, there is the will to eradicate it with the proper methods in order to bring more unity and equality to our society. (Quoted in de La Fuente 2001:88)

Rafael Duharte Jiménez (2001:65–85) and Alejandro de la Fuente (2001) have argued that the 1990s have seen the emergence of new forms of racial discrimination. While black Cubans are well represented in the workforce as a whole, new jobs in commercial enterprises are disproportionately occupied by white Cubans. De la Fuente attributes this to "the pervasiveness of a racial ideology that portrays blacks as lazy, inefficient, dirty, ugly, and prone to criminal activities. In times of scarcity and growing competition for resources, this racist ideology justifies the exclusion of an important population sector from the benefits of the most attractive sector of Cuba's economy" (2001:80). Growing racial polarization is also noted by Hammond: "This situation threatens to resurrect social divisions between black and white Cubans. Afro-Cubans are not only less likely to have relatives who have left the country, but are less likely to be hired by managers of the hotels co-owned by foreigners" (1999:24).

The combination of an expanding tourism industry and a re-emergence of racial inequality have made the performance of Afro-Cuban religious folklore an attractive professional possibility for many black Cubans. Furthermore, in contrast to the concerns raised by Rogelio Martínez Furé and Victor Betancourt that commercial (mis)representations of Santería are harmful to the religion's integrity, Bettelheim (1991:75) points out that many performers view their work not only as an economic necessity but as a genuine religious expression. I will conclude the chapter by considering some of the strategies employed by individual religious practitioners to resolve conflicting economic and cultural allegiances, but it will help to first inform the discussion with a brief look at the dynamics of cross-cultural interaction.

An Island of History: The Practical Dimension of Cultural Transformation

When musicians and dancers are offered folkloric jobs in convertible peso–paying hotels, their decisions to accept or not, as we have seen, involve more than financial considerations. Artists may accept these invitations with the goal of celebrating their religious beliefs in a context of sacred public performance, or may refuse them because of community commitments or spiritual convictions. Cuban anthropologist Lázara Menéndez Vázquez has argued that to grasp the emotive power of contemporary Afro-Cuban religions one must appreciate that the *transgression* of established religious customs has played a crucial part in contemporary processes of Cuban cultural reproduction and rejuvenation (2002:15–16). Santería's adaptation to changing economic circumstances is a good example of this, she says, because however "impure" its contemporary forms of representation may be, they demonstrate that "innovation and transgression do not constitute an exception to the rule. . . . [T]ransgressions of limits constitute particular ways of relating oneself to the sacred" (1995:40). Accordingly, the efforts of some groups to reconstruct a "pure" Santería based on its practice among Yoruba people in Nigeria fall short of their goal because, besides the fact that Cuba has had very limited contact with Nigeria since slavery, these efforts fail to recognize the legitimacy of adaptive forms of religious expression (1995:39). Santería's flexible nature, she suggests, is concisely embodied in the simple act of presenting cakes, along with more traditional offerings, to the Santería deity

Obatalá: "To defend the existence of a cake for Obatalá is to preserve a space for mutation, which is produced independently of our will, by the daily influence of contemporary forces on the way traditional popular culture functions. All those who defend, openly or in private, the Yorubization of Santería, should think about the responsibility of assuming a posture that tends toward the depersonalization of such a rich and complex phenomenon, and toward a devaluation of its other paths" (1995:50). Africanization for Menéndez Vázquez, or "Yorubization," in her terms, is only one of Santería's many, equally legitimate, paths of development. To the extent that folkloric representations of Santería are considered sacred acts of worship by performers, they constitute another path, and should be seen as an adaptation—but not subversion—of tradition. For a growing number of religious practitioners, like the Santero in the example below, there is, "no fear of contamination":

How is it possible to ignore the mixes, the hybridizations, the impurities, when one sees a Santero or babalawo in the street with a T-shirt that reads "Tribal Sport," wearing on his protected head a sort of headdress or cap whose embroidery recalls the Arab world; wearing proudly an iddé [consecrated bracelet] around his left wrist, half of whose beads are red and black to represent the colors of the saint that rules his head, and the other half green and yellow to represent his post as a priest of Ifá; carrying a stack of books, among which one sees the Bible, and identifying himself as Cuban Yoruba? His attitude does not signify the profanization of religion, but rather, simply the acceptance of an inexorable reality: that times change. (2002:25)

This flexible understanding of tradition avoids the pitfall of attributing precise, often essentialized, cultural characteristics to scientifically distanced "others." Such reductionism, she writes, is evident in the work of Bascom and Herskovits and leads ultimately to a fossilized view of cultural heritage: the true culprit of unreflective commercial folklore (2002:15–16). Alternatively, a dynamic and engaged view of culture that probes what Menéndez Vázquez calls the "zones of conflict"—a concept that resembles Renato Rosaldo's (1989) "borderlands"—allows a more sensitive appreciation of cultural change and historic adaptation.

Menéndez Vázquez not only recognizes the constantly evolving nature of cultural traditions but also identifies the influence of encompassing political and economic conditions on the way they evolve. She acknowledges, for instance, that the loyalty that individuals feel toward their community may restrict their performance of sacred songs in a hotel or nightclub, but she also recognizes that such a decision would not have to be made at all if tourism had not brought the new hotels and commercial opportunities for folkloric performance in the first place. The hard facts of economic policy, regardless of the political culture that brought them into being, have forced people to confront new situations and to make unprecedented decisions. This predicament has brought with it the unavoidable consequence that concepts such as "community," "loyalty," "respect for tradition," and "the sacred" have taken on meanings that were previously not possible.

The "functional revaluation" of these categories, to coopt Marshall Sahlins's (1981) term, may tell us as much about the resilience of cultural traditions as it does about their transformation under the pressures of global capitalism. For Sahlins, the process of contact between two alien societies, even when one comes to politically or economically dominate the other, does not require that the dominated party abandon its ways in favor of a new cultural modernity. On the contrary, when people are confronted by foreign expectations and understandings (situations he calls "structures of the conjuncture"), they tend to incorporate the new experiences into enduring conceptual structures. To illustrate this point, he cites the example of British sailors arriving for the first time on the shores of Hawaii. Their reception by Hawaiians, and the patterns of trade and exchange that ensued, unfolded according to local cultural scripts: "The interests [that Hawaiians] severally displayed in the European shipping followed from their customary relationships to each other and to the world as Hawaiians conceived it. In this sense, Hawaiian culture would reproduce itself as history. Its tendency was to encompass the advent of Europeans within the system as constituted, thus to integrate circumstances as structure and make of the event a version of itself" (Sahlins 1981:50). This process eventually led to conflict between Hawaiian chiefs, commoners, and women, in turn rearranging their relationships to each other and transforming their society: "The complex of exchanges that developed between Hawaiians and Europeans, the structure of the conjuncture, brought the former into uncharacteristic conditions of internal conflict and contradiction. Their differential connections with Europeans thereby endowed their own relationships to each other with novel functional content. This is structural transformation. The values acquired in practice return to structure as new relationships between its categories" (1981:50).

The situation in contemporary Cuba is not dissimilar: opportunities to earn convertible pesos by performing previously guarded sacred music and dances have been met with reconfigurations of traditional religious practice. Africanization and folkorization are two of these reconfigurations, and as in Hawaii, the divergence has caused internal conflict. Naturally, both stage performers and proponents of Santería's Africanization consider their own activities to be sacred and in keeping with tradition, but they tend not to extend this validation to each other. As Sahlins puts it, "People are criticizing each other. Besides, their different interpretations of the same events also criticize each other, and so allow us a proper sense of the cultural relativity of the event and the responses to it" (1981:68).

If we accept Sahlins's argument that "an invention of tradition entails some tradition" (1999:417), we arrive at an account of transformation in Afro-Cuban religions based on the incorporation of new economic forces and opportunities into persisting, albeit adapting, norms and structures of religious practice. That is, local culture not only survives; it also shapes the course of history. But Sahlins has not escaped criticism, and two contentions in particular may be useful for the case at hand. In an evocative review of anthropological approaches to culture, Adam Kuper takes issue with Sahlins's emphasis on cultural over material forces and, parodying Sahlins, writes, "Earthquakes, the rough intrusion of conquistadores, even capitalism, must be translated into cultural terms, mythologized, before they can affect peoples' lives" (1999:17). Kuper concludes by arguing: "No worthwhile theory of change can exclude objective economic interest and material forces, the social relations that constrain choices, the organization of power, and the capacity of people with guns to impose new ways of thinking and acting on those without them" (1999:199). If Kuper were studying Cuba, he might argue that Santería has been significantly transformed by the tourism industry, which itself has been promoted by the state out of sheer economic necessity. Ironically, this position resembles that of the revolutionary Cuban ethnologist Argeliers León, who argued that popular traditions "transform because of their use, often deformation, by the capitalist companies that are managed by the dominating class" (quoted in Baltar 1998:362). In this light, the emergence of Africanization on the one hand, and of folklorization as promoted by the Casa del Caribe, the Asociación Cultural Yoruba de Cuba, and entrepreneurial artists on the other, appears not so much as the adaptive survival of traditions but rather as their perversion, degeneration, and collapse.

The onus thus returns to foreign interests and objectives in Cuba, and a second criticism of Sahlins. To approach a balanced understanding of Cuba's socioeconomic trajectory it is as crucial to explore the motivations and expectations of tourists, development agencies, and institutions (foreign and Cuban), as it is to explore local reactions to them. To not treat the problem from all sides leaves the analysis incomplete at best and ethnocentric at worst, which, of course, was a major—perhaps the major—criticism of Sahlins's account of social transformation in Hawaii. In that context, Gananath Obeyesekere leveled against Sahlins the accusation that in explaining Hawaiian reactions to British sailors as predetermined by their traditional understandings, he portrays Hawaiians as helpless servants of culture, "incapable of commonsensical inferences and a reflective form of practical reasoning" (Obeyesekere 1997:194). For Obeyesekere, as is suggested in the title of his book, *The Apotheosis of Captain Cook: European Mythmaking in the Pacific*, British sailors followed cultural scripts (in their case of superiority, dominance, and rationality) as much as anyone, while Hawaiians dealt with the foreign intruders as rationally as anyone would in such circumstances, from maximizing trade opportunities to finally killing Captain Cook.

Obeyesekere's contention is illuminating in its inclusion of all parties in a process of cultural retention and adaptation, and it is worth noting here a theoretical overlap with Ortiz's transculturation, which made a similar, though less publicized, intellectual contribution sixty years earlier. As Fernando Coronil puts it in his introduction to the 1995 edition of Ortiz's *Cuban Counterpoint*: "A contrapuntal perspective, by illuminating the complex interaction between the subaltern and the dominant, should make it difficult to absorb one into the other, completing, however unwittingly, the work of domination" (1995:xi). Viewing cultural transformation in terms of interaction and engagement rather than in terms of responses to contextual constraints destabilizes the assumption that the internal dynamics of subaltern communities will inevitably be (or have already been) assimilated into the strategic objectives of national governments and global markets. Unilateral models of this sort fail to acknowledge the integrity and resilience of cultural traditions, which is precisely what a transcultural perspective seeks to avoid. I would like to conclude the chapter with a brief look at how commercial, political, and religious pressures converged in the daily pursuits of Miki at the Old Havana temple-house. The manner in which he managed to overlap economic interests stemming from tourism with spiritual loyalty to his religious community suggests a process of cultural transformation driven simultaneously by the objectives of the nation state and local vigilance toward threats of cultural cooption.

Hidden Exchanges

Between the extremes of cultural survival and breakdown exists a margin of possibility in which the mutual influences of Santería and tourism—their transculturations—become visible. As my teacher Miki shows in the following narrative, spaces of interactive mutation often function to reconcile distinct cultural and economic objectives:

PLAYING THE PART

When a film crew arrives from England, Italy, Spain, Greece, or the U.S. to film the music and dance of rumba and batá, religion always figures in prominently. Today's group, chaperoned by a guide from the Ministry of Culture, was from England. The filming involved Miki [my first teacher of batá drumming] being "the authoritative babalawo": an interview in full ceremonial regalia plus a mock consultation with Orula [the Santería deity of divination]. It interested me to see just how "mock" the ceremony was because of Miki's reaction to a Cuban television serial (telenovela) last night. In the weekly episode of *Violetas de Agua* (Water Violets), a pregnant woman decides to become initiated in Santería, despite the protests of her husband, so that she might give birth free of complications. As the last stage of her initiation she is "presented" to the batá drums, which are played to bring the goddess Yemayá into her head. Miki observed that although the three drummers were sitting on the wrong side of each other, the ceremony was accurately reproduced for the camera. Then, he and his mother together angrily condemned the program for televising "sacred" and "secret knowledge."

After his performance for the English film crew, I asked Miki what other babalawos might say if they saw the film, which involved killing a pigeon for Orula. "Don't worry, it's all an act!" he said. "I mean, look: this is what I used for Changó [the deity of thunder and drumming]." He was pointing to a conga drum, over which he'd draped a red cloth to make it appear as the container of Changó would appear in a real ceremony. "And look," he went on, "is that Orula?" He was talking about the collection of small seashells held in his palm. Although there were sixteen of them, these were not the cowry shells of Orula. "Also," he continued, "I didn't say the real words. Look: 'Omi ani wana . . . Carlos Manuel y su Clan [a Cuban pop music group] . . . afri añeñe . . . Los Van Van, Isaac Delgado [more pop music groups].' Any babalawo who sees this on TV will laugh and say,

A British film crew recording a folklore performance at Miki Alfonso's temple of Santería, Havana, May 2002. Photo by the author.

'Oh, that Miki is a cabrón!' [literally "bastard," but employed in popular usage to mean "cunning"]. And besides, anyone would do the same for $200 U.S."

I've never heard Miki justify his actions in such depth, particularly to me, so I was surprised he went into so much detail. And then I realized that there were others in the room, including a babalawo and two elderly Santeros. I think the elaborate explanation was more for them.

—Havana, April 2001

In this episode Miki made much of his skilful construction of an apparently authentic experience out of invented words, objects, and actions, and he identified this accomplishment with the cunning skill of a cabrón. In Erving Goffman's (1969) terms, Miki successfully set up a "working consensus" that reconciled the distinct perspectives and priorities of his interviewers and his religious elders. But while Miki creatively engineered this maneuver to guide the outcome of the situation at hand, it was the hand of tradition that guided his creativity. As the ancient Ifá divination parable of Otura Niko demonstrates, babalawos have employed a technique of selective restraint to regulate the transmission of sacred knowledge since long before the recent wave of international attention on Cuba. The day I was sworn to the batá drums, the story was narrated to me by the babalawo Rolandito Maseda in Santiago de Cuba as follows:

Otura Niko was learning to play the batá drums. He was improving well; so well that his teacher knew that Otura Niko would soon be more proficient than him. One day Otura Niko asked his teacher to give him the final secret rhythm, but his teacher refused. Otura Niko asked again and again until his teacher finally relented, saying, "Come to my house for dinner tonight and I'll teach you the final lesson." That night the two sat down to dinner; but only the teacher got back up. He had poisoned and killed his student Otura Niko for trying so hard to take knowledge that can only be given.

As my own proficiency on the batá drums improved, my various mentors and their colleagues made sure I knew this story well. One evening in Havana its lesson came to life during an initiation ceremony that I was attending with Miki and one of his local students. After the student and I had each played, faithfully adhering to musical rules we had learned over the months, Miki congratulated us and then sat down to play the mother drum, or iyá. We observed Miki's impressive performance, thunderous and electric yet sensitive to the authority of the singer, but noticed a number of differences between the way he was playing and the way he had taught us. On the way home that night we asked him about this and he admitted what we suspected: not only had he taught us an altered version of the rhythm in our drum class, but he had no intention of teaching us the correct version. Then, to our surprise, he congratulated us for learning an important lesson: that life experience, not classroom experience, is the best teacher. His lesson called to mind a pedagogic distinction made by Tomás Fernández Robaina: "There are those who advocate the creation of schools and academies where recent initiates can acquire this knowledge in the fastest, most direct way; others stick to the tradition of passing on this knowledge through direct tuition with a 'padrino' and experience gained through active ceremonial participation" (1997:2).

According to Martínez Furé, the pedagogic technique of withholding and disguising sacred knowledge is characteristic of African-based religions in Cuba (interview, 11 May 2001). This tradition of selective restraint is also recognized by Miguel Barnet, who notes that discretion is one of Santería's last defenses against total public exposure, or what he calls "horizontalization":

Just look at the number of babalawos these days: way too many. And you know what? I haven't heard the batá played properly in about ten years. The problem is that the batá is no longer a strictly sacred instrument. It used to be used in ritual contexts, whereas now you see it in every cabaret, with a ridiculous fifteen-minute-long *Meta Changó* [a signature rhythm of the deity Changó, patron of the batá drums]. That rhythm used to be played for half an hour, an hour, or even hours at a time.

So basically the purity of batá drumming and Santería in general have been diluted. There are one or two groups who still play batá correctly, like Ilé Tun Tun in Diez de Octubre: the group that also does the letra del año. By the way, there's another phenomenon that's weakened: now everyone wants the letra interpreted in their own city whereas it used to be done in one place. But notice that the guys in Diez de Octubre keep to themselves. They don't hire themselves out to cabarets like the others, and they play so much better.

Ilé Tun Tun and others like them are really the only way to prevent the horizontalization of an entire tradition because they maintain a vertical line for religious knowledge to be passed on. Otherwise it will be increasingly diffused horizontally to the entrepreneur babalawos and the hotel cabarets for tourists. (Interview, 27 March 2002)

A "vertical" pedagogy of religious tuition obliges teachers to reveal meaningful lessons little by little and sometimes not at all, requiring new initiates to learn actively and patiently over a period of time. An abundance of time, though, is one of the few things that foreigners generally do not have in Cuba. As a result, students of Santería music and dance, even those who become initiated in the religion, study their material hard but often have no opportunity to test the worth of their knowledge. As Marta Vega, director of New York's Caribbean Cultural Center, put it, "Foreigners are very rarely, if ever, allowed access to the most important sacred information, even if they get initiated. Many people go home mistaken, never realizing this" (interview, 20 May 2003). While Martínez Furé points out the dangers of learning "deformed" knowledge from unqualified, inexperienced teachers, this second kind of misinformation—the intentional kind—can result from studying with religiously orthodox, highly experienced teachers.

Central to these encounters are the efforts of their protagonists to write each other into their own scripts of social reality. Those foreigners who buy tickets to folklore cabarets, perhaps following the suggestions of friends or holiday entertainment brochures, experience performances that locals often consider to be sacred spiritual occasions. Other visitors attempt to buy religious knowledge directly from Santeros and babalawos, many of whom purport to reveal religious secrets even as they disguise and guard fundamental information. With copies of their lessons recorded on minidisks and videocassettes, most foreigners return home from Cuba—like the British film crew—satisfied that they got what they came for.

Miki's strategic engagement with the tourism market allowed him to successfully make a living while staying within the boundaries of his religious tradition. Drawing from both personal creativity and religious tradition, he managed to simultaneously build lines of external cooperation with the state tourism sector while maintaining a sense of internal privacy and community integrity. In Lin's (2001:67) terms, he acted as a "bridging" individual, whose capacity to navigate fluid, overlapping relationships put him in a position to mediate the concerns and priorities of distinct communities. His actions therefore represent neither the meticulous breed of religious orthodoxy practiced by Ifá Iranlowo and Ilé Tun Tun, nor the erosion of culture decried by Martínez Furé and critics of the Casa del Caribe and the Asociación Cultural Yoruba. Rather, his tactics resemble the way a growing number of Afro-Cuban religious practitioners make use of opportunities arising from foreign tourism. Indeed, what this approach may represent is an emerging grassroots response to the classic problem of balancing internal community loyalty with external collaborative linkage (cf. Light and Karageorgis 1994, Portes 1998:16–17, Portes and Sensenbrenner 1993, Wilson 1987, Woolcock 1998:158).

While this chapter has identified the capacity of self-proclaimed cabrones like Miki to build these kinds of overlapping, transcultural relations, the next chapter will consider the ability of such people to mediate between their communities and the state. The arrival of foreign NGOs interested in supporting community initiatives since the onset of the Special Period, coupled with a growing emphasis on administrative decentralization, has widened the representative capacities of certain "natural leaders." Leaders of Afro-Cuban religions have begun to figure into these developments, increasingly assuming the formidable task of articulating local needs to official institutions while representing state development objectives—from prevention of drug use and prostitution to promotion of foreign tourism—to their communities. Once again, the difficulty of reconciling broad community interests with more narrow commercial aspirations has been a defining problem.

2

STATE DECENTRALIZATION
AND THE COLLABORATIVE
SPIRIT

This chapter discusses the participation of Afro-Cuban religious communities in decentralized health and welfare projects in Havana. I am interested in how the incorporation of unregistered community groups into registered projects can widen spaces for civic participation at the grassroots even as it reconfigures preexisting forms of informal mutual aid. Recent projects have sought to address urban problems ranging from housing decay to drug abuse and prostitution, boost education and health services to disadvantaged sectors, and generate profits from the tourism sector. Social networks at the grassroots have functioned to stimulate popular participation in such projects, and local ideas have contributed to identifying solutions to emerging problems. Nevertheless, the creative potential of neighborhood projects has generally been constrained by legal restrictions limiting their capacity to manage finances and to reap the rewards of their commercial activities.

The 1992 amendments to the constitution and the 2000 Law Decree 91 of the popular councils provided new mechanisms for expanded local administration and management, but these advances have not generally translated into stable channels of upward communication due to financial restrictions, meticulous auditing procedures, and political entrenchment. Continuing limitations on local economic management reflect official concerns about corruption stemming from the strong influence of informal social ties at the grassroots. These concerns are born of the decentralization process itself; the creation of local administrative branches capable of recognizing and engaging with independent neighborhood actors has to an extent opened state institutions and their community initiatives to the pervasive pull of informal social allegiances and black market exchange. Ironically, the legal restriction of local managerial capacities has provoked the development of informal lines of cooperation between local state representatives, nonstate project participants, and their wider communities.

Informal circles of communication and exchange have gone some way toward compensating for ineffective "linear" mechanisms for converting local interests and objectives into official requisitions and policy outcomes (cf. Cohen and Arato 1992:556). The expansion of alternative unregistered mechanisms, however, has produced neither widespread grassroots opposition to the state nor political apathy, as it has in other contexts (cf. Foley and Edwards 1996:48). Rather, the combination of top-down structures of official authority and bottom-up modes of unofficial communication has produced neighborhood welfare strategies that exhibit a curious interdependence of state and nonstate inputs (Henken 2006, Ritter 1998). The juxtaposition of state legal authority and community social capital in emerging projects has endowed both sectors with parallel responsibilities for protecting local welfare and influencing the way local initiatives take shape.

The participation of Afro-Cuban religious groups in official development projects is a good example of this process because, unless they operate through registered institutions like the Casa del Caribe and Asociación Cultural Yoruba (which most do not), their networks of local exchange and social influence operate informally. The popular legitimacy of these communities derives not from official recognition but rather from their ability to protect local material and spiritual interests. By collaborating with decentralized state institutions local religious leaders have augmented their capacity to build community initiatives that respond to these interests. Local leaders typically hold no official authority to manage their projects' commercial development, but they have often accomplished social welfare goals by using official recognition as a platform for mobilizing popular participation.

I begin the chapter by advancing a set of conceptual propositions about how state-led community development initiatives, much like the state-affiliated religious institutions discussed in chapter 1, have set out to harness local social capital to support their objectives. I then present some background on the contemporary decentralization process and introduce two of its institutional protagonists in the sphere of community development: the Oficina del Historiador de la Ciudad (Office of the Historian of Havana) and the Grupo para el Desarrollo Integral de la Capital (Group for the Integrated Development of the Capital or GDIC). Seeking to implement high-impact health education, housing construction, and crime prevention programs, both organizations have engaged Santería communities to make use of their powerful channels of grassroots communication and allegiance while generating income from tourism through the promotion of folkloric religious performances. The second part of the chapter presents three case studies of such projects, focusing on the efforts of their leaders to mediate community and state interests.

The research for this chapter involved thirteen months of residence in Miki Alfonso's Old Havana temple-house, where I studied religious batá drumming. This experience was the sole basis for the third case study, which offers the most detailed look at the role of interpersonal exchanges in the formation of a neighborhood development project. As the research progressed, interviews with government officials became more frequent, and some of these officials were directly involved in building projects with religious communities that I had initially come to know for artistic reasons. The consequent interactions of artistic, religious, and development specialists ultimately became the focus of this phase of research because of the potential of these relationships to result in effective, socially inclusive collaborations.

The Rise of the Local

Across Latin America, the decentralization of basic services since the 1980s has shifted responsibility for public welfare away from national governments to local administrative branches, private service providers, and transnational NGOs (MacDonald 1995:32). Driven by economic globalization, this process has fragmented national development strategies through the delegation and commercialization of government services, which in many regions has prompted the formation of grassroots self-help associations committed to small-scale community welfare, bringing neighborhood management squarely into the heart of Latin American politics (Fernández Soriano 1999: 168, Friedman 1989). While some self-help groups have subsisted independently through networks of black market exchange, others have collaborated in neighborhood support projects in symbiosis with local governments (Hagopian 1998:104). In this way, state activity has proven indispensable in some contexts, albeit with increased sensitivity to local interests in the design and implementation of economically viable social welfare strategies.

In 1990 Cuba's centrally administered system of basic social services began to erode, resulting in the growth of locally managed neighborhood welfare projects built on the collaboration of decentralized state development institutions with a diverse range of community self-help groups.[1] Government initiatives in Havana during the past decade have relied heavily on the participation of informal community organizations and their social networks to confront problems such as drug use, prostitution, and housing decay. Urban development institutions have therefore approached leaders of Afro-Cuban religions to galvanize the support of their extensive social networks and to capitalize on their ability to generate revenue from the tourism sector through folkloric performance. This has mainly occurred in Havana's poorest urban neighborhoods, where Afro-Cuban religions have historically matured and responded to community needs, sometimes in collaboration with the Catholic Church (Domínguez 1989:46, Portuondo Zúñiga 2000). Haroldo Dilla Alfonso notes the tremendous potential for collaboration between state development initiatives and Afro-Cuban religious communities given that these popular religions "serve as very effective informal networks for passing along information and for socialization at the community level. Today there is a tendency to involve Afro-Cuban religious authorities in cultural promotion and other aspects of local development in certain neighborhoods. These religious assemblies clearly possess a considerable ability to mobilize people, an ability that is bound to increase in the future" (1999:33).

Collaboration with local government institutions has augmented the mobilizing potential of Afro-Cuban religious communities, but the realization of this potential has required a level of creativity and initiative that goes beyond what is "handed down" by the state. For unregistered community groups, institutional ties significantly reduce the risk of their projects being closed down by local authorities and can simultaneously equip them with sufficient official recognition to lodge formal requests for state resources. Nevertheless, the reorientation of neighborhood initiatives to the tourism market has not generally been accompanied by the creation of official channels for communicating local needs to municipal and provincial authorities and for facilitating local economic reward. Worse still, the goal of revenue creation for the central state has often been imposed on urban development institutions from above and assumed priority over more humanitarian project goals.

The combination of these opportunities and constraints has given rise to the expansion of unofficial mechanisms for resolving daily problems. Stemming in part from religious kinship relations, informal channels of communication and resource distribution have augmented the capacity of decentralized projects to respond to community needs. The emergence of effective informal mechanisms around official development projects has to an extent allayed local concerns about the cooption of community activities and made collaboration with the state more appealing. For the central state, the local distortion of administrative regulations is a small price to pay for the incorporation of independent circles of mutual aid into larger official structures of governance. The consolidation of informal channels of communication across the local "public-private divide" may in fact provide community groups with externally oriented modes of engagement that allow state institutions to engage them constructively and harness the productive potential of their social capital.[2] Furthermore, the consequences faced by governments that fail to engage with local circles of solidarity and allegiance range from social fragmentation to rising underground antistate sentiment.

For the central state, the crux of the problem is that neighborhood associations, from women's support groups to religious congregations, typically direct their allegiances, loyalties, and energies not so much to the good of the general public as to the good of their own specific community, a problem Putnam identifies in his distinction of "bridging" (generally beneficial) from "bonding" (more introverted) forms of social capital (2000:22–23). Ethnicity, class, and historical experience play a crucial part in defining the boundaries of community membership, and weighed up against these social bonds, public-spirited citizenship often takes second place. Thus, while "high levels of social capital, reflecting reciprocal bonds of trust, cut horizontally across classes and ethnicities" (Rotberg 2001:2), it is also true that bonds of trust originate from, and often remain confined within, class and ethnic identities. This has become evident in Eastern European postcommunist societies, where inward-focused circles of social trust and solidarity have seriously impeded voluntary participation in public initiatives (M. Howard 2002). For the Cuban state, opening up circles of local trust—or at the very least integrating them into wider projects—validates its larger claim to authority and public representation.

Network theorists have long been interested in the ways social circles at the community level intersect with structures of authority at the macro level (e.g., Alexander et al. 1987, Blau 1964, Collins 1981, Huber 1991). Such intersections have been critical to the political influence that informal networks have exerted on government and private sector institutions in Europe and Latin America (Alvarez 1997, Doyle and McEachern 1998, Slater 1985). Research shows that when networks of nonstate solidarity have coalesced into organized forms of political opposition, governments have generally sought to fragment them either by inciting internal rivalries and divisions, or by oppressing them overtly (Brecher et al. 2000, Carlessi 1989, Gregório Baierle 1998). The Cuban state clearly harbors concerns about the consolidation of

La Habana Vieja (Old Havana) and surrounding area

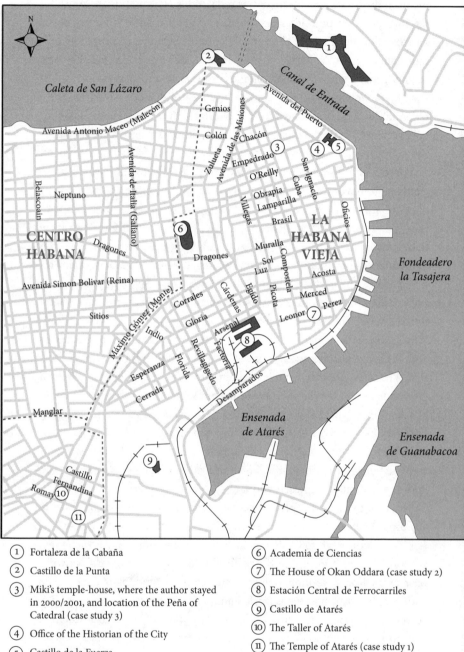

(1) Fortaleza de la Cabaña

(2) Castillo de la Punta

(3) Miki's temple-house, where the author stayed in 2000/2001, and location of the Peña of Catedral (case study 3)

(4) Office of the Historian of the City

(5) Castillo de la Fuerza

(6) Academia de Ciencias

(7) The House of Okan Oddara (case study 2)

(8) Estación Central de Ferrocarriles

(9) Castillo de Atarés

(10) The Taller of Atarés

(11) The Temple of Atarés (case study 1)

nonstate solidarity, but the three case studies I present below suggest a more engaged strategic posturing that has conciliated rather than contained local demands. This has involved the construction of new forms of engagement designed to harness productive capacities at the base in order to support the state's larger national development agenda.

The case studies exhibit an interplay of top-down and bottom-up forms of influence and exchange of information. From the top down, the projects benefited from legal legitimacy, but were also subordinated to an externally designed development plan. The emphasis on folkloric performance assumed by each project as it became "official" reflects not only the state's attempt to integrate local human resources into a national economic agenda, but also its careful supervision of links between community groups and foreign tour agencies. Nevertheless, case study 3 in particular shows that the formal legal power of the state is not impermeable to the informal social power of religious kinship. Afro-Cuban religions incorporate people in all occupations and income brackets, though this is typically less visible in official milieus. Case study 3 shows how a lack of official mechanisms for bottom-up influence was effectively compensated by unofficial religious links.

The first case study is from the popular council (consejo popular) of Pilar-Atarés, in the municipality of El Cerro and the other two are from the popular councils of Catedral and San Isidro in the municipality of Old Havana.[3] Each project attempted to address a range of community needs while generating income through music, dance, visual imagery, and other artistic representations of Afro-Cuban religions, reflecting the centrality of tourism to these projects and the opportunities it is perceived to bring. Gradually, each project became focused on the artistic performance of religious folklore as a central activity because of its commercial potentials. While attracting hard currency from tourists and generating an enthusiastic sense of collective purpose, folklore performances and related commercial activities nevertheless came to replace rather than complement the original project goals. The neighborhood welfare objectives of all three projects were undermined as a narrowing focus on folkloric shows for tourists stifled the participation of their wider communities. The map on page 72 identifies the locations of the three case studies.

The case studies show state agencies and community actors united in commercial pursuits but often pursuing divergent outcomes. For the state, revenue from tourism has largely replaced Soviet aid, and "folklore tourism" has proven particularly profitable, resulting in (and from) extravagant promotion campaigns by Cuban tour agencies, dance companies, hotels, and museums (Daniel 1995:61–62, 127; *Granma* 1987:10; Jatar Hausmann 1999:49, 141). The situation resembles that described by Joel Kahn in East Asia, where the commercial promotion of local traditions is a central project of governments attempting to tap the global tourism market (1997:105–106). Similarly, particularly in the 1960s and 1970s, the Brazilian government tried to incorporate Afro-Brazilian religious communities into registered folklore spectacles both to profit from tourism and portray an image of social inclusion and racial harmony in Bahia (Crook 1993:92–93, Ireland 1991:42). The Cuban government's incorporation of Afro-Cuban religious communities into official projects not only promotes tourism and the notion of social inclusion (as the first case study shows) but also helps to preempt unregistered economic activity, a goal that one Cuban development agency characterizes as "formalizing the informal" (Coyula et al. 2001:12).

But the regulation of informal economic activity is a delicate affair, which often carries unintended consequences. The role played by the black market in the daily lives of most Cubans is neatly summed up by the vernacular adage "El que tiene amigos tiene un central" ("He who has friends has a sugar factory"). In the projects described below a reorientation away from networks of informal economy and exchange to the tourist market effectively narrowed the ability of the projects to function for the benefit of their wider communities. Commercial activities, whether licensed by the state or condemned as illegal, therefore inhibited the development of participatory public-private collaborations. Nevertheless, having gained a degree of legal legitimacy, two of the three projects later revived their community welfare activities by building local participation through unregistered religious support networks.

Conditioned at once by legal recognition from above and by informal social power from below, the participation of religious communities in official projects suggests their growing capacity for civic participation. Paradoxically, the state's controlled empowerment of Afro-Cuban religious groups has both reduced the threat of nonstate organization at the grassroots and facilitated the expansion of unregistered support networks. One result of this is a growing interdependence of state and nonstate actors as they assume shared responsibilities for finding and maintaining a balance between commercial opportunity and community welfare. The challenge this raises for both sectors is to forge and maintain functional public-private relationships that give projects stability and confidence, without which even the most democratically designed initiatives tend to lose sight of their goals.[4]

From National to Neighborhood Decentralization

When the rebel government of Fidel Castro took control of Cuba in 1959, it inherited from the Batista regime a system of civic administration that did little to balance the needs of urban and rural provinces. With a mere 8 percent of Cuba's rural population able to access health services, a more equitable structure of resource distribution was one of the Castro government's first priorities (Uriarte 2001:2). Centralized administration of health, education, housing, and other services did much to benefit Cuba's disenfranchised masses, which the government encouraged to participate in large-scale campaigns (Eckstein 1994:22–23). Public volunteers were the backbone of the 1961 National Literacy Campaign, which taught 700,000 Cubans to read and write within one year, reducing illiteracy from 23 to 4 percent of the population (CIEM 2000:79). The similarly grandiose Social Microbrigade Movement of the mid-1970s and early 1980s enlisted the efforts of ordinary citizens to collectively construct their own housing, significantly easing the strain of rural migration to Havana that characterized the city's development in the first half of the twentieth century (Benítez Pérez 1999:49, Pérez Alvarez 1996:1).

While centralized strategies addressed some of the country's most pressing problems, locally elected representatives of provincial and municipal governments, as late as the mid-1970s, had very little authority to design and implement legislation according to the particular needs of their constituents. Ironically, the legislative system of the time was called Poder Local (Local Power), but consisted of a powerful national government whose provincial and municipal branches amounted to "administrative entities with little real power" (Dilla Alfonso et al. 1993:28). To address the problem a new system called Poder Popular (Popular Power) was created in 1976. One of its first actions was to pass Law Decree 1304, which replaced Cuba's 6 colonial-era provinces (created in 1878), 58 regions, and 407 micromunicipalities (created in the early 1960s) with a new system of 14 provinces and 169 municipalities (Communist Party of Cuba 1976). These reforms, which were designed to facilitate Cuba's integration into the Soviet economic system, also resulted in wider channels of popular political participation through a system of indirect elections and a higher degree of self-management and communication between local government institutions. The move toward decentralized governance likely drew inspiration from Allende's Popular Unity government in Chile, which from 1971 until the coup of 1973 made remarkable advances in facilitating the integration of organizations at the neighborhood level into community justice and law enforcement programs (Friedman 1989:227).

The onset of economic crisis in Cuba following the disintegration of the Soviet Union provoked further administrative decentralization, particularly in Havana. In 1988 trade with Socialist Eastern Europe had accounted for 87.4 percent of Cuba's imports (mainly of medicines, oil, gasoline, food, and heavy equipment required for sugar cane production, mining, and agriculture) and 86.4 percent of exports (CEE 1999:415). As tourism came to fill the economic void left by the withdrawal of support from Eastern Europe, the physical location and historical patrimony of some parts of Cuba made them key areas of commercial activity while others, less impacted by tourism, remained commercially undeveloped.

In the mid-1990s significant inequalities began to reemerge between— and within—zones more and less integrated into the U.S. dollar economy, requiring a system of local governance more sensitive to the growth of problems such as drug use, prostitution, and rampant black markets. A mechanism was needed to harness and coordinate the productive capacities of locally operating state industries, branches of mass organizations like the Federación de Mujeres Cubanas (Federation of Cuban Women, or FMC) and the Unión de Jovenes Comunistas (Union of Young Communists, or UJC), and unregistered community self-help groups. The government recognized that the collaborative participation of a wider variety of civic actors would stimulate greater local responsibility for dealing with emerging problems (Coyula et al. 2001:6).

To facilitate this process, in the early 1990s Havana's 15 municipalities were subdivided into 93 popular councils (subsequently expanded to 105), each charged with overseeing the productive integration of its locality (República de Cuba 2000:5). At present, each municipality contains between 5 and 8 popular councils, and each of these is staffed by a small number of volunteer specialists (usually less than 8) from local state businesses and institutions, who among themselves elect a salaried leader. Since their creation the popular councils have functioned mainly to promote horizontal communication between influential actors in their territories, advise neighborhood organizations about the legal requirements for their operations, identify social problems at the community level, and construct plans for their solution.

According to a delegate of Old Havana's Popular Council of San Isidro, the capacity for social intervention is the most valuable of the councils' functions: "They're very friendly, open places and they have the trust of the population. In my territory I heard about a young woman with a reputation for seeking out tourists, so I took personal responsibility for talking with her and then I found her a job. I could have denounced her or turned her over to the police, but that's not my job as a delegate. I and the other delegates are here to build trust in our neighborhoods even as we uphold the law" (interview, 2 April 2002).

The establishment of the first 93 popular councils and their subsequent expansion to 105 were developments welcomed by those favoring Cuba's political decentralization, but their effectiveness has left much to be desired. The problem is that for all the influence that popular councils may exercise in promoting dialogue and cooperation, they manifest the same problems as the weak provincial and municipal governments of the early revolution. That is, they have no resources or money of their own to carry out projects or offer assistance to the organizations and actors they coordinate. In the words of one Cuban development worker: "Popular councils are very creative and committed, but go and visit a delegate and ask him what projects he's carrying out. He'll show you a list of projects his team has designed to solve community problems then throw his arms up in frustration because he doesn't have any money for the necessary materials or services to implement them" (interview, 6 May 2002).

Decentralization, it seems, means different things to different people. A delegate of the Old Havana Popular Council of Belén explained: "The concept of decentralization is very two-faced in Cuba because the decentralization of administration, which amounts to the state washing its hands of responsibility for problems, is very different from the decentralization of money and resources. The first is very fashionable; the second doesn't exist" (interview, 4 April 2002).

For this delegate, the decentralization that has taken place at the neighborhood scale, at least in terms of urban planning, has been administrative rather than economic. The same problem has begun to provoke debate at the municipal level. When the city of Havana became one of the country's fourteen provinces in 1976, it was divided into fifteen municipalities, each one governed by a municipal assembly. Just as the Castro government in its early years sought to reduce socioeconomic inequalities between the island's provinces, it has also discouraged the economic divergence of Havana's municipalities through centralized collection and redistribution of income earned by profit-generating entities such as factories, hotels, restaurants, and other businesses. The municipality of Regla, for example, has a number of factories and industries, yet has a relatively low population. If left unregulated, the relative wealth and standard of living of Regla's citizens would soon rise above that of its more densely populated, less industrialized, municipal neighbors. To prevent this, profit-generating entities are managed by centralized ministries, to which they are required to submit their incomes for nationally planned redistribution.

This basic strategy of Cuba's planned economy has allowed for the reinvestment of earnings from the tourism industry and other profitable enterprises in activities of high national priority like citrus fruit cultivation and Internet development. However, while centralized economic management maintains the revolutionary principle of municipal and provincial equity, it nevertheless poses obstacles to the growth of local industries, which could otherwise be an important catalyst for economic stimulation. Indeed, despite the potential advantages of less regulated local economic activity, legal mechanisms to support autonomous financial management even of small profit-generating initiatives remain weak and noncommittal.

There are two institutions that have to an extent transcended these kinds of bureaucratic restrictions through a combination of legal flexibility and local sensitivity. These are the Group for the Integrated Development of the Capital, or GDIC, and the Office of the Historian of Havana. The two organizations are at the forefront of decentralized planning and development in Havana, designing and implementing projects that address emerging social and physical problems in the inner city. Their commitment to working face to face with residents and incorporating local perspectives into development plans marks a significant step away from the Castro government's orthodox administrative strategy of attending to urban needs through centrally planned ministries of health, education, sport, and so on. This kind of decentralization reflects Cuba's economic situation: effectiveness can no longer be attained through fully subsidized universal coverage; instead, efficiency has become crucial (Uriarte 2001:iii). This is especially true as living standards and personal incomes become increasingly diversified, requiring more streamlined delivery of services to vulnerable sectors such as senior and disabled citizens, single mothers, and unemployed youth. The government's emerging interest in synergistic collaboration with target communities has improved the efficiency of social service delivery over the past decade and has simultaneously attracted the interest of foreign NGOs and private donors, who typically require the participation of local actors in specific projects as a condition of funding.

With legal permission to receive and use foreign donations, the Office of the Historian and the GDIC have distinguished themselves from other de-centralized administrative bodies, like the popular councils. While the proj-ects of popular councils are locally designed, their effectiveness is often compromised because of limited access to centrally controlled resources, resulting in what one Cuban development worker has called "the passive inertia of state centralization" (Pérez Alvarez 1998:10). As Armando Fer-nández Soriano notes, the decentralization of resources since the early 1990s has lagged behind the decentralization of responsibility for local planning, reflecting the reluctance of the central state to cede authority to its local branches and institutions (1991:181). The Office of the Historian of Havana and the GDIC enjoyed unusual leeway in this regard, and have attracted support from foreign NGOs as a result.

The GDIC and the Neighborhood of Atarés

The GDIC was founded in 1987 as an advisory body to the City of Havana provincial government, bringing together an interdisciplinary team of ex-perts in community planning and development. According to Coyula and Pérez: "The Group has supported a new, alternative model of urban develop-ment that would be more decentralized and participatory, promoting the reappraisal of neighborhoods as clearly identified territories. This should allow for the breaking of big metropolitan problems into smaller units that are easier to handle, and encourage the participation of residents in dealing with their own issues" (1996:2).

The GDIC's main strategy has been to set up talleres de transformación integral del barrio (centers for integrated neighborhood transformation, or TTIBs) in Havana's most impoverished, marginal zones. The first three were set up in 1988 in the urban neighborhoods of Atarés, Cayo Hueso, and La Güinera, and by 2002 there were twenty-two talleres in operation across Havana. The Group estimates that the talleres are now directly impacting more than half a million people, over 23 percent of the capital's population (Coyula et al. 2001:9). Created to "bridge the widening gap between state structures and community life" (GDIC 2001:1), the talleres try to "stimulate the most positive cultural values of a neighborhood, maintain its traditions and keep its culture alive, and at the same time, encourage new ways of acting and thinking that are socially positive" (Coyula et al. 1999:4). In this way they aim to promote a sense of solidarity and belonging within neigh-borhoods so that residents take on a heightened sense of personal respon-sibility for their physical and social condition.

The GDIC hires local residents to staff its talleres since it is they who are most familiar with the area's problems and social mechanisms for dealing with them. This strategy has proven successful in community welfare projects in developing countries around the world and is described by Michael Moore (working in Taiwan) as enmeshment: "Staff are so much part of local society that they can neither escape uncomfortable censure if they are seen to be conspicuously performing poorly, nor ignore representations made to them by members" (1989:1742). Since the resident staff of the talleres usually have little prior knowledge of development strategies and management, they receive "capacitation" training courses from the GDIC. One of the goals of these courses is to equip new employees with strategies for responding to the specific demands of their communities in a manner that sustains the wider objectives and integrity of the GDIC. Following their training, employees are expected to actively contribute to the planning of projects that promote the welfare of their communities. "The bottom line," says the GDIC's former director Gina Rey, "is that local development initiatives must come from the base and not be imposed from outside the neighborhood" (interview, 25 March 2002). The GDIC's sensitivity to neighborhood issues is reflected in a survey conducted by its taller in the neighborhood of Atarés in 2001, a translation of which is provided on page 81. While the full range of GDIC projects cannot be discussed here, an example from the Popular Council of Atarés offers insight into the process of public-private relationship building in Havana.

Atarés is located in the municipality of El Cerro, which, despite its proximity to Old Havana, has not attracted any significant tourism of its own. Although it was not officially recognized as a metropolitan district until 1856, it originated in the mid-eighteenth century as a residential settlement for low-income workers from nearby cigar factories and the Havana docks (Buscarón Ochoa et al. 1996:3). Still bearing its marginal reputation, Atarés measures only 0.3 km square but houses more than 12,500 people (predominantly Afro-Cuban), and the already cramped living conditions are worsened by a high incidence of physical decay (Dilla Alfonso et al. 1999:104). In 1999 official unemployment stood at 11 percent, much higher than most surrounding districts, but the majority of residents—even those who are officially employed—earn the mainstay of their income through small-scale, unregulated trade and exchange.

The objective of this survey is to know the social problems of your block, and in this way achieve better preventative social work based on reliable details that describe the reality that our neighbors live in.

We hope for and need your cooperation and assistance, thank you.

GENERAL DETAILS:

Circumscription _____ CDR no _____ Block _____

Delegation _____ Block (street address) _____

1. What are the social problems that disrupt your block?
2. Are there children lacking attention from their families? Yes_____ No___
   If so, how many? ___ If possible write their first and last names _____
3. Are there young people between 16 and 24 years who neither study nor work?
   Yes ___ No ___ How many?___
   a) If so, can you say why? ___
   b) If possible write their names and last names ___
4. Are there women who don't work? How many? ___
   Are there men who don't work? How many? ___
5. Are there prostitutes? Yes ___ No ___ How many? ___
   Are there pimps? Yes ___ No ___ How many? ___
6. Are there families with social indiscipline? Yes ___ No ___ How many? ___
7. Note any other details you consider important.

Note: Write responses on the back if necessary.

According to Gina Rey, the GDIC's former director, a University of Havana study found that Atarés harbors a tremendous capacity for economic growth through small industrial activities. This potential for financial self-sufficiency, she explained, is based on strong social solidarity among local residents and could significantly reduce the demand Atarés places on the city's already insufficient resources:

Many residents of Atarés don't even like to leave the neighborhood because of the strong networks of support, friendship, and kinship that exists there. Some of these people are influential informal leaders in their community, often through the black market economy and religion, but many have no formal education. People that are more formally educated tend to be more upwardly mobile and likely to leave Atarés, either to return at the end of the workday or not at all. The result is a very strong web of informal community networks and ties in the neighborhood.

To bring people into legal employment it's logical to create local jobs and work centers. We've tried to do this with a ceramics workshop that produces goods for local consumption, like religious statues and objects, which have high demand in Atarés. The effect of employing people—especially single mothers—in this way is extremely positive since, otherwise, these folks may devote their energy to informal activities that are destructive. In the worst cases this means selling stolen goods, using drugs, and resorting to prostitution.

Now, you'd think small economic initiatives like pottery production are something the state would support. But it doesn't. Why? It has to do with insecurity about local autonomy, especially economic self-sufficiency. For the state, everything must go through the ministries' vertical power structures that are centrally directed. These local economic initiatives are seen as a threat to the system. Also, new initiatives require start-up resources that the state is expected to, but often can't, provide. It seems to me that insecurity about neighborhood initiatives is an outdated way of thinking in a context where local economies can actually take care of themselves through small projects like this.

The state company, Industria Local, which is responsible for monitoring and promoting local production of goods, has not viewed the initiatives in Atarés at all favorably. It sees them the same way it saw a ceramics workshop in San Miguel de Padrón—also set up to stimulate the local economy—which it recently shut down. The company's objectives simply do not include the creation of locally self-sufficient employment. This, of course, goes totally against the goals of NGOs like Norwegian People's Aid, which helped finance the Atarés ceramics workshop with the hope that the project would become self-sufficient, keeping the money inside the neighborhood.

We saw a similar process in Atarés in the early 1990s with a foreign donation of portable cement building-block machines, which were extremely helpful in construction projects because they could operate right there at the site of work. But the state didn't want local—uncontrolled—production of anything, so it took the machines away and put them in a large factory to centralize the production of materials for the entire mu-

{ A view from Old Havana toward the Cove of Atarés (Ensenada de Atarés),
{ March 2002. Photo by the author.

nicipality. It would have been so much more effective to leave the machines on site and use them for specific projects instead of macro objectives. (Interview, 25 March 2002)

The issue of centralized administration of locally generated income has emerged as a key area of contention since the early 1990s. A position that is gaining support among Havana's urban planners is for moderate reform that would allow municipal governments to manage the incomes of their respective territories at varying rates, depending on their needs and potentials for growth. Increased administrative autonomy of municipalities and popular councils seems to make sense given the recent growth of neighborhood self-help initiatives across Cuba, and particularly in Havana (Dilla Alfonso et al. 1999). Miren Uriarte reports 170 officially registered community-based projects operating in Havana in 2001, and there are no doubt many more operating unofficially (2001:iv).

Community initiatives have emerged with agendas ranging from environmental care programs to self-esteem support groups for women, and they are usually organized informally rather than through traditional vertical channels. While many neighborhood organizations have related themselves cooperatively with local governments, they have faced a series of difficulties arising from bureaucratic impediments to autonomous management. As with the popular councils, inadequate control of resources has been a major obstacle to their development. Nevertheless, the desire of grassroots associations to be directly involved in the planning and development of their localities has been increasingly voiced in the public accountability (*rendición de cuenta*) street forums held regularly by locally elected officials of Havana's municipal assemblies (Fernández Soriano 1999:180).

A SNAPSHOT OF INFORMAL ECONOMY IN ATARÉS

Sitting with a friend in the front room of his mother's two-room house in Atarés, I've come to expect the constant flow of visitors. Though they come in and sit down and chat and tell jokes, they have economic as well as social objectives. The men and women of all ages arrive with coffee, beer, chicken, eggs, bread, and other items that they sell at a lower price than the [national] peso shops, if the peso shops have these items at all. Some informal merchants go door to door, while others sell to passers-by along the main road, calle Monte, which connects Atarés to Old Havana. It takes about half an hour to walk to Atarés along Monte from the Capitol building in Old Havana, where most of the shops only sell in dollars. About half way to Atarés the dollar shops become more sporadic as the national money shops—often with nothing on their shelves—become more common. Approaching Atarés even the peso shops seem to fizzle out, replaced by men and women sitting on the floor with sheets or blankets laid down in front of them, covered with cassette tapes, notebooks, underwear, and other merchandise, ready to be bundled up instantly should a policeman or inspector come along. Other merchants work in couples: one stands alert with a bag full of T-shirts, beer, or soap, while the other approaches potential customers with two or three items in hand, less likely to attract attention than if carrying the bag.

A friend told me how her uncle makes a living in Atarés. Working at the shoe factory only pays 240 pesos (U.S. $9) a month. The shoes are made for sale in national money, but Jorge has an arrangement with the security guards to let him take two boxes (of 20 pairs of shoes each) home with him per month if he smuggles out a third box, which he gives to the guards. He takes the shoes to the dollar stores on Calle Monte and makes a deal with the person at the counter: they can sell the shoes for whatever they want if

Jorge gets U.S. $10 per pair. If the manager finds out then it's up to the counter staff to give the manager a cut of their profit.

—Havana, February 2002

Recent studies indicate that a wide range of Atarés residents participate in religions of African origin, particularly Santería, Palo Monte, and Abakuá (Barbon Díaz 2000:10, Nuñez González 1997:5). This does not necessarily reflect the wider trend of religious growth in Cuba over the past decade reported by Chauvin (1997:10), Eckstein (1994:122), Olshan (1997:10), Ramírez Calzadilla (2000:137–138, 192–193), Wall (1997:579), and others, but it may indicate a more visible and public form of participation in a variety of religions—particularly those of African origin—since the decision of the Fourth Congress of the Cuban Communist Party in 1991 to open party membership to religious believers (Rogelio Martinez Furé, interview, 11 May 2002; Miguel Barnet, interview, 27 March 2002; Castro Flores 2001:56). It is likely that this political opening and the wider trend of religious growth have reinforced each other, with the result that religious organizations, particularly those that are able to establish connections with official institutions, currently enjoy a capacity for civic action unknown in Cuba for over four decades or, in the case of Afro-Cuban religions, ever.

Foreign interest in Afro-Cuban religious folklore has also grown since the early 1990s, resulting in a number of initiatives in Atarés designed to take advantage of emerging economic opportunities. One institution that has shown enthusiasm for these kinds of projects is the Anthropology Center of Atarés, administered by the Department of Ethnology of the Ministry of Science, Technology, and Environment. In the early 1990s the Anthropology Center's team of researchers conducted a series of pioneering studies into racial relations in urban zones of Havana, the results of which remain largely unpublished. One of these studies, conducted in 1996, resulted in the design of a project that proposed to draw foreign tourists from Old Havana to an existing temple of Santería in Atarés. With the official objectives of generating employment and reinforcing a local sense of identity, the proposed project would renovate the house of the Herrera sisters, who were recognized as important figures in the development of the esteemed carnival group Los Marqueses de Atarés, founded by their father in 1937 (Nuñez González 1997:4). Based on the research of the Anthropology Center in 1994 and 1995, the resulting "ethnographic museum" would display ceremonial Santería objects and operate as a market for the sale of religious dolls, paintings, and cuisine. Folkloric performance would also play an important role. The museum's centerpiece was to be an altar to the Virgin of Las Mercedes, the biggest in Atarés, on whose feast day, 23 September, a sizeable congregation had gathered for years to worship the Santería deity Obatalá, who is often compared to—and is visually represented as—the Catholic Virgen de las Mercedes.

The Anthropology Center intended to sustain the house as a bona fide temple of religious observance even while selling entry to tourists. The project would not have been the first to bring the sacred and profane together in Atarés; in fact, the staff of the Anthropology Center cited examples of other nearby religious shrines that were catering to tourists interested in Afro-Cuban folklore. The proposal even speculated that resistance to the project from the local religious practitioners would be unlikely because most devotees of Santería in Atarés were becoming accustomed to foreign voyeurs (Nuñez González 1997:5).

For a number of reasons the center never became a reality. Some locals point out that the house had a reputation as a hub of black market activity and for taking advantage of foreigners, which at one point had led to the incarceration of one of its residents. This did not help the project's prospects, since to be legally viable it would need to be a secure location for tourists. Reflecting on the failure of the proposal, its writer speculated that neither the popular council nor the municipal government of El Cerro could convince the city government to pay the estimated U.S. $2,500 price tag. Furthermore, since the house was not linked to any official Cuban institution it could not legally accept foreign donations.

With all other options exhausted, the researcher took the project to the GDIC's Taller of Atarés, but the taller already had its hands full developing a similar project, also in conjunction with the Anthropology Center. The following case study describes that project and offers insight into the process of public-private relationship building in Havana. The project demonstrates how a commercial embrace of tourism can obscure a project's commitment to community welfare, but also how nonstate actors and institutional authorities can collaborate to protect neighborhood interests.

Case Study 1: The Munanso Tutuka Ensasi Cultural Center of Atarés

One of the GDIC's first talleres was set up in Atarés in 1988. Among its initial projects was building a working relationship with Francisco "Tato" Castañeda, an influential priest of Palo Monte and Santería, whose house was operating as an important temple for the congregation of locals. The GDIC intended to influence the temple's extensive religious community by asking the priest to distribute antidrug information and to encourage people to work as volunteers in construction projects and the maintenance of local clinics and schools. Living in the neighborhood, the taller's director recognized that the temple had significant social influence in Atarés and that it was already involved in the welfare of its larger community. Its engagement with community interests reflected Santería's practical, hands-on orientation to the social and material challenges of daily life (Brandon 1993:103, Cros Sandoval 1979, Pedraza 1998:25).

Santería encourages its followers to take heed of lessons conveyed through sacred stories that describe the adventures and exploits of supernatural figures called orichas (Ramos Bravo 1999:63). These figures serve as mythical role models, whose actions demonstrate the importance of social cooperation, interdependence, honesty, and respect for elders.[5] A favorite parable of many Santeros concerns the two warrior saints Ogún and Ochoosi. Although the two are considered brothers, the story recounts how fierce sibling rivalry exacerbated the personal shortcomings of each. Ochoosi, an unparalleled archer who never missed a target, frequently lost track of his prey because of his inability to move quickly through the forest undergrowth. Conversely, Ogún was hopeless with the bow and arrow but an expert with the machete, enabling him to cut a swift path through even the most dense vegetation. It was only when their village fell on hard times that the brothers put personal differences aside and agreed to cooperate, benefiting not only themselves but the entire community through their unique combination of talents. In Atarés, where voluntary participation and cooperation in community life bring significant social and material rewards, such stories play an important role in framing the logic of decentralized neighborhood self-help initiatives. As Liudmila Ramos Bravo puts it, "We can affirm that the values present in Santería and those formed by the Revolution do not contradict, but rather reflect each other" (1999:63). In 1988 the taller of Atarés set out to identify where its goals overlapped with religious values present in the neighborhood and proposed to build the project with the temple accordingly.

The project was one of the first instances of direct official collaboration between a state development agency and a grassroots Afro-Cuban religious community, and Fidel Castro himself came to meet the priest to mark the collaboration's significance. As a first step toward popular education the GDIC renovated and painted the entire temple-house on the condition that its residents (the priest, his wife, and granddaughter) work with the Atarés Anthropology Center to turn the living room into a public museum to display ceremonial objects of Santería to local and foreign visitors. Religious music and dance performances by the priest's granddaughter, Freila, became a feature of the exhibition. In 1993 the temple became the Munanso Tutuka Ensasi Cultural Center (referring to a deity of the religion Palo Monte, who is often compared to the Santería deity Changó and depicted as the Catholic Saint Barbara). In conjunction with the Anthropology Center, a number of documentaries about Afro-Cuban religions were filmed at the house, and the esteemed Cuban anthropologist Natalia Bolívar Aróstegui and colleague Carmen González Diaz de Villegas based portions of their study of Palo Monte, *Ta Makuende Yaya y las Reglas de Palo Monte* (1998), on the Atarés temple.[6]

Soon, regular tours of the neighborhood, featuring a stop at the temple, were being conducted by the taller to show foreign visitors an example of participatory, decentralized community development. As expected, many visitors were impressed by the tour and some started to leave donations. Before long, NGOs such as Oxfam, Global Exchange, Norwegian People's Aid, and the Australian Conservation Foundation also began to express interest and some donated money to the taller for its community work. The temple was very successful in its role as a feature of the neighborhood tour, so much so that its museum alter ego and performance work for foreigners became the focus of its relationship with the taller. While it continued to operate as a focal point for the religious activity of locals, its capacity for building links between the taller and the larger community were left undeveloped, as were its potential activities in drug prevention and social welfare.

But Freila, the priest's granddaughter, was not satisfied with the folklorization of the temple, which in her opinion did not bring any significant benefits to the community. Following the death of her grandfather in late 2001, she became the project's director and started to refocus the temple on its original goals. To promote its wider social capacity she started to organize activities at the temple-cum-cultural center, such as recreation days for neighborhood children, religious education for locals interested in Santería, and, through her religious contacts, public conferences on natural medicine, community health, and other neighborhood issues. Freila continued her work with the taller as the cultural center's guide, but she developed these community activities of her own accord. This required a level of understanding and trust with the taller, which was neither obliged nor authorized to approve the establishment of these independent initiatives, however much

Francisco "Tato" Castañena, the priest of the Atarés temple, presented by Antonio Castañeda (president of the Asociación Cultural Yorubá), meeting Fidel Castro. Courtesy of the Munanso Tutuka Ensasi Cultural Center and Freila de la Caridad Merencio-Blanco.

they reflected the project's original mandate. Freila clearly appreciated the taller's willingness to "look the other way":

> Even though the taller isn't run directly by the government, it still has to do what he orders [as is customary in Cuba, while saying the word "he," Freila traced out the shape of a long imaginary beard extending from her chin, leaving no doubt about "his" identity]. What preoccupies me is that the taller has been ordered to make money, which is why it has started this folklore-development-tourism project with us. But you see we can't just think about economics. Our community is more than its economy. . . .
>
> We work with the taller because it's an organization that has a positive influence in the neighborhood. The people who work there understand what I'm trying to do even though I'm doing it without a license. Actually I'm hoping the taller will give me the materials I need to expand the center and build a second story on top of the the casa-templo [temple-house], where my ahijados [Santería godchildren] can stay during their ceremonies. (Interview, 29 June 2001)

Together with Freila's commitment to her community and her independent spirit, the taller's initial involvement in project design and the resulting official relationship gave the temple a legal legitimacy and security that was crucial to its later achievements. Without this affiliation with a state institution such a project would be closely monitored and susceptible to centralized managerial regulations, which in this case would be enforced by the Ministry of Culture. The project's accomplishments thus resulted from the productive interdependence of the temple and the taller, for it was this cooperative relationship that solidified its capacity for social action. While the taller's commercial objectives differed significantly from Freila's, the project brought these objectives together into strategic collaboration for the benefit of the state, the residents of the temple-house, and the wider community.

It is likely that Freila's ongoing work as a tour guide for the GDIC earned her a measure of administrative freedom to pursue her larger goals and that, conversely, her propensity for creativity and relationship building influenced her decision to continue serving the GDIC. The project benefited from its official connection to the GDIC, but it also benefited from a variety of informal understandings between Freila, her community, and the taller. Her discomfort with the project's folkloric orientation provoked Freila to develop its wider social potential together with the participation of her religious support network. Her unofficial influence also extended into the taller, which afforded Freila sufficient space to pursue her wider objectives by quietly approving her recreation and education initiatives. Ultimately the combination of these official and unofficial inputs yielded productive results.

Old Havana and the Office of the Historian

While tourism has yet to expand in earnest in Atarés, quite the opposite is true of the municipality of Old Havana, which, with approximately 102,831 residents packed into 4.4 km square is, like Atarés, one of the city's most densely populated zones (UNOPS 2001:4). Attracted by its colonial and early-twentieth-century architecture, foreign visitors are awed by the crumbling edifices and then, coming face to face with their tenants, get invited for coffee into cramped apartments that often have no running water and leak gas from rusted pipes. In 1994 the Cuban government created the tourist agency Habaguanex, which is administered by the Office of the Historian of the City, to reinvest profits from Old Havana tourism into the municipality's neglected infrastructure.

Dr. Eusebio Leal is the Office of the Historian's director and Old Havana's equivalent of mayor. An accomplished writer of poetry and researcher of Latin American history, he argues that tourism has been an important characteristic of the city for centuries. While the Office's rapid construction of hotels, entertainment venues, and shops that operate exclusively in U.S. dollars is resented by many locals, who get paid in Cuban pesos, he views these developments as "a recuperation of the capacities the city has historically enjoyed. It's very hard to create ways for foreigners and Cubans to mix in clean, healthy environments. Most Cubans really do want genuine cultural interchange, and we're looking for ways to promote this . . . We're trying to preserve schools and houses, create jobs and encourage true participation, for which we've created dynamic fiscal structures that allow reinvestment of profits in the historic center" (interview, 29 April 2002). Following the 1993 collapse of the *Colegio del Santo Angel* (an eighteenth-century merchant's house recognized by UNESCO as a World Heritage Site), Dr. Leal exercised extraordinary diplomatic skill in arranging the implementation of these fiscal structures through Decree Law 143, making the Office of the Historian the only state institution in Cuba able to control spending, profits, and general economic management at the municipal scale (Hill 2007:59).[7] Autonomous financial management liberates the Office of the Historian from the orthodox economic model that requires other municipalities to surrender their incomes to centrally governed ministries, which budget according to national, rather than municipal, priorities. It is a move toward decentralized administration of resources that many progressive Cuban politicians and social commentators would like to see applied to their own municipalities, notwithstanding the diversification of living standards—Old Havana is a case in point—that this implies.

Like the GDIC, the Office of the Historian has a variety of strategies for encouraging the participation of local residents in development initiatives. According to Manuel Coipel, a sociologist at the Office of the Historian, there are two main approaches: collaborative assistance to preexisting, self-directed community projects, and the creation of new projects in consultation with Old Havana residents (interview, 2 April 2002). For the latter scheme the Office of the Historian holds public meetings in each of Havana's seven districts (the popular councils), at which local residents and community leaders identify neighborhood problems and suggest solutions, a method of participation that follows the model of the public accountability (*rendición de cuenta*) meetings held by locally elected members of the city's municipal assemblies. Neighborhood needs and project plans are drawn up on a street-by-street "map of risks and resources" and the most useful, cost-effective projects are selected for implementation (Rosendo Mesias, co-ordinator of the United Nations Program for Local Human Development [PDHL] in Havana, interview, 27 February 2002). The Office of the Historian's finances for this work come from profits earned by state businesses in Old Havana, joint ventures with foreign investors (the state retains owner-ship of at least 51 percent of any such enterprise), and from the United Nations Development Program, which since September 1998 has brought into effect a multilateral matching-funds scheme through the PDHL that by 2003 had contributed over U.S. $8,500,000 to projects on the island (UNOPS 2003).

Described below are two recent projects in Old Havana that developed collaborative links between Afro-Cuban religious communities and the Office of the Historian. Both projects strove to balance commitments to their respective communities with opportunities for commercial growth from tourism. Interestingly, the first case shows how a project became focused on tourism on the advice of the Office of the Historian, whereas the second shows how the Office of the Historian pressured a project to refocus on its community when it perceived a growing unregulated market for tourists as socially destructive.

Case Study 2: The House of Okan Oddara

In the Old Havana Popular Council of San Isidro, which houses 11,556 people in forty-two city blocks, the Office of the Historian established a community center in 1995 to build links with the local community and its informal leaders (TRIBSI 2001a:1). The strong influence of Santería in the neighborhood soon became apparent as the center identified a number of emerging grassroots initiatives based on natural medicine, cuisine, art, and performance of religious folklore. One such project, the House of Okan Oddara (Yoruba for "Noble Heart"), was founded by a San Isidro Santero, Felipe, in the communal space outside his tenement house apartment in November 1999. Concerned about growing social delinquency among local youth, he developed a cooperative project with a nearby elderly gardener so that neighborhood children tended the garden in return for vegetables that Felipe taught them to cook and prepare in traditional Afro-Cuban recipes. He also identified certain medicinal plants in the garden linked to the prac-tice of Santería and taught his young recruits about their religious properties and uses. In this way, Felipe sought to stimulate the children's creativity, constructively occupy their free time, and introduce them to the moral teachings and social values of Santería. The project attracted much local interest and soon expanded to include a neighborhood waste-recycling project, painting workshops, and musical rehearsals, all of which were discussed and presented—still without any official support—at a weekly community arts festival. The festival drew the attention of local artists and artisans, who began to display photography and sculptures for the appreciation of the community and for small bartering and trading in national currency.

While neighborhood enthusiasm for the weekly festival abounded, its organizers felt that to maintain it they would need to improve the house's conditions. Lighting inside and outside the space was needed, as were kitchen implements, paper and crayons for the art workshops, musical instruments, a sound-mixing board with a microphone and loudspeakers, and a hydraulic motor with pipes to give the building running water. In late 2000 Felipe made contact with the Office of the Historian's San Isidro community center, with which he worked on a formal proposal to the Office of the Historian requesting funds or, if none were available, then a license that would legally recognize the project and permit it to generate its own funds. Along with a description of the project's history, activities, and objectives, the proposal also included a "code of principles to guide our steps into the future, ensuring that our initial motivations remain true and guarded" (TRIBSI 2001b:7).

The code of principles confirmed the project's commitment to the social and environmental needs of the community and recognized neighborhood solidarity as the project's most valuable source of inspiration and guidance. Furthermore, it stated that any income earned through self-financing—whether Cuban pesos or U.S. dollars—would be reinvested in the improvement of the project's physical conditions and operational capacities. But in its attempt to gain official endorsement, the code of principles also made a significant departure from the project's original goals. Principle number 5, for example, stated that "the cultural space, devoted to the project, will not be used except for the artistic promotion of local performers." Meanwhile, no mention was made of community knowledge about natural medicine, cuisine, the promotion of local artisans, and education about social values. The proposal was worded this way on the advice of the Office of the Historian's neighborhood community center because the project's chances for funding would improve if it showed promise as a tourist attraction. According to an Office of the Historian employee, the Okan Oddara project needed to "professionalize" before receiving any sort of license or official patronage.

Felipe took up the challenge of "professionalization" enthusiastically, so that by April 2002 his group of young performers was rehearsing dances of Afro-Cuban folklore daily. In line with principle number 5, they became the focus of the weekly festival, both because of their growing artistic proficiency and because, under the gaze of the Office of the Historian's San Isidro community center, the prohibition of unlicensed vending (even to locals) discouraged the participation of neighborhood artisans. As the House of Okan Oddara focused itself on the goal of folkloric performances for tourists, the project was not able to maintain its original community-based activities. This was the situation in May 2002, and Felipe believed that until the project's security was guaranteed through a license for independent management or through funding from the Office of the Historian, it would remain exclusively committed to "artistic professionalization." According to an employee of the San Isidro community center, if the project ever managed to enter an officially subsidized relationship with the Office of the Historian, the community center would oversee the revival of the gardening activities and expand the House of Okan Oddara project to once again involve the wider San Isidro community. Such a collaborative relationship would give the project the stability and confidence necessary to refocus on its original neighborhood welfare ambitions.

The case of Okan Oddara suggests that a particularly challenging phase in the maturation of such projects is the establishment of a consensual legal framework for reconciling state and community interests. By reaching out to the San Isidro community center, Felipe opened potential avenues for acquiring new resources, but simultaneously compromised his project's autonomous humanitarian focus through a commitment to artistic "professionalization." Both Felipe and the community center staff aspired to revive the project's social welfare activities, though in a form that incorporated these into the economic agenda of the Office of the Historian. While the House of Okan Oddara appeared to be traveling gradually along a path toward legal recognition and community participation, an effective integration of state and nonstate inputs was still some distance away.

Case Study 3: The Peña of Catedral

In early 1999 a group of elected representatives of the Old Havana Popular Council of Catedral, together with officials from the Office of the Historian, approached a family living in a local solar (or tenement house, where a number of families live together in small adjoining units) and asked it to start a weekly *peña* (public performance) of Afro-Cuban folkloric music and to participate in a neighborhood health education campaign. The family was well known in religious circles because its mother, Felicia Alfonso, was a powerful Santera with many ahijados (godchildren) and her two resident sons were practicing priests of Ifá. She was also the street's Committee for the Defense of the Revolution (Comité de Defensa de la Revolución, or CDR) representative, making her a woman with an unusually wide range of friends and contacts.[8] One of Felicia's sons, Miki, had been trained in the ritual music of Santería and rumba by the renowned Pancho Quinto, with whom he had toured in South America. Through Pancho Quinto, Miki came to own a set of consecrated batá drums, which he and his group were frequently invited to play at the ceremonial celebrations of Felicia's extended religious family. These religious affiliations gave the weekly peña a wide base of popular support, and it wasn't long before it expanded to involve numerous local residents, musicians, and Santeros.

Neighborhood parents started bringing their children to Miki during the week for music lessons so that they too might participate in the weekly gathering. With Miki the children started to learn about the place of music in Afro-Cuban religions and the social and moral values that underpin each of the deities of Santería (orichas) and their songs. According to Felicia:

Our peña is one of the only opportunities in Old Havana for locals to come together to enjoy music for free and buy mojitos [cocktails] for three pesos [about 15 U.S. cents]. These days it has become hard for Cubans to enjoy themselves in Old Havana because, with the increase of tourism, most things are sold in dollars: like mojitos, which cost three U.S. dollars in public bars. The popular council asked us to provide recreation for locals, which we're doing, and they've also asked us through the CDR to distribute pamphlets to the population about healthy living and the threat of AIDS.

When I moved into the solar in December 2000 the peña was officially operating in line with Felicia's objectives, but news of the weekly performance had started to circulate among the growing number of foreign visitors eager to get off the tour buses and mix more closely with locals. To accommodate them, unlicensed tour guides, commonly called *jineteros*, or "riders," for their skillful manipulation of tourists and their dollars, started making the peña a regular port of call.

The eight families residing in the tenement house had already been selling home-made pastries, potato chips, and rum mojitos for small prices in

The babalawo Miki Alfonso's neighborhood students dressed as the deities (orichas) of Santería. Photo by the author.

national currency to Cuban spectators, but when tourists started to come regularly a dual economy emerged whereby foreigners were charged a one–U.S. dollar entrance fee and sold refreshments at inflated prices. One resident, who had a telephone in her apartment, made it available at a dollar per call and she charged the same for the use of her bathroom. Video recordings were permitted at a negotiated rate, and soon it was common to see local women leaving hand-in-hand with foreign men, who often appeared to be twice their age. Complications started to arise when jineteros began to demand commissions, and on several occasions the police intervened in some drug-related disputes. By January 2002 the peña was a long way from its original goals: it was no longer a space solely for the recreation of locals, and the social values promoted by the health education pamphlets and Miki's classes for children were being visibly undermined.

These developments did not go unnoticed at the popular council and the Office of the Historian. When I interviewed one of the Office of the Historian's sociologists about the peña, he mentioned that these kinds of problems significantly damage a community group's chances of receiving a license for legal operation and for building collaborative relationships with government institutions. Without such official support a project not only becomes incapable of growth, it becomes susceptible to closure. The peña's organizers received the same message through the CDR, which called twenty-one of its neighborhood leaders to a meeting at the solar to discuss the issue and formulate a plan of action. As both CDR representative and organizer of the peña, Felicia assumed responsibility of reforming the weekly gathering.

Living in Felicia's house, I learned that the peña's political ties extended far beyond the CDR. One of the many Santería godsons of Felicia worked in the popular council, giving him three important resources: up-to-date information about the peña's official standing, access to a computer and a printer, and direct contact with the local delegate. Furthermore, a number of the peña's musicians, also connected to the solar through religious kinship, were well-established members of the National Union of Cuban Writers and Artists (Unión Nacional de Escritores y Artistas Cubanos, or UNEAC). These connections were activated in tandem: a proposal was written up by Felicia and her sons, edited and printed out by her godson at the Popular Council, and presented to both a UNEAC projects committee and the delegate of the popular council. The proposal emphasized the peña's commitment to three activities: the creation of a much-needed recreational space for local residents, the instruction of neighborhood children in music and social values, and community education about health issues through the distribution of health education pamphlets and public lectures.

Felicia and her family hoped that the proposal would be passed on to the Office of the Historian, where it might secure a license for the peña to legally generate income and earn the solar a new plumbing system. A meeting with representatives of the Office of the Historian in April 2002 revealed that the peña would be supported so long as its "safety and legality" were maintained. In the meantime, the Office of the Historian and the popular council would wait and see if the peña honored the commitments of its proposal. The same message came to Felicia through the CDR, further motivating her to clean up the weekly gathering. From now on, no more known jineteros would be allowed in, nor women known to go "fishing" for foreign men. Those suspected of selling marijuana or other drugs were banned, as was the sale of telephone calls to foreigners. Interestingly, dancing in the style of *abakuá* (a semireligious brotherhood with ethnic links to southeast Nigeria) was also banned because of abakuá's reputation for encouraging machismo, pride, and generally hot-blooded behavior (or *guapería*). The surreptitious sale of mojitos and other refreshments continued, though moderation was enforced through selective service, and, to the disappointment of many, dilution with water.

The author saluting the Santería deity Elegguá at the Peña de Catedral, Old Havana, 2002.

A number of public activities organized through Felicia's religious connections further aided the peña's makeover. First, she was interviewed on Radio Havana about the importance of "rescuing traditions" and presenting them to the local and foreign public in a safe environment, and then a television documentary on traditional music was filmed. It featured Miki's band and was broadcast around Cuba and on Cubana Airlines flights arriving in Havana. Within a week of the radio broadcast, a local artist with religious ties to Miki painted murals of Santería icons on the inside and outside walls of the solar, helping the house get the cover story of the Ministry of Culture's glossy *Salsa* magazine in May 2002.

These activities made the peña widely visible to Cubans and foreigners and, along with the reforms promised in the proposal, saved it from being shut down by the Office of the Historian. This threat of closure and, conversely, the Office of the Historian's capacity to provide material assistance, clearly motivated the peña's reformation. The project's rebirth, though, resulted not only from state intervention but also from Felicia's personal efforts, which drew significant strength from her grassroots network of religious allegiance. The diverse individuals who came together in this collaboration were united, despite their distinct aspirations and objectives, by a common desire see the peña survive.

Project Summaries and Conclusions

The three projects discussed in this chapter presented valuable opportunities for the GDIC and the Office of the Historian to involve high-risk communities in activities ranging from health education to the construction of schools and clinics. But the path toward participatory collaboration between the government development agencies, the projects, and their wider communities was obstructed when commercial opportunities from tourism were given higher priority than neighborhood interests. In Atarés the GDIC's taller worked with the religious temple on an innovative plan to build community support for its antidrug and other social programs. But the plan was sidelined when the temple proved successful as a folklore museum for the enjoyment of "folklore-development tourists," helping the GDIC to acquire much-needed foreign donations. However, taking advantage of the temple's official affiliation with the GDIC, the granddaughter of the late project director worked through informal channels to recommit the temple to the original goals it developed with the taller.

Meanwhile, the House of Okan Oddara, while noble in its original plans to educate neighborhood youth about gardening, natural medicine, social values and art, had to streamline these activities in hope of an official contract with the Office of the Historian that prioritized folkloric dance performances as a potential source of revenue from tourism. According to its directors, the project would remain focused on this activity until achieving the formal support of the Office of the Historian or a license to generate profits from small trading. Either result would tighten its relationship with the San Isidro community center and give it the stability and confidence to reactivate its community-based activities.

Finally, the peña of Catedral also neglected its original commitments to community education and neighborhood recreation when tourism brought opportunities for a small, unregulated marketplace that soon escalated to involve drugs and prostitution. In such a context, pamphlets about healthy lifestyle choices and the religious education of local children were tragically undermined. Clearly the illicit nature of the peña's informal economy—both socially destructive and financially covert—was the key reason for its problems with the Office of the Historian and the popular council. Ultimately, the threat of closure and the possibility of assistance from the Office of the Historian led the peña to recommit to its original social goals and reform its approach to tourism.

The revival of the temple of Atarés and the peña of Catedral resulted from functioning, if not always smooth, collaborative relationships between state institutions and nonstate actors. Although the peña's reformation was motivated by the Office of the Historian's power to shut it down, the state's contribution to these initiatives was not only regulatory. Government participation was just as important in the original design of both projects and their subsequent legitimacy, as it was in the physical maintenance of the temple of Atarés. The state thus played an indispensable collaborative role in the temple and the peña, which may have never developed their community welfare potentials without official intervention.

According to Eusebio Leal, balancing community and commercial interests has become central challenge in the development of Old Havana:

Tourism is here to stay, and it will increase a hundredfold when the blockade is abolished. North Americans want to come here because we have something they don't: art, architecture, and historic traditions all within Old Havana. . . . Economically, I calculate that for every one Cuban employed in tourism, ten people live. The point is to use tourism as a mechanism for development, which other countries have demonstrated is possible. That said, we reject the idea of turning our historical center into a theme park and novelty show; instead we work to improve schools, living conditions, participation, and jobs. (Interview, 29 April 2002)

The three cases examined in this chapter demonstrate some of the complexities of this plan and indicate the often unacknowledged importance of "informal" religions in shaping the public-private collaborations that are proving central to its unfolding. Each of the initiatives discussed above was already functioning as a hub of religious activity before developing collaborative links with the government's urban development institutions, and the official projects that eventually resulted from these links were largely based on harnessing the social capital infused in preexisting religious kinship networks. The subordination of humanitarian project goals to a more narrow focus on folkloric performance illustrates the powerful financial appeal of the tourism industry, which in each case left local capacities largely untapped. But the return to more community-oriented activities such as dissemination of health and education information in case studies 1 and 3, and the strong potential of a more inclusive outcome in case study 2, suggests that community commitments and loyalties can also be powerful motivating factors.

Freila and Felicia's use of official recognition as a platform for mobilizing wider religious contacts demonstrates both the strategic utility of fluid, overlapping relationships for integrating multiple agendas, and the formidable civic potential of Afro-Cuban religions at the grassroots. Indeed, the public health presentations organized by Freila in Atarés and Felicia's promotions of the peña at the popular council and through media publicity all took advantage of interpersonal allegiances generated from religious solidarity. Clearly participation in "informal" religions in Cuba is not limited to the poor, "popular classes," but rather cuts across occupational and other socioeconomic categories into the formal sector, blurring any tidy distinction of the public and private spheres. It is remarkable that despite a lack of effective "linear" mechanisms for converting local needs into official modes of representation, overlapping circles of state and nonstate social capital, mediated by community leaders, have begun to produce relatively stable channels of vertical collaboration. Indeed, the formation of semiofficial projects like these is a good example of how nonstate sectors, in collaboration with local officials, have begun to carve out new spaces of civic participation from the bottom up.

For the central state this kind of engagement with the population not only channels local energy into official projects but, equally important, lends credibility to its claim of stewardship over civil society. The next chapter will consider this claim, particularly in light of state interactions with foreign NGOs, which are growing in number and influence in Cuba. While governments in socialist and postsocialist settings harbor a unique capacity to bring about favorable conditions for popular participation in voluntary civic initiatives (M. Howard 2002:168), foreign NGOs in Cuba and elsewhere have often not recognized this potential. A key problem in the Cuban context, I will argue, is the way the term "civil society" is defined and operationalized, for, as Jorge luis Acanda González puts it, "within civil society is where the destiny of our revolution is at stake" (2003:8).

3

SUSTAINABLE SOVEREIGNTY:
INTERNATIONAL NGOs
AND CIVIL SOCIETY IN CUBA

The economic revitalization programs discussed in the previous chapters rely in large part on foreign financing and development aid from international NGOs. A recent United Nations document identifies over two thousand functioning Cuban–foreign NGO collaborations (UN 2000:9), and considering the attempts of the Cuban government to reinsert the island into the world market, the frequency and depth of foreign development initiatives and commercial activities are bound to increase. Cuba differs from other emerging economies in the extent to which the central government maintains an active role in regulating the flow of resources and avenues of collaboration both domestically and internationally. Foreign investors are permitted no more than a 49-percent share in commercial joint ventures, and international development agencies are subjected to the meticulous background investigations and constant scrutiny of the Ministry of Foreign Investment and Economic Collaboration (MINVEC). They are also required to work closely with state-affiliated partner organizations, ranging from centrally governed ministries to local NGOs, which often limit collaborative development activities to a slate of predesigned projects.

A high level of legal regulation has enabled the Cuban state to coordinate the efforts of international development agencies more strictly than authorities in postsocialist Eastern Europe, where service duplication and a lack of interagency communication have slowed the formation of nationally and regionally integrated strategies for economic recovery and social development (Economist 2000:26, Ishkanian 2001). Nevertheless, the rapid changes of the 1990s have exposed some serious shortcomings of central planning and top-down control of resources, which have not been adequately sensitive to emerging problems at the community level, even when projects are locally designed (Fernández Soriano 1999). Working in an environment that is regulated from above to simultaneously protect national interests and promote formal sector commercial expansion, international development NGOs have faced challenges in Cuba that are becoming increasingly relevant around the world as governments in East Asia and Latin America experiment with strategies for stabilizing domestic economic environments and attracting "sticky" foreign investment (Jarvis 2004:10).

Monitoring the relationships of foreign NGOs with the Cuban state opens a useful window into the state's claim to represent national interests and maintain stewardship over civil society within its institutions and organs of popular participation (see Harnecker 1999:120). Two particularly illuminating aspects of these relationships are the negotiation of Cuban and foreign perspectives about the need of NGOs to work independently with neighborhood associations, and the process of balancing the interests of target communities with the pressing need for commercial competitiveness. By way of four case studies I will suggest that the state's claim to represent the popular foundations of civil society has been weakened by market-oriented policy objectives that tend to prioritize institutional financial viability over local needs, though the evidence also shows how social welfare at the grassroots can be enhanced through well-designed commercial initiatives.

The first case study illustrates the difficulty of arriving at a mutually acceptable framework for defining the responsibilities of foreign NGOs in relation the Cuban state and local community groups. The case shows how each of these party's priorities were addressed on paper through the goal of "building civil society," but also that the meaning each party attached this objective varied considerably. Different understandings of "civil society" resulted in funding delays so severe that the project was almost abandoned altogether.

The next three case studies focus on the challenge of reconciling state and foreign NGO approaches to balancing community welfare with commercial growth. Generating hard currency has become vital to the Castro government's political and economic legitimacy: to act with authority in development initiatives it must appear to be at least as capable, efficient, and financially viable as foreign partner organizations. The second case study shows how these priorities surfaced in the production of an Australian subsidized environmental educational magazine, whose commercialization by a Cuban state-affiliated NGO raised Australian concerns about the publication's alienation from community issues and popular readership. The third case study takes us on a visit to the Santa Ifigenia cemetery of Santiago de Cuba, revealing how its gradual transformation into a tourist attraction— with the support of foreign NGOs—has benefited state-operated tour companies but done little for the cemetery or its employees. The fourth case study involves an Italian NGO's efforts to set up a cultural center in Santiago de Cuba, and the state's somewhat distinct interest in exploring the center's commercial potentials. Interestingly, this final case study suggests that the state's commercial ambitions can support local interests by bringing new opportunities for education and employment.

Foreign NGOs and Civil Society in Cuba

Over a decade ago a detailed report by Gillian Gunn entitled *Cuba's NGOs: Government Puppets or Seeds of Civil Society?* observed that many of the Cuban organizations that refer to themselves as NGOs are in fact embedded within the administrative structure of the state, and more committed to reinforcing state authority than building truly "nongovernmental" initiatives (1995). Five years after the appearance of this report the director of Oxfam America's Cuba program, Minor Sinclair, observed the same phenomenon, though he described it not as political contradiction but rather as an "integrated approach" to state-society relations: "In broad terms, they [Cuban NGOs] have not looked to substitute or compete with the State in the delivery of services. . . . They look towards an integrated approach, by engaging the citizenry and yes, by engaging the government, in the task of development. . . . NGOs, as part of civil society, have a vital role in reverting the economic crisis" (2000:2, 8). The main difference between the two accounts is Sinclair's understanding of the Cuban NGOs, however connected they may be to the state apparatus, as "part of civil society." Thickening the plot, the Cuban sociologist Rafael Hernández then argued that alongside domestic NGOs, civil society organizations ranging from recreational groups to religious associations also have their rightful home within the state bureaucracy:

> In the case of a socialist society like Cuba, many of these organizations are found not in the private but in the state sector. This situation has led some observers—especially those who still confuse civil society with free enterprise—to jump to the conclusion that those organizations are nothing but tentacles of the state bureaucracy, divorced from civil society. The news for those given to such thinking is that in a socialist society like Cuba, the universities, professional and religious associations, community and labor organizations, and cultural and academic publications are

also spaces of civil society where the cultural and ideological variables in the equation of hegemony are daily reproduced. (2003:128, emphasis in original)

Reading these accounts one is left wondering how Cuban organizations, particularly the "nongovernmental" kind, can belong simultaneously to civil society and to the state. At the core of this problem is that the meaning of key terms seem to have undergone what Roland Barthes (1967) might call a "semiotic shift" from their original connotations. In other words, the march of time—or perhaps "dash" since the early 1990s—has put the reality experienced by Cuban grassroots associations out of step with the established meaning of terms such as "civil society," "participation," "sustainability," and even "state."

For Antonio Gramsci (1971) civil society existed in symbiosis and interpenetration with the state. That is, schools, workplaces, and practically any form of social organization operated—or should operate—under state hegemony as vehicles of popular education and national solidarity. This perspective, rearticulated in Joel Migdal's (2001) notion of "State-in-society" and Akhil Gupta's (1995) "blurred boundaries" between state and society, draws on what Rafael Hernández (2003:27) identifies as a holistic tradition stemming from Marx and Hegel to include the state and civil society in "the same equation." The more positivist North American tradition, by contrast, separates the two, as for example in the work of Immanuel Wallerstein, who writes that "Society is one half of an antithetical pair whose other half is the State" (quoted in Hernández 2003:137; also see Acanda González 2003:4). To pit state and civil society against each other, concludes Hernández, is an "abuse of this concept [civil society], especially by writers who study Cuba from afar. . . . This reductionism has little to do with the majority of recognizable uses of the concept in theoretical work" (2003:28).

A more integrated view of state-society relations does seem to be warranted in the Cuban case, particularly considering that laws adopted from 1976 to 1985 to institutionalize the revolutionary process codified the state's efforts to control civil society (Crahan and Armony 2006:13). Nevertheless, recognizing the political significance of religious communities, professional unions, and the informal sector to this debate, Margaret Crahan and Ariel Armony have argued that it is necessary to go beyond both the Cuban and U.S. approaches: "Civil society in Cuba is neither an exclusive space for the maintenance of the existing order nor an exclusive space of political opposition to the regime" (2006:30).

Considering the ambiguous status of Cuban civil society, it is not surprising that different definitions of the term have come into use. Such linguistic uncertainty, however, is not unique to Cuba, for as Jenny Pearce writes: "The same language and concepts are used by all, from the World Bank to Southern NGOs and grassroots movements. The reluctance to clarify the distinct meanings invested in these concepts, however, reflects collective collusion in the myth that a consensus on development exists" (2000:15–16). One result of this collusion is that goals such as civic democratization and participatory empowerment may have generally been too readily associated with civil society, with the result that "you won't find anyone who has a bad word for civil society. Everyone sees it as a thoroughly good thing!" (Keith Tester, personal communication, 4 August 2004). Writing in 1992, Tester was among the first to suggest that civil society may be best understood as "an imagination," with a variety of applications and strategic uses (Tester 1992:125). Indeed, when the practical implications of the concept are unpacked, Tester's observation is borne out in the distinct, even contradictory, ways the term is used to describe and prescribe how governments regulate their economies and manage social affairs. International debates about the meaning of civil society reflect this ambiguity:

Civil society is so often invoked in so many contexts that it has acquired a strikingly plastic moral and political valence. The recent renaissance of the term began with anticommunist dissent in Eastern Europe, which gave civil society its association with opposition movements and "parallel polis" to the state. . . . Civil society is sometimes conceived as spontaneous growth, prior to and independent of government, and sometimes as dependent on government for legal structure, robust recognition, or outright fiscal support. (Rosenblum and Post 2002:1)

Linguistic ambiguity, writes Hernández, also characterizes the Cuban case: "Today, words like 'market' or 'democracy,' 'civil society' or 'transition' display a . . . frozen state. Each one alludes to a global referent that is homogeneous but serves to differentiate. Whatever the critical examination they may deserve as concepts, these terms are frozen into a state that has little to do with their original meaning" (2003:122).

The fact that markedly different, even contradictory, scenarios can be represented with the same terms has important practical consequences in Cuba, where the notion of civil society has been employed to describe everything from a space for the expression of popular interests with "the active participation of the authorities" to anything that is "in counter-position to the state" (Reció et al. 1999; see also Azcuy Henríquez 1995; Dilla Alfonso 1993, 1999). As Ariel Armony has argued, structures of power and authority in Cuba are determined largely by the question of how the state relates to civil society, that is, "whether civil society in Cuba should be construed as being within or outside the State. This problem is not merely theoretical or terminological: this conundrum has vital implications for the organizing of hegemony in Cuba . . . It is important to ask, what are the tactical advantages of the phrase "civil society" in Cuban discourse? What is the legitimacy that actors can gain from "being part" of civil society?" (2003:22, 25).

Actors ranging from community organizations to Cuban state institutions clearly have much to gain from "being part" of civil society, not least the capacity to attract the recognition and funds of foreign development agencies. Aware that civil society has become internationally perceived as "a legitimate area for external intervention" (Edwards 2004), the Cuban government maintains significant control over the channels and destinations of international funds, with the aim of directing their flow to organizations that are administratively and ideologically connected to the state. As a result, the objectives of development agencies and the donors who finance them, which are usually stated officially in terms of strengthening civil society and building democracy, are often implemented with much more involvement of the Cuban state than openly acknowledged by anyone concerned (Cisneros 1996:7–8, 18). The U.S. State Department has attempted to minimize this possibility by requiring U.S. NGOs to demonstrate the independence of their Cuban counterparts when they apply for legal permission to operate in Cuba. This requirement, in the North American tradition, understands Cuban civil society as oppositional to state interests, a view that is embodied in the Cuban Democracy Act (Track II policy), which, despite its ineffectiveness to date, officially seeks to "reach around" the Castro government to support the growth of independent organizations (González and Nuccio 1999:33).

Guarding against the empowerment of domestic oppositional organizations is a key factor influencing the Cuban state's insistence on authority in development planning. As Alfonso Quiroz puts it, "Attempts to enhance the autonomy of non-governmental associations in Cuba have been regarded as suspicious and possibly contributing to foreign efforts to undermine the socialist character of the Cuban system" (2003:56). Raúl Castro articulated this concern in a 1996 speech to the Central Committee of the Cuban Communist Party, when, as Joseph Scarpaci et al. write, "he emphasized that the

Cuban concept of civil society is not the same as that in the United States, and he claimed that some foreign NGOs in Cuba, 'attempt to undermine the economic, political and social system freely chosen by [the Cuban] people. . . . [Their] only aim is to enslave [Cuba]' " (2002:165).

The approaches that foreign organizations take to dealing with the Cuban state have both provoked and responded to these suspicions. At one extreme are organizations like the Ford Foundation, which according to one of its program officers, maintains strict distance from Cuban state institutions:

> Ever since the Ford Foundation was accused of funding the 1960 Kennedy election campaign, we've been required to prove that our grantees satisfy a set of "due diligence" regulations. In Cuba this requirement is applied with extra care because we have to make sure that partner organizations are independent from the state. This affects the kinds of projects we can fund. . . . One recent project was to provide resources for a female symphony orchestra in Santiago de Cuba.

> Some educational and humanitarian aid agencies are less constrained in choosing who they work with. The organization Global Exchange, for example, gives a lot of autonomy to its on-site employees, who have pioneered a form of close person-to-person contact and developed really strong grassroots relationships. Global Exchange does this because technically it is a private organization with an educational and humanitarian mission. But I think its enthusiasm for building relationships with Cuban institutions comes at the expense of really investigating the backgrounds of those institutions. In other words, Global Exchange has no "due diligence" regulations. As a commercial enterprise, it only seeks to satisfy the requirements of its customers. (Interview, 15 May 2003)

Governed by "due diligence" regulations, the Ford Foundation is clearly not at liberty to develop collaborative projects with Cuban state institutions. Global Exchange, on the other hand, works with governments—socialist or otherwise—around the world to promote grassroots development, community activism, and cross-cultural understanding through face-to-face contact, despite a history of legal difficulties with the U.S. State Department. The director of the Global Exchange Cuba Program described the organization's links with Cuban state institutions in terms of respect for the country's political sovereignty:

> We bring ordinary U.S. citizens to Cuba to show them the reality behind all the U.S. media propaganda, and we always conduct these "reality

tours" through Cuban host institutions. Many of our groups arrive at hospitals and other locations with backpacks full of antibiotics and want to be directly involved in the donation; to see with their own eyes the delivery of goods. We tell our customers to ask their Cuban chaperone about this before handing things over, because this kind of direct giving can aggravate inequalities and encourage a sort of dependence. That's why the Cuban government calls the Economic Crisis a cancer, for which tourism is the chemotherapy: it can work as a short-term cure, they say, if it doesn't kill us! (Interview, 25 April 2003)

While Global Exchange treads a middle ground between direct community engagement and collaboration with the Cuban state, the eleven United Nations bodies operating in Cuba represent the most explicit form of cooperation with Cuban authorities. The director of the U.N. Population Fund (UNFPA) in Cuba spoke of the benefits and limitations of this relationship:

We always work through the Ministry of Foreign Investment and Economic Collaboration [MINVEC], which operates very effectively as a coordinator of foreign donors and investors. It can do this precisely because it has knowledge of all the foreign initiatives in Cuba. And so it directs funds to the projects that need them most. Following MINVEC's instructions, we turn over resources to a designated ministry, be it health, education, environment, or whatever, and then the project is out of our hands. So we never deal directly with the population or community groups. If I went, for example, to a hospital as a U.N. representative to assess its needs or to talk about a donation then I'd get into serious trouble with MINVEC. (Interview, 25 February 2002)

The testimonies of these three development workers indicate intense contradictions underlying international approaches to engagement with Cuba. My case studies of two projects undertaken by an Australian NGO show how these contradictions surfaced in distinct approaches to promoting community empowerment and commercial growth, ultimately reflecting alternative political interpretations of "civil society" and "sustainability." The two case studies look in some detail at how the NGO attempted to reconcile its hands-on approach to community development with the requirements of state-affiliated partner organizations. The way the projects developed reflects the ongoing claims of Cuban institutions to represent and maintain stewardship over civil society interests, but also how the state's increasingly commercial orientation has weakened the validity of this claim.

Case Study 1: The Australian Conservation Foundation
and the Politics of Plant Life

In the four years following the withdrawal of Soviet support, total economic activity in Cuba was reduced by 40 percent, so that by the mid-1990s Havana residents were consuming only 20 percent of the FAO's recommended vegetable intake (Jatar Haussmann 1999:xv, 38; ACF 2000:5). From 1993 until 2001 the Australian Conservation Foundation (ACF) developed a series of programs to help compensate for these losses in inner-city Havana through the dissemination of a horticultural technique called permaculture. Originally developed in the early 1970s by Tasmanians Bill Mollison and David Holmgren, permaculture integrates the cultivation of nutritional and medicinal plants in such a way that diverse organisms benefit each other as they grow (Caridad Cruz 1997:2). Shade-dwelling plants are grown beneath taller plants, whose seeds and shade-giving leaves fall to the ground in autumn. These are consumed by free-range chickens, which fertilize the soil for a productive harvest the next year. The result is ordered chaos: plants of remarkable diversity planted not in regimented rows but in seemingly arbitrary —though carefully planned—positions relative to each other. The technique's use of small spaces is well suited to the cramped conditions of urban Havana, and the Cuban government has supported the project by contributing open tracts of public land free of charge to anyone willing to cultivate them.

The ACF's Cuba Project coordinator, Adam Tiller, remarked that the symbiosis of organisms in the permaculture model metaphorically reflects the ACF's political philosophy: just as the plants flourish through their natural interdependence, grassroots community groups are most effective in addressing local needs when they are allowed to collaborate on neighborhood welfare projects without being overly regulated by the state (interview, 23 September 2000). While there is some evidence of this in the decentralization of Cuban community welfare projects in recent years, the activities of foreign NGOs like the ACF are much more thoroughly policed. Their primary legal obligation is to cooperate with state-affiliated partner organizations, which vary widely in terms of flexibility and transparency. After eight years of directing the ACF through such partnerships, Tiller noted, "We have always done much better dealing with small organizations, and that's something I would insist on if I could go back and start over" (interview, 9 August 2002).

One of the larger organizations that the ACF dealt with was the Instituto Cubano de Amistad con los Pueblos (Cuban Institute for Popular Friendship, or ICAP), which is the Cuban government's primary mechanism for handling international donations. Having secured foreign funds, ICAP takes sole responsibility for assessing national development priorities and designing projects. In this way it insulates Cuban citizens from foreign contact by positioning itself as the sole intermediary between donating agencies and target communities. Many donor organizations are content with this arrangement because it relieves them of complicated tasks like analyzing project budgets and evaluating reports of project outcomes in Spanish. ICAP, they feel, can do this more effectively. Most Cuban solidarity and friendship groups around the world also adopt this form of support as an expression of respect for Cuba's national sovereignty.

While ICAP offers a relatively simple mechanism for foreign donors to support Cuban development projects, it has drawn criticism from inside and outside Cuba. Concerns have been raised about ICAP's exclusion of community input in its centrally planned projects, but even sharper criticism has focused on ICAP's lack of transparency. Prior to 1989 ICAP's ambassadorial activities earned it national prestige, along with a generous budget allocation. The Special Period precipitated ICAP's fall from grace, both in terms of its capacity to finance domestic projects and its ability to keep pace with the changing expectations of international development institutions. According to a Norwegian NGO officer: "ICAP is more concerned with politics than development, and it's just not up to speed on the rules of neoliberal cooperation. For example, it has no transparency at all. You can't let anything go unspoken with ICAP, so you have to say, 'It is a requirement of our funders that every dollar is accounted for'" (interview, 17 March 2002). An inside perspective on this problem was offered by a woman employed by ICAP in the mid-1990s, the most austere years of the economic crisis:

> Listen, at ICAP we used to take whatever came through the door: pens, books, calculators, clothes. I got this sweater from there. I used to bring books and stationery home and send my daughter out to sell them. I think the Italians sent us these things to forward to other ICAP offices and then on to schools in the countryside. It wasn't a problem when my boss found out because she was worst of all: she took more than anyone; she was just trying to feed her family. Life has become a bit easier since then and now ICAP is more careful. . . . Those were very difficult years. (Personal communication, 26 February 2002)

The ACF's relationship with ICAP came about because of a project that involved a third organization, the Melbourne-based Australia-Cuba Friendship Society (ACFS). Since 1983 the ACFS has collaborated with ICAP on a variety of projects, such as an annual "work brigade" program. This has usually consisted of forty to sixty Australian men and women who volunteer their manual labor to ICAP projects. Recent brigades have sent Australians to pick fruit in the rural town of Caimito, thirty-five kilometers outside Havana, where ICAP has constructed a self-contained village for foreign volunteer workers. The brigade also participates in educational tours of development projects in urban Havana. In January 2001 I caught up with the annual ACFS work brigade during its visit to the GDIC's Taller de Transformación in Atarés (see chapter 2), where I had been unofficially working as a volunteer at the time.

TOURING ATARÉS

This afternoon the 51 Australians from the ACFS finally arrived on a large bus from Caimito to visit the taller. They looked pretty tired and sunburned. As usual [visits from foreign delegations and tour groups were not uncommon] we set out a large circle of chairs in the taller, and the local artisans set up their tables with paintings and sculptures to sell. Silvia [the director of the taller] spoke about the neighborhood development projects and got the visitors ready for the walking tour. Yesterday I asked Silvia if she'd like me to interpret but she said that ICAP had provided an interpreter, who was a specialist in urban development issues.

We started the short walking tour. The man from ICAP was emphasizing the point that foreign donations are needed to upgrade the Atarés sewerage system and to repair buildings. When we came to my favorite part of the tour, the casa-templo [temple-house of the Afro-Cuban religion Santería, discussed in chapter 2], the group had to break up to fit in the museum/living room. Freila [the priestess of the temple] did the explanation of the main saints and sang a song about Yemayá. Someone asked what Yemayá represents and Freila said, "Ella es la patrona del mar" [She is the patron of the sea]. The ICAP interpreter said, "Yemayá is the patron of evil." Freila noticed the error and said in perfect English, "The patron of the sea, not of evil." The ICAP man looked disgruntled and explained that he thought she said "mal" and not "mar." Fair enough, I thought, since many Cubans pronounce their Rs like Ls; but shouldn't a specialist in urban development, who must have some knowledge of popular religions, know that Yemayá is the goddess of the sea and not of evil?

Walking back to the taller I spoke with some of the Australians, who were full of questions about the economic management of the taller, the inclusion of women in projects, etc. I answered as well as I could. They ate the buffet meal that had been laid out for them at the taller, got back on the bus, and left. It was good to speak English again, or so I thought. But Alfonso [a taller employee] told me that I was on thin ice: "You shouldn't talk to the foreigners; they don't need to know everything you know." Then Silvia called me into her office. She told me that it had been a pleasure getting to know me for the past two months but that my request to work with the taller, which I had lodged the previous year, had been rejected. . . . I think I have seriously underestimated the importance of insulating foreign tour groups (especially those working with ICAP) from daily life in Cuba.

—Havana, January 2001

After little more than two months in Cuba, when these events took place, I was clearly not yet sensitive to the delicate balance governing NGO-state-community relations. Without realizing it I effectively upset this balance by momentarily assuming the role of mediator between the foreign visitors and the local community, presenting an alternative, potentially conflicting view to that of the ICAP interpreter. The content of my dialogue with the Australians, though supportive of the taller's projects, was irrelevant in the shadow of this fundamental transgression of protocol. Over the next four months my contact with the taller was sparse, mediated by its parent organization, the GDIC, where I was working as a project report translator. Owing largely to the good will of the taller staff, I eventually resumed my visits to Atarés, though with considerably more tact.

Although the Australian visitors may have been personally interested in community welfare, popular participation, and perhaps even the political currents conditioning their experience of Atarés, the ACFS program that they were part of was not designed to critically examine these issues. As ACFS president Joan Coxedge pointed out, the organization's relationship with Cuban authorities does not accommodate potentially intrusive inquiries into the dynamics of Cuban civil society and governance (interview, 23 March 2000). But a year earlier, in 1999, the ACFS had become involved in a more locally engaged project in collaboration with the ACF. The project concerned a small community-operated center called the Proyecto Comunitario de Conservación de Alimentos, Condimentos, y Plantas Medicinales (Community Project for the Conservation of Foods, Condiments, and Medicinal Plants, or PCCA). Based in the Havana municipality of Marianao, the center had been working through neighborhood committees for the defense of the revolution (CDRs) since 1996 to conduct public workshops on the benefits of homemade medicine and inexpensive methods of food preservation. The center's commitment to community welfare was reflected in its publicity brochure, which stated that it "does not commercialize the products that it creates" and that it "operates without monetary ambitions and without charging for its training and educational programs" (PCCA 2000).

Impressed by this commitment the ACFS began to raise money in Australia to donate to the PCCA, but since it functioned primarily as a solidarity organization the ACFS was not officially registered as an NGO in Australia, and was therefore ineligible for the support of the Australian government's Agency for International Development (AusAID). This is where the ACF came in. According to ACFS president Joan Coxsedge: "We joined forces with the Australian Conservation Foundation because we discovered that through AusAID the project would then attract two dollars for every one we raised, with the result that our $7,000 was augmented by $14,000 from the government. ICAP is looking after the funding management of the scheme" (ACFS 2000:2). Taking advantage of its preexisting relationship with Aus- AID, the ACF wrote a project application requesting Australian government funds to match the amount raised by the ACFS. The project was referred to as "Fruit for Family Nutrition in Havana, Cuba, 1999–2000" and the PCCA as part of the "National Association of Amateurs for Botanics and the Protection of Nature," or ANABPN (as it is referred to in the excerpts below). ICAP, the proposal said, would simply act as the intermediary "funds transfer agency." The application characterized the project in terms of AusAID priorities such as "sustainable development," "capacity build- ing," and "strengthening civil society." The application was successful and enthusiastic project planning commenced late in 1999. In an interview three years later Adam Tiller told me that at the time his primary concern in dealing with ICAP was to "elicit transparency," which he attempted to do in letters and emails to ICAP like the following:

The project process is quite straight-forward and uncomplicated. . . . [W]e are very pleased that ICAP is able to play its role in this project, as we believe that ICAP brings another level of accountability and legitimacy to the international assistance process, as well as a long and trusted part- nership with the Australia-Cuba Friendship Society, indicated by its flaw- less track record of annual financial and organizational arrangements over the last 15 years or so. We also appreciate that this decade ICAP has established itself in a significant role as a coordinating international network and clearinghouse for [the] setting up and funding of aid and development projects in Cuba. (Email to ICAP, 23 September 1999)

But for ICAP this was not business as usual: it was accustomed to receiving donations and distributing them as it saw fit, and not accustomed to acting as a "funds transfer agency" for a specific project. Nevertheless, after some months of negotiation an ACF officer based in Havana sent an email to Melbourne: "The money can now be sent, and should be as quickly as possible, to the account of ICAP, who will pass it on to the PCCA/ANABPN" (email to ACF, 24 April 2000). The project money was divided into two installments, the first of which, AUD $12,000, was sent to ICAP on 23 May 2000. This was where the problems began.

ICAP never acknowledged receipt of any funds, and despite the efforts of the ACF field officer and ANABPN staff, the situation remained unresolved for over two months. On 1 August, the ACF attempted to reverse the money transfer, but was unsuccessful. Later that month, the director of ICAP's Australia and Asia Division visited Melbourne and Sydney to work with the Cuban Olympic team and to promote ICAP to Australian donors. In a meeting with an ACF officer she noted that banking problems are common, and that a more reliable method of sending money would be to give her cash to carry on her person. A different Australian donor, she explained, had recently given her AUD $10,000 for her to take in her suitcase. "I told [her]," said the ACF officer, "that I didn't think that this was appropriate for the ACF's situation!" (email to ACF, 9 September 2000). It was decided that a bank draft would be more appropriate for her suitcase, but even this would not be possible because the original funds had still not been recovered. An email from the ACF accounts clerk noted: "With regard to payment, I cannot repay the first part of the payment until I have had it refunded. . . . We are waiting for the first payment to show up before sending any more funds as we don't want 2 lots of payments to go missing" (email to ACF project staff, 24 August 2000). The missing funds were not recovered in time to send a bank draft with the ICAP officer, but finally, after the ACF employee in Havana coordinated a meeting with the manager of the Cuban Commercial Bank and the donation supervisor of ICAP, the money transfer was reversed. It was decided that the project funds would be divided into three installments and sent as bank drafts, with ACF staff visiting Cuba on three separate occasions.

Prolonged negotiations with ICAP about the format and handling of the funds resulted in a delay of almost two years before the first two installments arrived in the hands of the PCCA community project, and this was only possible by passing the money through a special branch of ICAP that supervised its spending. I visited the PCCA/ANABPN community center in March 2002, by which time the third installment had still not arrived. Its director told me her understanding of the situation:

> To be honest we're not looking for any financial support from foreign NGOs. What we're doing is already working fine. You have to understand that this is a community project. Everything we do has its base right here in the neighborhood, and from here the project has expanded right across Cuba. Too much collaboration with foreign donors, NGOs, and tourists can damage our community focus. Dealing with foreign agencies requires a huge amount of time and energy, and detracts from our community work.
>
> I'll give you a simple example that ought to be close to home for you: over six months ago we were supposed to receive a [U.S.] $6,000 donation from the ACF, with which we were going to buy a computer and some books for the center. For some reason the ACF never sent us the money. I'm sure it has to do with bureaucracy at some high level of administration, but really no one knows exactly what happened. So the end result was a loss of valuable time and energy, which we could have used much better here in our community.
>
> We don't refuse these kinds of donations, but nor do we ask for them. . . . The mass organizations like the FMC and the CDRs, and the Ministry of Agriculture all help us by printing our pamphlets and distributing them around the country, so it's natural for us to work with the state. Why try to invent a new set of relations and networks when we can use those already in place? (Interview, 8 March 2002)

In a context where state organizations like the Federación de Mujeres Cubanas (Federation of Cuban Women, or FMC) and CDRs provide the supporting services necessary for the functioning of the PCCA and the dissemination of its educational materials, its director did not appear to be concerned about strengthening civil society and reforming modes of community participation. By contrast, ICAP was extremely concerned about protecting state authority, particularly its own role as the supreme intermediary of international relations: "Everything," it wrote, "should be sent through ICAP, both ways" (ICAP fax to ACF, 16 July 2000). As the ACF on-site officer explained, ICAP was not content to act in the capacity of a "funds transfer agency": "ICAP got very upset that the ACFS and ACF weren't corresponding enough with it. What was actually happening was that the ACF was in charge of the ACFS donation and was trying to work directly with the PCCA. But since a portion of the money was from the ACFS, ICAP felt that, like previous donations, it should be able to use the funds according to its own priorities" (interview, 24 March 2002).

Since the function of ICAP is to receive unconditional project donations it was not accustomed to dealing with the specific project requirements of the ACF. But underlying the methodological differences of the two organizations was the larger conceptual disjuncture of Cuban and Australian government approaches to "building civil society," which found practical expression in delayed financial transactions and confusion on the ground about the workings of "bureaucracy at some high level." Ultimately the ambiguity of the term "civil society" enabled the ACF to write project renewal proposals that claimed, in line with AusAID strategic goals, that civil society was indeed being strengthened through community empowerment and participatory project design (ACF 2000:4, 15). Needless to say, an AusAID progress report is not the appropriate place to debate the definition and usage of civil society. Indeed, a key result of this project was that the collaborating parties emerged from it having promoted their own distinct interpretations of the term. By positioning itself as the sole representative of local development needs, ICAP advanced a view of civil society as integrated into and dependent on the central state. The ACF, on the other hand, mindful of Australian government funding criteria, did not dispute AusAID's (2003) definition of civil society as a key mechanism to "create demand for greater accountability and transparency in government."

In promoting a vision of "independent" civil society, institutions like AusAID follow the lead of organizations like the World Bank and the Inter-American Development Bank, which since the early 1990s have prioritized the promotion of civil society around the world because of its "democratizing" potential. But as Ariel Armony points out, development agencies may be misguided in this pursuit since there is nothing about civil society that is inherently democratic (2004:4). Indeed, Armony's evidence suggests that civil society is a terrain of struggle and inequality, often dominated by economically powerful sectors. The growing number of international development agencies and government aid programs that have adopted the fortification of civil society as a primary objective may therefore set out from an erroneous position. "Policy," Armony concludes, "has been running ahead of research" (2004:213).

In Cuba the increasingly problematic mandate of organizations like ICAP is to minimize the negative consequences of international engagement. This has become more difficult not only because of the attempts of foreign NGOs to empower independent civil society, but also because the post-Soviet Cuban state and affiliated domestic NGOs have themselves increasingly prioritized international commercial competitiveness above specific local welfare concerns (Mesa-Lago 2000). Cuba continues to maintain a high comparative level of support for public services, but the commercialization of development initiatives to facilitate domestic growth and international economic integration raises the question of how genuinely the state can continue to claim stewardship over civil society. The next three case studies examine how foreign NGOs can become caught up in this problem.

Case Study 2: Se Puede—"It Can Be Done"

Despite their often conflicting visions of state–civil society relations, one goal that most governments and development NGOs have increasingly in common is the building of political legitimacy through commercial effectiveness and management strategies adopted from the corporate sector (Salskov Iversen et al. 2000). For Karl Marx, capitalist expansion resulted not only from an ability to develop new technologies or even to generate income through trade, but also from a capacity to create new commodities out of goods and services that were previously not for sale (1981 [1867]:445–448). Contemporary development financing institutions promote this entrepreneurial spirit by emphasizing the need for transparency, democratic governance, and grassroots participation, not as ends in themselves but as means to marketization and commercial competitiveness (OECD 1995:13–15; World Bank 1993, 1997). This has prompted some researchers to argue that even when the commercialization of services is not an explicit operational goal, NGOs since the 1990s have implicated themselves in a "new colonialism" that mystifies processes of social marginalization through a rhetoric of global economic integration and sustainability (Petras 1999:434). While global inequalities may have been legitimized and even exacerbated through deregulated privatization schemes supported by neoliberal governments, international corporations, and affiliated NGOs, a dire need for hard currency has made Cuban institutions themselves a key proponent of market reform. A second scenario involving the ACF shows how the commercialization of community services can have social costs, but also that these costs have become a generally accepted consequence of "sustainability" in a market-driven world.

From 1994 until the ACF's withdrawal from Cuba in 2001, its main official partner organization was the Fundación de la Naturaleza y el Hombre (Foundation for Nature and Mankind, or FNH). According to an FNH publication, the organization is "a civil, nongovernmental, cultural and scientific institution dedicated to researching and promoting environmental programs and projects, in particular those that relate to society and culture" (Caridad Cruz 1997:4). Like other Cuban NGOs, the FNH is in fact closely tied to a central state ministry, in this case the Ministry of Agriculture. One of the ACF's primary projects with the FNH was the regular publication and circulation of a short magazine called Se Puede ("One Can," or "It Can [Be Done]"). Financed by the ACF with a grant from AusAID, the first seven issues were dedicated to practical matters like popular recipes, home medicinal remedies, and permaculture gardening techniques. Articles were written by a combination of FNH specialists and community permaculture activists, and since it was sold at 5 national pesos (about U.S. 20 cents), it circulated widely among Havana gardeners, reaching an estimated 50,000 people in 1997 (Caridad Cruz 1997:3). By encouraging readers to grow their own gardens the magazine's populist orientation was central to the ACF's strategy for making permaculture self-sustaining in Havana, in line with AusAID project guidelines.

Also in the interest of project sustainability, the FNH gradually assumed editorial authority as Se Puede's readership grew. But the FNH had always been more interested in the philosophical implications of environmental awareness than the technical details of planting gardens; that is, it saw its mission as ideological: from "the awakening of citizens to the generation of values and principles . . . the defense of life, and not only from the biological point of view but also the psychological, sociocultural, economic and political" (FNH 1997:2). This orientation surfaced in Se Puede when the FNH made its first executive editorial decision: to start replacing the magazine's practical content with naturalist poetry by the FNH's deceased founder (and close friend of Fidel Castro), Antonio Núñez Jiménez. Around the same time the new editorial committee unveiled its strategy for making Se Puede self-sustaining: "When the [next issue of] the magazine is finished, we will proceed to its distribution and commercialization by the company Copretel. Once this is done the magazine will be available to anyone who is interested. . . . [It] has the potential to reach 150,000 readers" (Caridad Cruz 1997:7, 9).

Along with a 300 percent increase in the magazine's price, these editorial innovations did not please the ACF, whose 1998 progress report to AusAID noted:

> The focus of the magazine [has been] altered from that originally conceived by Cuban and ACF staff in 1994. Articles with a general environmental theme have been introduced, in addition to the articles on practical food and household solutions. The committee is also promoting a more intellectual/scientific and commercial presentation, with the aim of increasing its economic viability, including international sales to earn scarce foreign currency income. These changes, however, may be compromising the original core practical, educational and populist aims of the magazine. (ACF 1998:2)

Pressure from the ACF eventually led the FNH to reintroduce community-authored content in the magazine, though this amounted to little more than a "letters to the editor" page. According to the ACF Cuba project director, Adam Tiller, the situation reflected a fundamental paradox of sustainable development: "It's like Cronus and Zeus. At some point you have to respect the autonomy of the thing you helped create. We put years of work into *Se Puede*, but ultimately it's the FNH's project, and it's important that we don't try to impose our priorities on the FNH. One of our goals from the beginning was to help the FNH to develop sustainable projects . . . [and] for better or for worse we accomplished that goal" (interview, 15 May 2000).

The evolution of *Se Puede* suggests that sustainability and commercialization have become kindred ambitions in the global era. Indeed, the future of the Cuban state depends very much on how successfully it relinks itself with the currents of international trade, an objective made no simpler by the U.S. trade embargo. The FNH's commercialization of *Se Puede* was an attempt to introduce a Cuban commodity to the world market: a survival strategy deemed necessary despite its social cost and regardless of how much it deviated from the wishes of its foreign benefactor. Ultimately the magazine was a collaborative project underwritten by the shared ambition of sustainability, though the meaning of the term ranged from self-sufficiency to profit maximization according to the interpretations and objectives of the collaborating parties. As in the previous example, this semantic flexibility resulted in a functioning alliance that adhered to key project reference terms while allowing participants to pursue distinct interpretations of those terms. Unlike the previous example, though, the official mediation of domestic-

En Cuba: Grupo de Orientación a la Familia
sobre Permacultura
Calle 158 # 107, altos, esq. Primera A
Reparto Náutico, Playa
Ciudad de La Habana, Cuba
Tel/Fax: + 53 7 336090

$5.00

Saber y hacer
sobre plantas
medicinales

Maria Mercedes Garcia Negrin.

The front cover of an early issue of *Se Puede*, which focused on natural medicinal remedies. Courtesy of the Australian Conservation Foundation Cuba Project.

international relations did not facilitate the state's claims of representation and stewardship over local interests and civil society so much as its pursuit of economic targets.

The achievement of sustainability—sometimes social, sometimes economic—across a range of projects resulted in the ACF's withdrawal from Cuba late in 2001. By that time permaculture "skills transfer" programs had been effective enough for the FNH to run its own training course. According to the ACF on-site officer, her three years in Cuba had been a successful, though uphill, battle. She felt that the ACF's basic objectives had been accomplished, even though there was still much to be done in the area of promoting dialogue and interdependence between community groups. The reality of this ongoing challenge suggested itself to me metaphorically one bright afternoon as we sat in her Central Havana permaculture garden. She had just returned from a month of researching organic farms in the western province of Pinar del Río, and while she was away some local project trainees had looked after the garden. As we sat there chatting on a bench I was struck by the diverse colors of the fruit bushes, medicinal plants, and vegetable patches, which her new recruits had neatly arranged, to her dismay, into perfect rows and columns.

The Office of the Conservador and the Commercialization of Development

The above scenarios suggest that state mediation between international NGOs and community associations has become critical to the Cuban government's political and economic authority. Intensifying international engagement has required Cuban partner organizations to deal with increasingly diverse foreign agencies, but also seems to have provoked a growing, perhaps excessive, attention to appearances. A Norwegian development worker commented on the Havana Office of the Historian's expenditure on office equipment:

> You've seen the office building from the outside: a beautifully restored 19th century colonial mansion with the original masonry exposed. But what a contrast on the inside: the most powerful, flashy, up-to-date computers, zip drives, scanners, you name it. And all paid for by the UN. I think they try to present an image to foreigners—especially NGO workers—that they are up-to-date with the latest gadgets and as equipped as anyone in the world for the tasks at hand. This is fine until you walk half a block in any direction and find people living in collapsing houses with power cuts and water that runs once a week, if that. (Personal communication, 30 March 2002)

The development worker's concern was that the Office of the Historian allocates an inordinate portion of its U.N. funds to projecting itself as an agency of international standards. Whether or not this is true, there does seem to be growing international pressure on domestic agencies in developing countries to present a sanitized, technologically advanced image, even if this means compromising operational outcomes and disrupting local culture (Economist 2000:26). As a Nicaraguan NGO officer puts it, "Do we measure results or are we content to be visible in high circles by slickly using some of the electronic gimmicks that have come to represent citizenship in many countries?" (Bendaña 1998).

LOOKING GOOD

Today I met with a sociologist at the Office of the Historian of Havana to discuss strategies for encouraging local participation in one of the Office's community projects. . . . We arranged to meet again the following week, so I scribbled down the appointment in my diary. He scribbled down the appointment in his Palm Pilot. When I arrived at the temple-house [where I was living at the time, only two blocks away from the Office of the

Historian], Felicia joked that she would have to raise my rent. Office of the Historian staff and their foreign colleagues, she said, are a class above average people. Felicia's son, Miki, was in the main room with some friends, watching a flickering video of Waterworld. "Felicia, he knows that," he called, "that's why he wears his nice shirt when he talks to Eusebio" [the director of the Office of the Historian]. He's right, I thought to myself. Then, Kimbo [one of Miki's friends] said, "What is it with people in Old Havana? Eusebio with his money, Adrian with his clothes, and Miki with his gold teeth!" Everyone laughed. Kimbo was right: we were all conscious of maintaining appearances.

—Havana, May 2002

Clearly the interactions of foreign and national development agencies are shaped by more than project objectives and outcomes. Attention to appearances, particularly technological capacity, seems to be a growing characteristic of development culture. What is at stake is the projection of modernity, and while contemporary conceptions of modernity may vary regarding the function of the state, private enterprise, and civil society, what they tend to have in common is a sense of legitimacy based on commercial effectiveness. This is as true in Cuba as anywhere else, and not only in Havana.

Like Havana, Santiago de Cuba has an Office of the Historian, but its responsibilities are more academic than economic. The institution that encompasses the Santiago Office of the Historian is called the Office of the *Conservador* (conserver), which resembles the Havana Office of the Historian more closely. The activities of the Office of the Conservador focus primarily on the physical conservation of the city's historical center, but its duties extend far beyond restoring monuments and architecture. While the Office controls 2 percent of hard currency revenue earned within Santiago's historical center, most of its income consists of donations from foreign NGOs. Like the Office of the Historian of Havana, it serves as a Cuban partner organization for external agencies interested in projects ranging from architectural design to health education. According to the director of the Office of the Conservador, Omar López Rodríguez:

Our projects range from physical restoration to social development. We're a very effective channel for foreign financial cooperation and NGO intervention: UNESCO donated [U.S.] $50,000 to our archaeology-based restoration project in 1999 and last month we initiated cooperation with PDHL [see chapter 2]. We also collaborate with French and Italian NGOs.

Santiago is different from Havana. People here have a more defined sense of identity, which is reinforced through an open lifestyle: they mix a lot in the streets and usually leave their front door open. This can help our work in terms of participation and education, because people generally want to be involved in their communities.

Housing is a problem in Santiago, so I would prefer that an NGO pay for new housing before the restoration of, say, a park or church. We're careful with the resources that we have: we don't restore a person's house, for example, without also educating residents about the historical value of the architecture. That way they take a stronger sense of ownership and protect the city against vandalism and neglect. The patrimony of the city, you see, is inside each of its residents: caring for the city means caring for themselves. (Interview, 24 April 2002)

Two further case studies, both involving Santiago de Cuba's Office of the Conservador, show how projects initially dedicated to popular education can develop commercial priorities. Case study 3 describes how the commercial development of the city's main cemetery attracted the interest of foreign NGOs and state-owned tourist agencies, but left cemetery staff unrewarded. Case study 4 permits a more optimistic conclusion: that when projects are designed with local needs in mind, commercialization can stimulate local education and employment.

Case Study 3: Resting, but Not in Peace—
The Phantom Guides of the Santa Ifigenia Cemetery

The guides at the Santa Ifignia cemetery are proud of their detailed knowledge of the symbolic design of tombs and the biographies of the individuals they house. "This is cultural history," explained Ariadna, "and the lessons and values are visible right down to the epitaphs. We regularly show around groups of schoolchildren, who have to memorize the lessons and stories for class. For example, the first two burials here were a young aristocratic white woman and an African slave: you see, in death we're all equal" (interview, 23 April 2002). Ariadna had studied history at Universidad de Oriente and had been working in the cemetery for seven years; her colleagues were similarly experienced. Periodically the cemetery staff worked with a team of historians from the Office of the Conservador to publish booklets about the lives of historical figures buried in the cemetery. Ariadna hoped that the provincial government's Department of Common Services, which manages

Santiago de Cuba

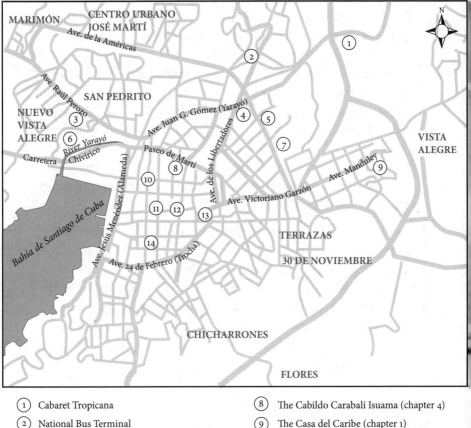

1. Cabaret Tropicana
2. National Bus Terminal
3. The Santa Ifigenia Cemetery
4. Plaza de la Revolución
5. Teatro Heredia
6. Vicente Portuondo's temple-house where the author stayed in 2001, 2002, and 2006 (chapters 1, 4)
7. La Universidad de Oriente

8. The Cabildo Carabalí Isuama (chapter 4)
9. The Casa del Caribe (chapter 1)
10. The Peña Deportiva Félix Roque Pécora (chapter 4)
11. The Cuban-Italian School-Workshop
12. The Office of the Conservador
13. Plaza de Marte
14. Cathedral of Santiago de Cuba

the cemetery, would allow staff members to set up a gift shop to sell these booklets and other items as a way to augment their monthly salaries (250 pesos, roughly U.S. $10). The resulting revenue, she said, could also be invested in tourism promotion and used to maintain the cemetery grounds. A chronic lack of funds had recently led the Department of Common Services to deal with the cemetery's overcrowding problem through a rather unusual recycling plan: remains were being dug up after two years of burial and packed in concrete blocks to make space for new arrivals. The concrete blocks were then used to build a new, expanded perimeter wall around the cemetery.

But overcrowding was not the cemetery's only problem. Resources were needed to maintain and restore important tombs and to promote the cemetery as a clean, hospitable, tourist-friendly environment. But stretched to its financial limit in 2002, Common Services was in no position to invest in gift shops or tourism promotion. The predicament resulted in the intervention of the Office of the Conservador, which, in a move to take a more active role in the cemetery's financial management, solicited the assistance of foreign NGOs to restore important tombs (Omar López Rodríguez, interview, 24 April 2002).

The Office of the Conservador also collaborated with a range of tour operators to promote the cemetery to foreign visitors, but the benefits of this initiative did not trickle down to Ariadna and her colleagues. This, she explained, was because the big state-owned tour companies were monopolizing the industry:

> We cemetery guides are gradually being made obsolete by the tour guides of agencies like Rumbos, Cubamar, Horizontes, Mercatur, and especially Cubanacán. They bring in groups of tourists to snap a few photos and, even though the tour guides don't know anything about the cemetery's history they don't consult with us so that they can keep all the tips.
>
> It's kind of paradoxical that we who stuck it out in university receive miniscule salaries, while those who quit and got into tourism in the 1990s reap all the benefits. But this also has to do with a change in tourism that I've noticed: these days they don't come to learn so much as to relax and meet women. They don't even want to learn what we could teach them. Some of us joke that we've become the ghosts of this cemetery. (Interview, 23 April 2002)

As I left the cemetery a Cubanacán bus pulled up in front of the entrance, but only seven of the fifty or so tourists went inside the cemetery with a

Cubanacán guide. Some stood around the bus chatting, but most peered through the fence to take photographs. This way they avoided paying the one U.S. dollar entrance fee. Less than ten minutes later the visitors reboarded the bus, whose engine had never stopped running. The Santa Ifigenia cemetery was an appropriate addition to the site-seeing itineraries of Cubanacán and other tour operators, whose customers welcomed the opportunity to snap some passing shots of Cuban history. But the employees of the cemetery played no part in the enterprise, forced instead to participate as invisible witnesses to a process of commercial expansion beyond their control.

Case Study 4: The Cuban-Italian School-Workshop

Despite the difficulties of integrating commercial growth with community welfare, where possible the Office of the Conservador has sought to harness the power of international collaboration to do precisely this. One of its most significant ongoing collaborations is the Escuela Taller Cuba-Italia Ugo Luisi (the Cuban-Italian School-Workshop, named after the Italian architect Ugo Luisi). The project, which commenced in 1999, has a total cost of U.S. $1.5 million and is funded 70 percent by an Italian NGO called the Association for Participation and Development (APS) and 30 percent by the Santiago de Cuba municipal government through the Office of the Conservador. The aim of the project is to enroll young people, who are past school age but "unlinked" to further education or employment, in a two-year course that teaches the theoretical and practical skills of conservation work. Of roughly 250 applicants each year, the school accepts 25 to 30 new students.

As with most foreign-financed projects in Cuba, the school-workshop was initially proposed to the APS by the Santiago de Cuba city government in conjunction with MINVEC. The first official action was to define the responsibilities of the APS and the Office of the Conservador in a letter of cooperation. Vincenzo Diliberto, the APS on-site officer, explained that while these conditions, or "reference terms," are worded very specifically, there is some room for flexibility: "MINVEC has called me a number of times recently, instructing me to follow the guidelines more closely. They say I have to buy this or that number of TV sets from this or that company, but I often prefer to follow my own judgments; after all I'm achieving results, so no one can really complain" (interview, 20 April 2002). But while flexibility may have sometimes worked in Vincenzo's favor, other times it has proved frustrating:

In June 2001 I went home to Italy for three months. In the months leading up to my departure I worked extremely hard to secure cement, paint, tools, and a roof for the school. Getting these resources was the hardest part, so I was expecting the construction work to proceed smoothly in my absence. When I came back, not only had nothing been done but all the materials were gone. I found out that the city government had reallocated the resources to its new social work school, which is a very public and politically significant project. Apparently their school wouldn't have been finished in time for Fidel's televised visit if they hadn't taken our cement and our roof. (Interview, 17 January 2002)

While MINVEC's flexibility may have caused occasional setbacks, the project has also profited from MINVEC's ability to arrange the tax-free importation of specialty items such as books and videos from Italy. These items, explained Vincenzo, are the building blocks of his ambition to expand the school into an Italian cultural center:

The APS has to be careful with this. Foreign NGOs are watched pretty closely to make sure they don't spread antirevolutionary ideas. The French cultural centre in Havana has had to work extremely hard to stay active. We're starting with the school but slowly introducing Italian books and a language course. Gradually we'll transform the school into a "Casa Italia" with a public library, movie screenings, and lectures on Italian culture. We want to educate people but first we need stable relations with the state. Today the school, tomorrow the cultural center! (Interview, 17 January 2002)

When I visited Vincenzo three months later he was pleased with the cultural center's progress:

The Italian language course has commenced with twenty-five enrolled students, and next week we're going to start a unit on Italian cuisine. I know Cubans love Italian food because when my mother came to visit a few months ago everyone on the block was stopping by to try the food. We want to strengthen links with Italy because the only experience most people here have of Italians is through tourism, and Cubans should know that there's more to Italian culture than chasing after women. (Interview, 20 April 2002)

Careful to proceed gradually in a sensitive political environment, Vincenzo was confident that his envisioned Casa Italia would eventually build new

{ New house on the block: The Cuban-Italian School-Workshop "Ugo
{ Luisi." Photo by the author.

understandings between Cuba and Italy. But the director of the Office of the
Conservador, Omar López Rodríguez, identified a different kind of contribution that the school-workshop might make, more in line with his own plans.
A fundamental task of his office, he said, is to generate income through
foreign collaboration, the restoration industry, and tourism:

> Generating income means commercializing potentially profitable proj-
> ects. The school-workshop, for example, could in future produce high-
> quality wood and metal products not just for its own restoration work but
> for sale to other projects and construction companies. . . . Another ele-
> ment of income generation, following Eusebio's model [Eusebio Leal,
> the Historian of Havana] is the opening of networks of cafés and gift
> shops. We've learned from Eusebio that foreign collaboration requires
> the presentation of a clean, acceptable face. These kinds of coffee shops
> could be very popular with tourists in Santiago de Cuba, and the school-
> workshop may be a good place to start. (Interview, 24 April 2002)

By the end of April 2002 the school-workshop was rapidly expanding its
cultural activities, and had just hosted a ball to commemorate the fall of
fascism in Italy. This was its first public party, but Vincenzo hoped that other
events from Italian history would be similarly celebrated. While still functioning primarily to educate locals in restoration techniques, the school-
cum-cultural center was progressing according to Vincenzo's plan. It seemed

only a matter of time before an Office of the Conservador gift shop might open next door to sell Italian memorabilia in dollars: something like Santiago de Cuba's house of French fashion, La Maison, in Vista Alegre, or perhaps a small restaurant serving Italian-style pizza and coffee. A gift shop and café at the school-workshop would resemble countless other developments shaped by the state's pressing need to earn hard currency. It would be a logical overlap of interests, at once delivering technical training, economic stimulation, and cultural education, and it already seemed to be under way.

Conclusion

International engagement has raised a series of challenges to traditional structures of political authority in Cuba. One of these challenges arises from the arrival of foreign NGOs committed to building grassroots initiatives in partnership with community groups, forcing the state to defend its legitimacy as the sole representative of citizens' needs. Functioning to broker the relationships of foreign NGOs with local community groups, state institutions like ICAP and MINVEC constitute the front line of this defense. This became evident when the Australian Conservation Foundation (ACF) attempted to collaborate directly with the PCCA community horticulture center. Wary of the ACF's attempt to "strengthen civil society," ICAP's mediation of the relationship ensured that the flow of resources remained firmly under state control. The financial confusion resulting from this level of regulation proved frustrating to the ACF, but ultimately it reflected an alternative interpretation of civil society that endorses state stewardship over community interest and national sovereignty. The project's eventual settlement of a mutually acceptable NGO-state-community relationship resulted from an integration of these political philosophies behind the practical goal of building popular participation through the PCCA community center, while the finer political details of "civil society" were never openly fleshed out.

A more entrenched and serious challenge to the state's claim of stewardship over civil society has emerged from its own efforts to integrate Cuba into the world economy. Policies seeking to enhance commercial competitiveness have often failed to protect local interests, effectively eroding the state's representative legitimacy from within. The ACF's relationship with a Cuban partner organization, the FNH, showed how conflicting social and commercial development goals surfaced in the production of the environmental magazine *Se Puede*. On paper both organizations agreed on the importance of project "sustainability," but the ACF's understanding of the term was based on generating local interest in permaculture training, while the FNH understood it to mean financial profitability. Ultimately the FNH's commercialization of the magazine was a sound economic strategy, but it did not reflect the interests of the local readership. Similarly, in Santiago de Cuba, the way the Office of the Conservador and its foreign donors renovated the Santa Ifigenia cemetery for foreign tourists benefited state-operated tour agencies like Cubanacán but brought no substantial benefits to local employees. Ariadna and her fellow guides were not averse to the cemetery's commercial development, but the way they were segregated from visiting tourists left them feeling like "ghosts": excluded and unrepresented.

The rapid establishment of countless economically oriented development projects like those discussed above has contributed to a situation in which popular interests have become less closely integrated into the objectives of state institutions. This is a problem faced by governments around the world, but its implications are particularly serious in Cuba because commercial development has rendered the state's claim of stewardship over civil society increasingly difficult to substantiate. The insistence of organizations like ICAP and MINVEC on mediating between community groups and foreign NGOs commissioned to strengthen "independent" civil society reflects this internal volatility and vulnerability. Therefore, projects that can provide concrete benefits at the local level while simultaneously stimulating economic productivity have become crucial to the legitimacy of the Cuban state. The Cuban-Italian school-workshop was an attempt to do precisely this. The project served the interest of its patron NGO in establishing an Italian cultural presence in Santiago de Cuba, complete with language courses, a movie library, and potentially even a pizzeria. But it also served the interests of the state and the local community by training students in the occupation of architectural conservation, producing a young workforce equipped with the technical skills necessary for the commercial production of construction materials and services.

Cuba's gradual reintegration into the global economy, reflected in the growing presence of foreign NGOs, raises questions about the impact of commercial expansion on community welfare and the relationship of the state to civil society. This chapter has argued that although the authority of the state continues to condition the evolution of community associations, economic streamlining and political reform have limited the state's ability to universally distribute material and ideological resources. It is necessary, then, to examine how economic spaces and social sectors that receive less attention from the state are being filled. At present, religious communities—

both Christian and Afro-Cuban—have shown the strongest potential to independently represent popular interests, though a critical problem has been the weakness of linkages and allegiances across traditional denominational boundaries. The final chapter considers the historical phenomenon of cross-religious interaction in Cuba, the contemporary political turbulence it continues to generate, and its influence on the evolution of civil society in Cuba.

4

PATRIOTIC SPIRITS:
RELIGIOUS WELFARE PROGRAMS
AND THE POLITICS OF SYNCRETISM

As Cuba adapts to the pressures of reinsertion into the world market, state subsidies and foreign investment have typically prioritized sectors with strong commercial potentials, such as tourism and nickel mining, while less profitable sectors, such as transport, housing, and health services, have fared less well. The community-oriented programs of foreign NGOs and domestic neighborhood organizations have helped to remedy this imbalance by easing pressure on the social service system to respond to emerging needs at the local level. This incremental shift of responsibility away from the state has reduced material shortages but has also rendered established structures of ideological and legal authority vulnerable to the encroachment of organizations operating less directly under the state's political hegemony. This is evident in the expanding community development programs of Christian organizations, which identify greater social engagement as an opportunity for evangelization and for gaining greater leverage with the state on issues from civil rights to media control.

Contemporary research on social capital and civil society makes a useful contribution to understanding such scenarios by clarifying how political authorities and community organizations can become enmeshed in intricate forms of material and ideological exchange (Armony 2004:34–38, 55; Federke et al. 1999:729, 738; Foley and Edwards 1999:165–168; Lin 2001:110–111, 141–145; Portes 1998:6–8, 15; Woolcock 1998:164–170). As Portes (1998:7) puts it, "The currency with which obligations are repaid may be different from that with which they were incurred in the first place and may be as intangible as the granting of approval or allegiance." Such a trade-off of tangible and intangible resources characterizes the relationship of the state to religious organizations in contemporary Cuba, the former offering greater space for community engagement and ideological diversity, the latter offering greater responsibility for local welfare (often backed up by material resources from overseas) and allegiance to state political authority. This process of exchange has been intensified by the deepening political implications of loyalty to the revolution at the grassroots, endowing religious social (and financial) capital with a high "exchange value" relative to civic concessions from the state.

While the state has encouraged religious groups to help confront local development challenges, it has also shown deep concern about the formation of cooperative relationships and cultural identities not directly subordinated to its political hegemony, for example, between Christian and Afro-Cuban religious communities. More open expression of religiosity, engagement with decentralized state institutions, and collaborative development work facilitate these relationships, further appreciating the value of religious social capital. As the previous chapters indicate, the state has attempted to slow this process by controlling and discouraging the formation of independent associations that could compete with its authority at the local level. The political sensitivity of the situation is reflected in public statements from socially active religious organizations that they acknowledge the civic authority of the state and are committed to working under it.

Because of their growing popular support and increasingly public character, religious groups have shown stronger potential than others to represent and advocate local needs. As Olga Portuondo Zúñiga (the Historian of Santiago de Cuba) explains: "In the range of official institutions created by the revolution, popular religious associations were never recognized, but now it's precisely these that are becoming the most active. Since the state's ability to maintain its institutions was crippled in the late 1980s, many of these organizations have surfaced to fill the void. They are flourishing because they give people social and economic protection as well as a sense of identity and historical direction" (interview, 19 April 2002).

The previous chapters have described some of the sociopolitical conditions framing expanding religious activism, identifying the importance of individuals capable of mediating between their communities and the state, the prevalence of informal lines of collaboration alongside more formally structured local welfare initiatives, and an overarching framework of state authority in development planning. Under these conditions it is possible to identify three factors shaping the potential of Christian and Afro-Cuban religious (or religiously affiliated) organizations to consolidate their representative capacities and strengthen their position as emerging civil society protagonists. These are their ability to protect the material and cultural interests of their constituencies, the extent to which they build formal and informal relationships across theological and cultural divides, and their willingness to engage productively with the state.

This chapter examines the organizational development of these civic prerequisites in three scenarios of religiously affiliated community activism. It begins with an analysis of Christian organizations as they take advantage of official permission to expand socioeconomic relief programs and build stronger congregations. These efforts have brought psychological, material, and even legal security into some neighborhoods, complementing the social service capacities of a weakened state sector. But they have also encroached on the state's ideological terrain through evangelical programs that encourage public reflection and debate on social issues, though always with statements of deference and respect for the revolution. Where these activities overlap with those of Afro-Cuban religious communities the state has shown concern about the potential emergence of unregulated interreligious solidarities. This concern surfaced during Pope John Paul II's visit to Cuba in 1998, as it has done historically on the feast day of Cuba's patron saint, the Virgen de la Caridad del Cobre. The Virgen's multireligious appeal still provokes political concerns, as I found during the annual procession to the Cathedral of El Cobre (near Santiago de Cuba) in 2001.

Eleven months in Santiago de Cuba also brought me into contact with one of the country's longest surviving community mutual aid organizations, the Cabildo Carabalí Isuama, which is discussed in the second part of the chapter. Founded in association with the Catholic Church in the early nineteenth century to protect the cultural and economic interests of enslaved and free black Cubans, the Cabildo went on to play a supporting role in both of Cuba's wars of independence from Spain (1868–1878, 1895–1898). Following the Revolution of 1959 it was official registered as a symbol of Cuban cultural patrimony, bringing it national recognition. As a state-subsidized cultural organization, the Cabildo's mutual aid functions became less prominent in the 1960s and 1970s, as did its expression of religious customs in response to the prevailing ideological pressures of the time. But according to the Cabildo's aging members, the strain of the Special Period has provoked a revival of the organization's mutual aid functions in the form of collective savings and a series of community welfare projects. Religious expression and cooperative relations with the Catholic Church have also reemerged in the Cabildo's public activities, though the open celebration of sacred ceremonies and symbols is always balanced with enthusiastic vocal and visual

endorsements of the revolutionary government. It is unlikely that the Cabildo will assume representative capacities in any way comparable to those it
once possessed, but its contemporary experience shows that a changing
political context has allowed it to develop the kinds of organizational prerequisites necessary for open civic engagement.

The chapter concludes with a case study of a neighborhood welfare organization in Santiago de Cuba that has also begun to show its civic potentials
through a combination of internal protection, external linkage, and an ability to work productively within the prevailing legal framework. By openly
reaching out to a socially diverse community, including religious believers
and homosexuals, the organization has engaged previously marginalized
constituencies in projects ranging from job placement to popular education.
This kind of local activism stretches the limits of the revolution's traditional
ideology, but more significant still is that the organization is owned and
managed by the state. With a blend of local and national loyalties at its core,
the organization is a good example of how state and nonstate influences are
converging to define the character of Cuban civil society.

Evangelical Alliances and the Collaborative Spirit

The activities of Cuban Catholic and Protestant congregations since 1990
reflect their evolving relationships with the Cuban government, but they also
carry the legacy of colonial-era loyalties in the long struggle for independence from Spain (1848–1898). Catholics such as Father Félix Varela (1787–
1853) campaigned vigorously for the abolition of slavery in Cuba, even traveling to Spain to warn the colonial authorities of slavery's potential political
consequences: "I am sure that the first person to mount the call for independence will have almost all of the people of African origin on his side. Let us
not fool ourselves: Constitution, liberty, equality, are synonyms; these terms
are polar opposites to the words slavery and inequality of rights. It is in vain
to try to reconcile these opposites" (Varela 1973:274). Together with other
Catholics Varela fought to introduce liberal political ideas into Cuba, from
citizens' rights to a republican government and independence (Crahan and
Armony 2006:8, Maza Miguel 1999). Following the Haitian Revolution and
the independence of Spanish colonies in the 1820s, Bishop José Díaz de
Espada y Landa (1802–1832) also attempted to promote republican ideas in
Cuba. An influx of conservative Catholic clergy at this time led to his expul-
sion from office, though he did successfully identify a sector of the Cuban
Catholic Church with the independence struggle (Crahan 2005:233). Nev-

ertheless, the church's official endorsement of Spanish rule in the nineteenth century—even as Afro-Cuban and Protestant groups were becoming identified with the independence movement—resulted in widespread anti-church sentiment (Aguilar 1972, Kirk 1989:30).

The year 1898 marked the overthrow of Spanish colonial rule in Cuba (and the Caribbean), but it also marked the arrival of diplomats, soldiers, and missionaries from the United States. The chronic inadequacy of infrastructure in the aftermath of the war gave easy entrée to Protestant schools, churches, hospitals, and orphanages, which played a central role in establishing U.S. hegemony in Cuba. As Louis Pérez Jr. puts it:

> U.S. control of Cuba implied responsibility for salvation and redemption in the religious sphere no less than in the secular one. Indeed, they were conceived of as being one and the same. National policy fused indistinguishably with evangelical purpose, and the distinctions were blurred early: no suggestion of conspiracy or even the need for formal collaboration, rather a convergence of ideological constructs and shared cultural norms that readily yielded common purpose toward similar goals. (1992:106)

The growth of Baptist, Methodist, Episcopalian, Presbyterian, Quaker, and other Protestant congregations was so rapid in Cuba during the first half of the twentieth century that by the 1950s they had outnumbered their Catholic counterparts in lay persons, preachers, and temples. Strong administrative connections with the neocolonial power facilitated Protestant expansion, but the conservative ideological commitments that accompanied these connections proved damaging in the wake of the 1959 revolution (Yaremko 2000). The revolution's restructuring of society reinforced Christian conservatism, which expressed itself in strong, though patently ineffective, challenges to the legitimacy of the government between 1959 and 1961 (Crahan 1979:156). According to Fidel Castro, Cuban Christianity (particularly Catholicism) was on an inevitable collision course with the revolution because its social and economic priorities in the first half of the twentieth century were utterly removed from the basic interests of the masses (Castro 1986:143).

For its part, the Catholic Church perceived ideological differences as paramount: "[Catholics] did not oppose themselves to the revolution because it confronted the interests of the bourgeoisie and the empire, but because it proposed a system of values, an interpretation of reality, a conception of the New Man and an educational project that were alternative to that of the Church" (Girardi 1994:109). Expelled from Cuba in 1961, the auxiliary bishop of Havana, Eduardo Boza Masvidal, went as far as arguing that the ideological underpinnings of the revolution were at odds not only with Christianity but with the values and ideals of all loyal Cubans: "We are helping the revolution enormously, and we want the great social transformations that Cuba needs, but we cannot want nor support the materialist and totalitarian Communism which would be the most blatant negation of the ideals for which so many Cubans fought and died" (quoted in Cardenal 2003:505).

The revolutionary government never outlawed religion, but it did restrict its expression in various ways. The 1963 nationalization of the education system, for example, had a profound impact on Catholic and Protestant organizations, which until then drew a significant proportion of their income, as well as recruits, from private religious schools. Tentative efforts toward rapprochement emerged in the early 1970s as some Christian leaders sought ideological reconciliation with socialist notions of social justice, but these impulses came from a relatively small circle of academic pastors, while official Protestant and Catholic voices sought security in a more apolitical perspective (Clemente et al. 1995:53). Meanwhile, unofficial voices in the Catholic laity were decidedly less passive, though equally ambivalent, calling for progressive integration into the revolution from some quarters and for civil dissent from others (Crahan 1982:8). These tensions culminated in an exodus particularly of young lay people from the church, provoked also by fears that outward expression of religious faith might incur state persecution in the form of professional and public discrimination (Büntig 1971:112–113, Clemente et al. 1995:53).

The late 1960s and early 1970s marked the beginning of an improvement in church-state relations, provoked in part by Fidel Castro's trip to Chile, during which he observed Christian organizations coexisting, and in some instances cooperating with, the Allende government. In the 1970s and 1980s activist Protestant and Catholic organizations in Chile, as well as in Nicaragua and El Salvador, demonstrated their commitment to progressive domestic agendas, or what the Communist Party of Cuba called "the tasks of the revolution in the construction of socialism" (Kirk 1989:155), giving rise to further improvement in church-state relations. The publication of Fidel Castro's *Fidel and Religion: Conversations with Frei Betto* in 1985 and Castro's subsequent meeting with Cuban evangelical leaders in 1985 and 1990 signaled a deepening of this rapprochement. This process continued into the 1990s, with the granting of permission for Christmas and Easter celebrations to be televised in 1990, the acceptance of religious believers into the

Communist Party in 1991, and the election of two religious leaders to the National Assembly in 1993.

The political leadership's tolerance for religious expression since the early 1990s constitutes both an official response to an increasingly religious population and an attempt to build support in a social sector where state influence was previously minimal (Eckstein 1994:25). This political agenda has been facilitated by the incorporation of Christian organizations into registered development initiatives as the state responds to the pressures of economic globalization. Looking internationally at a range of emerging economies, the Belgian priest and scholar Francis Houtart has observed that the weakening capacities of many governments, resulting from a globalizing "logic of the market," has provoked the consolidation of religious communities to protect the spiritual and material needs of disenfranchised communities (quoted in Alonso Tejada 1995:28–29). This has become evident across Latin America as religious organizations assume greater responsibility for protecting and advocating community interests, often more effectively than governmental and nongovernmental development agencies (Agüero and Stark 1998:123). The changing socioeconomic landscape in Cuba reflects this reality as Christian organizations, typically drawing financial support from donors in the United States and Europe, ease the financial responsibilities of the central state by providing concrete material benefits and services to growing congregations. The organization Caritas, for example, through its Catholic Relief Services division, invested more than U.S. $10 million into Cuban "living parishes" between 1993 and 1997, the years most severely affected by the economic crisis. Caritas officer Rolando Suárez Cobain explains that "because of shortages of medicine, for example, people in the parishes can identify their neighbors who need something like insulin, and we can try to get it to them" (quoted in Chauvin 1997:10). Committed to the well-being of their congregations, over fifty-four Christian organizations and community centers had emerged in Cuba by 1997, with over fifty thousand members (Wall 1997:579).

The establishment of organizations like the Centro Católico de Formación Cívico-Religiosa (Catholic Center for Civic-Religious Education), the Equipo Promotor para la Participación Social del Laico (Team for the Promotion of Lay Social Participation), and the Comisión Justicia y Paz (Commission for Justice and Peace) signals a strengthening Catholic appetite for social engagement in Cuba. By 1998 the Cuban Catholic Church was operating twenty childcare centers, twenty-one retirement homes, five hospitals, and numerous free medicine dispensaries (Orozco and Bolívar 1998:460).

The church's public voice has gained further reach through the circulation of new pamphlets and journals (currently over twenty), plus the revival of old ones such as the *Vida Cristiana*. Meanwhile, the multidenominational Christian Centro Memorial Dr. Martin Luther King, supported by the U.S.-based Pastors for Peace, has developed a public street lighting project in collaboration with the government's electricity provider in the popular council of Los Pocitos, and worked closely on social programs with the Psychiatric Hospital of Havana.

Perhaps no organization has been more active than the Centro Cristiano de Reflexión y Diálogo (Christian Center for Reflection and Dialogue). Founded in 1991 by the Presbyterian pastor Raymundo García Franco, the Centro has begun to deliver a variety of basic social services in the city of Cárdenas, assuming a large share of previously state-administered responsibilities (Margaret Crahan, personal communication, 12 May 2003). With funds from religious institutions in the United States, Canada, Germany, and Spain, the centro repairs public buildings; supplies state schools, hospitals, and nursing homes with fresh agricultural produce; and runs environmental care programs with its own newly purchased trucks and other heavy equipment (García Franco 2000:6).

Despite its considerable social impact, García Franco is careful to point out, "Our organization is a modest resource for the nation and our people that in no way competes with or substitutes the state. . . . [W]e respect the political authority of the government" (García Franco 2000:6–7). Nevertheless, researchers at Havana's Centro de Investigaciones Psicológicas y Sociológicas (Center for Psychological and Sociological Research, CIPS) detect a changing of the guard in the area of social service delivery, characterized by "religious organizations assuming roles and functions, particularly in basic services to the population, at a time when state social institutions cannot deliver them as they used to given the real limitations of the period" (del Rey Roa and Castañeda Mache 2002:99). Welfare activities, they write, have facilitated Christian evangelical efforts: "The distribution of medicine and other products, such as prizes for children's and young people's activities, produces a kind of attraction in participating communities at the grassroots, which could be characterized as the 'jabonización [disinfecting] of evangelism'" (2002:99). To the extent that church-related welfare programs respond to local demands, they serve to ease some of the pressure on the state to fund social services at the grassroots. But as the diary excerpt below indicates, religious welfare work can also consolidate potentially dissenting forms of nonstate solidarity:

Lismaray [the wife of my batá drum teacher in Havana], her friend Aimé, and I went to a Catholic service this evening. Aimé's brother was recently arrested for jineteando [illegally selling goods and services to foreigners] and so a service was held for him at the Old Havana Cathedral. About twenty people made up the congregation, many of them carrying clothes, containers of food, and other gifts for their loved one. Aimé said that some of these people were friends, others relatives, but most were connected to her brother through belonging to the same Santería rama [branch, or family of initiation]. The service was quick: an Our Father, a Hail Mary, and a short sermon by the priest about the value of helping others through difficult times.

Then there was a clear change of tone as the priest started instructing the congregation on the logistics of the visit: they would walk to the Dragones police station [about half an hour away on foot] in an orderly fashion and would light candles when they approached. After presenting the prisoner with gifts they had brought, they would sit with their candles lit outside on the steps of the police station until the morning. Since it's the middle of December it gets cold at night, so the priest gave each of us a blanket, to be returned tomorrow. Having been in Cuba for less than a month, and since I'm hoping to stay for almost two years, I decided not to join the group in case it might have consequences for my visa application. I was about to give the blanket back to the priest but Lismaray quietly suggested otherwise: "When we leave the church give it to me. We could use these at home: didn't you say you've been cold at night?" The priest finished handing out blankets and suggested that anyone with any money to spare should put it in the donation box on the wall after the service, because "that's how we can continue our community work." I told Lismaray that I wasn't carrying any money with me and she replied, "Oh, that's alright, neither is anyone else."

—Havana, December 2000

The congregation in this episode came together to publicly show support for a young man charged with taking advantage of foreign tourists. The march to the Dragones police station, organized as a religious activity, was peaceful and did not openly criticize any government policy or ideological position. But it did carry political weight as an organized nonstate activity drawing public attention to the plight of Aimé's brother and others in his predicament. The public spectacle of a candle-lit vigil on the steps of the

Dragones police station, regardless of its intentions, would surely have conveyed a vivid public message that organized protest is not an unthinkable avenue for expressing collective dissent.

While some of the marchers may have harbored this political objective, there is a range of other factors that condition how such events play out. From the state's perspective, a degree of tolerance for public protest conveys a message of official respect for civil rights to domestic and foreign political observers. In the case of small church-affiliated actions like the event above, it also conveys appreciation for larger Christian political cooperation and much needed contributions of material resources. Christian groups are aware, however, that this appreciation has limits, and most have kept their protest actions relatively small for fear of having their channels of international support blocked (Crahan and Armony 2006:35).

International linkages and material resources are central to the legitimacy of Christian groups in Cuba, and probably also factored into the episode in question. There is growing evidence that free gifts and material benefits (in this case, blankets) have made participation in church activities more attractive, causing some ministers to lament that unrealistic hopes for economic assistance and overseas travel are encroaching on the spiritual appeal of Christianity (Clemente et al. 1995:57). It is worth noting that exactly the same problem plagued Christian communities before 1959. Margaret Crahan quotes a Christian leader celebrating its resolution by the early 1970s: "Before, many became members of the church precisely to take advantage of the benefits of the primary schools and of the colleges, to be a candidate for a scholarship in the United States, to receive help—social and economic—from the church. . . . But people come to church now because of a profound religious conviction; we have members of greater quality" (Wallace 1973:7, quoted in Crahan 1979:167). Renewed concerns about the motivations of churchgoers reflect a resurgence of both material scarcities in post-1990 Cuba and a resurgence of Christian social activism.

But beyond its material dimension, this activism also responds to powerful psychological needs in the aftermath of the Soviet collapse. As Rafael Hernández puts it, "The discrediting of a bankrupt "real socialism" had an ideological effect, provoking disorientation and the loss of historically created referents for wide sectors of the population. . . . [A]wakening to the post-Cold War world was, for Cubans, like waking into an endless nightmare" (2003:101). Many previously nonreligious Cubans, writes Clemente, have filled this acute ideological vacuum by turning to God: "For many, their ideologies and associated values collapsed along with the Berlin Wall, and they were left empty, looking for shelter from the storm. From professionals and managers to militant communists, they approached the church with curiosity, anxiety, uncertainty, and in some cases fear, but today they are baptized believers, missionaries, and even pastors" (1995:56).

A growing recourse to personal spirituality is evident in both the growing size of Christian congregations and in an unprecedented enthusiasm for charismatic forms of worship, which offer a heightened sense of spiritual experience. Driven on by energetic live music, worshippers outwardly express spiritual emotions and speak without restraint about their personal experience of God. Ramírez Calzadilla notes that the public emergence of these practices has attracted practitioners of "popular religions" particularly to Protestant churches: "At the end of the twentieth century Protestant churches started to incorporate charismatic forms whose participatory and dynamic ceremonial style—involving experimentation, 'possession,' and healing—has generated popular acceptance conditioned by the resemblance of these practices to forms through which Cubans have traditionally expressed their religiosity" (2001:6). Christian liturgies have also introduced theater and dance programs that aim to convey moral lessons in a more accessible form, and the use of traditional Cuban musical instruments that facilitate a stronger sense of connectedness and locality among worshippers. On the train from Santiago de Cuba to Havana, a young woman told me how these kinds of performative religious activities influenced her recent conversion to Christianity:

SINGING THE LORD'S SONG

About ten minutes out of Santiago the woman sitting to my right turned to me and asked what book I was reading. I replied that it [was] a novel about a whale, called *Moby-Dick.* "Oh, that's interesting," she said, "but have you tried reading this book?" She was reading a leather-bound, red and gold embroidered Bible, so I took the opportunity to ask her a few questions about her faith.

Beatriz said she had become Methodist last year, and that since coming to know the Savior her troubled life—complicated by deaths in the family and her own depression—had finally started to make sense. She had previously gone to Santeros and babalawos in her home city of Guantánamo to cure her insomnia, but their "superstitions" and "high prices" had only depressed her further. Relief finally came when Beatriz's uncle (who was sitting across the aisle and also reading a Bible) took her to his church and introduced her to a new group of friends. "Until then," she said, "I was living a sinful life: going out with lot of boys and dancing regguetón" [a style of music, influenced by Jamaican dance hall, that is very popular, particularly in Cuba's eastern provinces]. "Do you not dance anymore?" I asked. "No, but I've started a rap band. Would you like to hear?" She took a notebook out of her bag and chose a song called "Me lo Dijo El Señor" [The Lord Told Me So]. Her rhymes were so well composed and delivered with such conviction and talent that people sitting in the surrounding aisles applauded when she finished, inspiring her to perform another one.

Beatriz asked me if I would like to visit her church in Havana. She [is] going to perform there next week and use the church's audio equipment, not available to her in Guantánamo, to record a tape. I said I'd like to visit and she gave me a bookmark illustrated with pictures of Jesus for me to contemplate while reading *Moby-Dick*. "Maybe I've done some good today," she said, "and so maybe it wasn't a coincidence that our seats were together." I agreed.

—Santiago de Cuba, February 2002

In a context where personal ambitions are often frustrated by a lack of resources and opportunities, Christian organizations offer an alternative space for self-expression and social recognition. Although Beatriz's conversion to Christianity was motivated by her desire to live a more satisfying and upright life, her enthusiasm for preaching her faith resulted largely from her church's support of her artistic talents. The growing attention of Christian authorities to the interests of young believers like Beatriz have made previously unattainable ambitions, such as traveling to Havana to perform and record music, a real possibility for thousands of potential converts.

This socially engaged orientation has brought new energy and numbers to Christian congregations, but it is less clear how strongly participants in emerging church-affiliated activities feel themselves to be loyal members of the larger Christian establishment. Despite the success of Christian community outreach programs, Cuban religious life remains characterized by a high incidence of home worship and informal practice, or what Ramírez Calzadilla calls, "spontaneous religion": "To consider only membership excludes believers who do not participate, resulting in a flawed profile of real religious presence in the population. Following such a model, an estimate cannot be made about the social weight of spontaneous religion, nor about expressions whose practitioners do not always recognize themselves as members of a religious group" (2000:82). Ramírez Calzadilla identifies three levels of religious belief, organization, and structure: first, spontaneous participation that has little or no formalized structure; second, semistructured individual or communal worship of miraculous figures; and third, organized institutional worship with specifically corresponding beliefs (2000:63). These forms of expression constitute an important part of both Christian and Afro-Cuban religions. Practitioners of Santería, for example, make extensive use of sacred objects and domestic shrines but also belong to meticulously structured religious communities that assign specific spiritual and ceremonial responsibilities to appropriately trained initiates. The organizational structures of Christianity are more widely and openly recognized than those of Santería, but many Christians also practice their faith away from churches, at homemade shrines and in informal gatherings. This folk dimension of Christianity has been integral to the religion's historical formation in Cuba and other Latin American countries, both facilitating and growing out of syncretic exchanges with African and Native American religious traditions (Levine 1992, Ramírez Calzadilla 2000, Ortiz 1993, Vallier 1970). As Fidel Castro puts it, "Cuba is generally considered a Catholic country. I do not accept this. Because the terms are confused. Many people were baptized in the Catholic Church. In general, when a priest would go to the countryside it was to carry out baptisms. . . . [Y]es, I can say that in the countryside the vast majority of the population are believers. But what have they believed in? Well, I think it is a sort of cocktail of all beliefs" (1982:55–58). Hugh Thomas (1971:1124) similarly observed that it is "hard to distinguish Afro-Cuban religion from lower class Catholicism," while Pablo Alfonso (1985) notes that "Cuba is not Indian, nor white nor black, but mulata [mixed]. Cuba is not Catholic, nor Protestant, nor atheist, but creyente [believer]."

Interreligious dialogue is a historic tradition that continues to shape the development of Cuban Christianity in the new millennium, and according to the eminent Catholic priest and scholar Carlos Manuel de Céspedes García Menocal, it is a heritage that should be embraced. Former executive director of the Cuban Council of Bishops and a vicar of the Archdiocese of Havana, Céspedes is the great-grandson of the legendary independence fighter Carlos Manuel de Céspedes, who declared the freedom of enslaved Africans in 1868. As Orozco and Bolívar note, "If today there is a Cuban priest respected by the leaders of Afro-Cuban cults, he is Céspedes" (1998:319). Calling for Catholic leaders to strengthen the popular bases of their congregations, Céspedes advocates the church's acceptance of believers of Afro-Cuban religions, "even in the most marginalized and delinquent sectors of Cuban society" (Céspedes 1995:17). Greater diversity and popular participation, he writes, are ultimately good for the health of the church: "I have the impression that today the Catholic Church enjoys a level of appreciation and attention in all layers of the social texture, probably more than at any point in the past one hundred and fifty years of our history. . . . I think that this appreciation will expand if the Catholic Church thoughtfully comes to terms with our growing *mestizaje* [heterogeneity]. . . . All of this for the cause of promoting a culture of tolerance and pluralism concomitant with human nature" (1995:21–22). Diversity, he continues, is also a question of political vision: "In a society like ours, ecclesiastic goodwill suffers difficulties conditioned by a centralized, vertical conception of the state. The transcendence of this situation through a conception that is more participatory, decentralized, and democratic would result in a better development of ecclesiastic life and spiritual growth for our people, in the direction of its own identity, culture, and idiosyncrasy" (1995:22).

But according to Fidel Castro, no institution has discouraged participation and diversity more than the Catholic Church, which was precisely the cause of its original clash with the revolution:

That's how the initial conflicts with the church began, because those [privileged] sectors wanted to use the church as a tool against the revolution. How was it that they could attempt that? Because of a factor that was characteristic of Cuba but not of Brazil, Colombia, Mexico, Peru, or many other Latin American countries: the church in Cuba wasn't popular; it wasn't a church of the people, the workers, the farmers, the poorer sectors of the population. Here, in our country, something that was already in vogue and which later became common practice in most of the Latin American countries had never been applied: that of priests working side by side with the villagers and workers, priests working in the fields. . . . [T]here wasn't a single church in the countryside, not a single priest in the countryside. (Castro 1986:147)

While the Cuban Catholic Church has acknowledged a historic "distribution of apostolic personnel that has privileged the middle and upper classes" (ENEC 1986:40), Céspedes would clearly like to turn this situation around. He is among a number of Catholic leaders calling for greater outreach and tolerance for "informal" and syncretic worship in order to strengthen the church's capacity to represent and draw support from more diverse sectors (Alonso Tejada 1995:24). This kind of gradual bottom-up consolidation could strengthen the church's legitimacy as a civil society protagonist, and may prove more effective than formal approaches to Christian institution building, which have long been by inhibited by a combination of legal obstacles, conservatism among religious leaders, and noninstitutional worship (Crahan 2000:26–27, Crahan and Armony 2006:34). Furthermore, building more dynamic and representative institutions through dialogue with other religious communities makes good sense in a society so long characterized by religious syncretism. Fernando Ortiz considered this historical legacy of ethnic mixing central to the formation of Cuban national identity (*cubanidad*), whose consolidation was embodied in the unifying symbol of Cuba's patron saint, the Virgen de la Caridad del Cobre (Ortiz 1929). The next section considers the Virgen's continuing ability to bring together followers of different religions, and the potential of such unions to represent public interests in an organized fashion.

The Virgen, the Pope, and the Politics of Syncretism

The Virgen de la Caridad del Cobre is probably the most widely venerated religious figure in Cuba, her popularity arising largely from the syncretism of the Catholic Virgin Mary with the Santería deity Ochún, the goddess of female sensuality. The Virgen's religious plurality hails back to the legendary discovery of her image on a wooden tablet by two native "Indian" Cubans and an enslaved African fishing off the north coast of the eastern city of Barajagua in 1613 (Portuondo Zúñiga 1995:8). Located for a time in a Barajagua slave hospital, the image was eventually brought to the mines of El Cobre in the mid-seventeenth century, where it was venerated by black and native mine workers together with white supervisors. In her unparalleled study of the Virgen de la Caridad, Olga Portuondo Zúñiga, the officially appointed Historian of Santiago de Cuba, notes that different depictions of the Virgen's apparition at sea reflect changing historical contexts, such as growing ecclesiastical pressure in the early nineteenth century to represent all Cubans in the image by replacing one of the native "Indian" sailors with a white one (1995:11).

Although the Virgen de la Caridad was not officially declared patron saint of Cuba until 1916, she has typically been depicted as a mixed race *mulata* since the mid-nineteenth century, in this way providing "a central trope through which Cuba has struggled over its claimed *mestizaje* national identity and its attendant anxieties about social crossings of race and class" (Brown 2003:224). The Virgen's mestizaje surfaced in a more overtly political form in the 1950s, when both pro- and anti-Batista forces appealed to her for assistance. Following the triumph of the revolution her statue was transported to Havana for the National Catholic Congress attended by an estimated one million Cubans, including Fidel, at which shouts of "Cuba si, comuniso no" rang out (Crahan and Armony 2006:6). To the present day the Virgen is characterized by heterogeneous interpretations, whose Catholic and Afro-Cuban character reflect the diversity of her devotees (Corbea Calzado 1996:7). Each year on the evening of 7 September, the eve of the Virgen's feast day, these diverse believers come together in their thousands for a twenty-five-kilometer processional walk from Santiago de Cuba to El Cobre. In 2001 I participated in the walk, and noted some observations along the way in my diary:

TO EL COBRE ON FOOT

By 7 p.m. there must be two or three thousand people gathered right here on the main road of San Pedrito. Everybody is waiting for the procession to officially begin. A group of my friends from the neighborhood has dressed in white and are going to do the [twenty-five-kilometer] walk, so we've brought four bottles of rum, made up the street by Oscar in his basement, to keep us going. My companions tell me that the walk will not be easy, but that for some of them that's the whole point: Daniel, for example, has made a promise to Ochún that he'll go the distance on foot because she helped him with a romantic problem last year. Vicente [my batá drum teacher], was worried about me going off on the walk, but as with so many occasions, his friends pointed out that I will be protected by his musical and religious reputation.

At last a man at the front of the crowd with a megaphone is getting the procession under way. He welcomes the crowd on behalf of the Cathedral of El Cobre and then says a Hail Mary, which the collective voice of the crowd repeats, with some exceptions. My friends, for example, are not the most solemn of participants. They're chatting away and laughing, drawing glares from more subdued participants. I notice as I look around that there are many light-skinned people present, many of whom are carrying Bibles. There are many more people with darker skin.

The crowd slowly moves forward along the road. We pass a number of shrines along the way, at which people stop to light candles and say Hail Marys and Our Fathers. These tend to be the people with fair skin. Their solemn manner is again at odds with that of my friends and other darker-complexioned participants, many of whom are having a great time telling jokes, singing, and clapping the rumba clave [the rhythmic foundation of the Afro-Cuban musical style called rumba]. Not far ahead we hear the sound of drums coming from a small house, its front door open. My friends—most of them accomplished percussionists—quicken their pace, heading for the house. It's a bembé [Santería musical ceremony with conga drums (tumbadoras) and calabash rattles (chekeres)] that's being held for Ochún, and so we join in: singing, clapping, and playing the tumbadoras and chekeres, and drinking rum. We leave after about fifteen minutes, content and energized for the walk that will take a good four or five hours longer.

We notice a lot of police cars along the way, and at one point one stops and three officers watch us pass by. One of them, with a video recorder on his shoulder, approaches us and puts the camera right on us. My friends are not worried by this. They just sing even louder and laugh and clap. This happens four more times before we arrive at El Cobre.

Only four of us remain when we arrive. The rest of the group jumped on trucks as they went on their way to El Cobre. Approaching the cathedral the road is crowded with people dancing to the latest pop songs, projected from loudspeakers mounted on trees. Vendors sell pizza, rice with pork, orange soda, beer, and rum right up to the church steps. Inside the cathedral is a different atmosphere altogether. People are kneeling or sitting in the pews, waiting for the service to begin. Its eventual commencement is signaled by a statue of the Virgen, which rotates on a motorized turntable to face the congregation. I notice about twenty minutes into the mass that a good number of people have fallen asleep.

—Santiago de Cuba, September 2001

Clearly the veneration of the Virgen brings a wide range of people into close proximity and shared activity. It is equally clear that within this shared activity they participate with distinct objectives. In some ways the procession resembles accounts from the seventeenth century, which describe extravagant food and drink, amusements, music and dance, and the participation of whites, blacks, and mulattos (Portuondo Zúñiga 1985:156). One particularly striking account was recorded by Fonseca: "At last the Holy Virgin's followers started a solemn procession, illuminated with wax candles, with the musical intonations of praises to the Holy Mary; at the same time, the blacks danced with their *atabillos* [drums] and other creations" (quoted in Corbeo Calzado 1996:8). The Virgen was, and still is, a symbol of collective identity, whose wide appeal seems to lie precisely in her semantic flexibility.

Corbea Calzado recorded the attendance of approximately 1,400 people at the procession to El Cobre in 1979, and over 12,000 in 1994 (1996:10). These numbers reflect a growing convergence of spiritual affinities and personal

The Virgen de la Caridad del Cobre (the Virgin of Charity from [the town of] Cobre), with three sailors at her feet. Courtesy of Tania Jovanovic.

objectives in the Virgen's annual celebration. Daniel, for example, endured the walk because he had made a promise to Ochún, and yet he waited in line like everyone else for the official procession to commence with a Hail Mary. The man with the megaphone, officially in charge of leading the procession on behalf of the Cathedral of El Cobre, gave the event an outwardly Catholic veneer by bringing devotees of Ochún and Catholics into apparently organized religious solidarity. The political significance of solidarity behind the image of the Virgen has been noted by John Kirk, who writes that the 1961 march to El Cobre "was intended by many as a show of force in political as well as religious terms" that escalated into an antirevolution protest and the subsequent expulsion of 130 priests from the island (1989:102). In the politically turbulent year of 1990, the specter of popular religious unity once again triggered official concerns that the procession to El Cobre might become an organized antigovernment protest, resulting in its suspension (Eckstein 1994:122). On the road to El Cobre in 2001, an abundance of police officers, some of them equipped with video cameras, indicates that to some extent the same fear persists.

Official concerns about religiously based political action in contemporary Cuba may not be unfounded. In Latin America and Eastern Europe the 1980s saw cooperating religious institutions and believers playing a crucial role in opening up authoritarian regimes to democratic reform (Wood 1997:307). In Poland, for example, the widely venerated image of the Black Madonna emerged as a national symbol of popular unity and even appeared on the lapel of the Solidarity Movement leader Lec Walesa when he signed the 1980 Gdansk accords, with an oversized pope souvenir pen (Osa 1996:69).

Rafael Duharte Jiménez notes that as early as the mid-nineteenth century the Cuban Catholic Church was intentionally using the image of the Virgen de la Caridad to consolidate popular support, particularly among believers of Afro-Cuban religions, "who were accustomed to the phenomenon of multiple depiction" (2001:69). Despite the diverging Catholic and Afro-Cuban interpretations of the Virgen, or perhaps because of them, her unifying image appears to have brought about a gradual process of interreligious dialogue resembling what Daniel Levine (1992) calls "linkage": the development of collaborative relations between legally registered, socially prominent religious organizations and locally influential popular religious associations. The political potentials of such solidarities are described by Christian Smith: "Religion can and sometimes does cut across class, occupation, and racial lines in ways that link people together who would otherwise remain isolated. Therefore, when religion, in these cases, lends itself to an activist cause, the social movement automatically benefits from the advantages that these cross-cutting social associations bring" (1996:20–21).

The notion of a well-integrated religiously based social movement in Cuba overstates the current capacities of the country's religious organizations, though perhaps not their ambitions. As González and Nuccio put it, "Catholic and Santería priests . . . are capable of attracting a mass following as a counter-elite" (1999:8). The Catholic Church in particular has sought to publicly present a socially integrated face resembling that described by Smith both in the yearly procession to El Cobre and during Pope John Paul II's visit to Cuba in 1998. In a meeting organized by the Catholic Cardinal Jaime Ortega to introduce the pope to leaders of other religions, no Santeros or babalawos were invited to attend alongside their Protestant and Jewish counterparts (Pérez Sarduy 1998:39). Ortega justified their absence by suggesting that initiates of Santería (whose religion requires them to be baptized Catholic) did not need to be represented independently of the church because "they have never felt foreign or even distant from us" (quoted in Orozco and Bolívar 1998:321). The explanation stood at odds with Ortega's previous descriptions of Santería as a collection of reductive folkloric traditions, an opinion echoed in the pope's declaration that "syncretic cults, while meriting respect, cannot be considered a religion per se" (quoted in R. González 1998:2).

At a time of global attention on the Cuban Catholic Church, Ortega's explanation was strategic: it painted a picture of national religious unity that was emboldened by the open recognition of Protestant Christians and a minority Jewish contingent but that would have been thrown utterly out of perspective by the recognition of Afro-Cuban religions, which are followed to some extent by approximately 70 percent of the population (Pérez Sarduy 1998:40). It was at this opportune time that the state's Centro de Prensa Internacional (International Press Center) presented news reporters with a babalawo, Enrique Hernández Armenteros, who offered an alternative perspective on the pope's visit. The move was interpreted by some as an act of political manipulation on the part of the state, intended to highlight differences and aggravate tensions between Santeros and Catholics (Orozco and Bolívar 1998:323–324; also see Tamayo 1998:1). The notion that the state sought to engineer a divisive relationship between the church and believers of Afro-Cuban religions is supported by researchers at Havana's Centro de Investigaciones Psicológicas y Sociológicas (Center for Psychological and Sociological Research, CIPS), who anonymously published a report in 1998 alleging that the Cuban Communist Party's acceptance of religious members in 1991 and subsequent modification of the constitution reflect an ongoing "process of political manipulations that seek to generate a religious conflict of churches" (CIPS 1998). It is worth noting that the man who piloted these legal reforms, Carlos Aldana, had long been critical of Catholic ambitions in Cuba: "Unfortunately, the Catholic hierarchy in Cuba is an extension of Miami thinking, an extension of a political stance that is basically annexationist. They are very identified with a program of capitalist restoration" (quoted in Orozco 1993:590).

The state's ability to draw attention to (and perhaps widen) cracks in public projections of religious unity is strengthened by long-standing animosities between official Catholic and Afro-Cuban religious leaders. Commenting on Ortega's reluctance to recognize Afro-Cuban religions, the director of the Asociación Cultural Yoruba de Cuba (Yoruba Cultural Association of Cuba), Antonio Castañeda Márquez, told me:

> I don't try to make links with the Catholic Church. When the pope was here there were some crazy babalawos who wanted to meet him. CNN

and other news channels came to ask me if I was going to officially represent Cuban followers of Yoruba religion. I said, "If the pope wants to meet us we're happy to talk, but I'm not asking him for this because we have nothing in common." Let's not forget that our religion was around long before Christianity. I have nothing against Christians and I respect all other religions. In fact I don't even ask people what religion they are when they apply to join our association.

The Catholics aren't as tolerant though. Remember, Cardinal Ortega said we're profane and that we're a cult of devil worshippers. It was a bad comparison, but he made it. And notice that afterward he took it back. After all it's our people who fill his churches, and have done for two hundred years. Go to church and see how many *collares* [Santería necklaces] are there! So he took his comment back because he realized that if he says things like that his following will evaporate!

Personally I don't think that would be a bad thing. Here in the association we've created a shrine for worshipping the orichas, but people still present iyawós [new Santería initiates] at church. It's a Cuban tradition. (Interview, 9 January 2006)

Castañeda notes that despite his differences with Ortega, the Cuban tradition of interreligious dialogue continues to develop at the grassroots. As Carlos Manuel de Céspedes puts it: "In other countries where syncretism is similarly present, a dependent of such sects can live their whole life without ever stepping into a Catholic place of worship and without ever having contact with a priest. In Cuba, this is not possible: from baptism (initiation) to the funeral (death), a syncretic worshipper requires the pastoral services of the Catholic Church" (Céspedes 1995:17–18). Ceremonial requirements, such as those that oblige Santería initiates to first be baptized in the Catholic Church and then regularly attend masses for deceased ancestors, lead to interreligious contact that can have political as well as spiritual consequences (R. González 1998:3). A good example is recorded in the diary excerpt presented earlier in this chapter, which described a Catholic service for an incarcerated man. When I recorded the event in my diary I was interested in the role of the church in providing congregations with scarce material resources and social services. It did not strike me as significant at the time that the congregation was made up largely of people connected to the incarcerated man through Santería. But the members of his rama (branch) had come together to protest the arrest of their religious brother in a way that they almost certainly would not have without church support.

The church's political capacity in such situations results largely from its official recognition as an established and clearly structured organization, a recognition that Santería communities do not share (Pedraza 1998). This is not to say that Santería and other Afro-Cuban religions are not structured in their hierarchies of authority, service, and responsibility. On the contrary, many of these structures date back to precolonial Nigeria and Benin and have been meticulously described in anthropological literature on the subject, starting with the works of Bascom (1969a, 1969b, 1980), Herskovits (1967), and Ortiz (1973 [1906], 1987 [1916], 1984 [1921], 1995 [1940], 1950), and extending through to the current ethnological research of institutions such as the Casa del Caribe. Furthermore, despite a history of discrimination preventing their official organization, Afro-Cuban religious communities are unified by certain sociocultural values and have engaged in political action since long before, and long since, Cuba's independence from Spain (Ramírez Calzadilla 2001:5). Black political activism has correlated historically with periods of rapid social transformation in Cuba, reflecting Lázara Menéndez Vázquez's (1995, 2002) observation that Santería has always adapted to its socioeconomic surroundings to protect the interests of its members (as discussed in chapter 1). Religiously based organizations like the Cabildo Carabalí Isuama of Santiago de Cuba (discussed below) not only protected the legal interests of their members in the colonial and republican eras but also played a crucial role in the "Aponte conspiracy" of 1812, the black uprising of 1835, and both of Cuba's wars of independence from Spain (Bettelheim 1991:69, Brown 2003:55–61, P. Howard 1998, Rushing 1992). Furthermore, the rebellion of 1912 relied heavily on Afro-Cuban religious imagery and the mobilization of religious networks to transmit resources and information. The 1912 movement was suppressed, but networks of Afro-Cuban activism persisted.

By the 1920s and 1930s some of these networks had evolved into organizations dedicated to securing professional and political opportunities for black Cubans (R. Moore 1997). Others went further, promoting a black-nationalist agenda premised on racial segregation (Fernández Robaina 1993:96). This project was ultimately subsumed by the larger, racially integrated labor campaigns organized in opposition to the rule of President Gerardo Machado (1924–1933). Throughout the 1930s and 1940s the National Federation of Black Societies and the Atenas Club both actively worked to consolidate the unity of Afro-Cuban workers, and by the late 1950s the lawyer René Betancourt was advocating the establishment of exclusively black cooperatives (Sergiat 1993:82–84). The Revolution of 1959 arrested this ambition, but the political activism of black organizations continued. In 1970, for example, employees of the Havana docks paralyzed the facility in a twenty-four-hour strike to protest the government's interference with *abakuá* brotherhoods (C. Moore 1988a:306).

Afro-Cuban political resistance emerged again in the mid-1990s, the most difficult years of the Special Period, as street protests erupted in Guanabacoa and other areas strongly associated with Afro-Cuban religions (Ayorinde 2004:158–160, cited in Crahan and Armony 2006:26). More recently, the growth of unregistered associations such as Ilé Tun Tun and Ifá Iranlowo and the efforts of state institutions to collaborate with Santería communities in neighborhood development initiatives indicate the unique political challenges and opportunities raised by the continuing strength of Afro-Cuban religions. As Rafael Hernández writes:

> At the level of civil society, the most widespread Cuban religions of African origin represent a network of relations and social mobilization more important than that of a Catholic Church that continues, in its structure, its ideological positions, and its social practice, to be relatively rigid and unrepresentative. Unlike the Catholic Church, Santería does not have a rigid national hierarchy, nor does it answer to the designs of a foreign power like the Vatican. Santería's hierarchies and modes of social organization are rooted in civil society itself, and they operate in a more democratic and popular fashion. If the associations and sites of worship of these popular religions were a breeding ground for political opposition, then the stability of the system would be broadly placed in question. (2003:59)

The church, says Hernández, is less representative of popular interests than Santería, but has a more officially recognized administrative hierarchy. Indeed, at the vigil outside the Dragones police station described earlier in the chapter, the church's official standing and legal legitimacy provided an institutional platform for the Santeros to protest the arrest of their brother. Mounting the vigil through the church made sense since an independent protest against the police would likely have provoked further arrests. As Ivor Miller has observed, outside of folkloric performance and participation in ethnological research, Afro-Cuban religions have not generally penetrated the public sphere either legally or culturally: "Like the proverbial black grandmother hidden from view in a family striving to 'pass' for white, Afro-Cuban religions remain hidden from view in polite society" (2000:32). The Catholic Church is comparatively more visible in public affairs, protected as it is by legally recognized networks of global solidarity that strengthen its capacity to represent and protect the interests of expanding congregations.

One of the church's bolder public moves in recent years was the 1995 publication of the El Amor Todo lo Espera (Everybody Awaits Love) declaration, which draws attention to "discrimination based on philosophical and political ideas, or religious creed" and concludes that "the only solution that presents itself is to resist" (Cuban Council of Bishops 1995:399). The declaration signaled the church's determination to "resist" what it viewed as prejudice endemic to the social structure and revealed its broader ambition to diversify society by opening new avenues of dialogue and spaces for civil action (del Rey Roa 2002:98). To promote this agenda the church hosted Pope John Paul II's visit to Cuba in 1998, which it hoped would revitalize the Catholic community and bring new opportunities for evangelization. To an extent the visit facilitated the church's ambitions, winning it new converts from among the thousands of onlookers who attended the pope's public masses, and affording it the opportunity to openly express its support for greater civil freedoms and social engagement. The pope voiced this political vision in his sermon in the Plaza de la Revolución: "A modern state cannot make atheism or religion one of its political ordinances. The state, while distancing itself from all extremes of fanaticism or secularism, should encourage a harmonious social climate and a suitable legislation that enables every person and every religious confession to live their faith freely, to express that faith in the context of public life, and to count on adequate resources and opportunities to bring its spiritual, moral, and civil benefits to bear on the life of the nation" (John Paul II 2003:635).

Despite such bold statements, many of the specific concessions pursued by the church and the Vatican to help them bring their influence to bear on the nation have not materialized. Greater leverage with the government through access to the press and expanded public engagement programs, for instance, has been slow to mature. The most dynamic area of activity has been the intensification of Christian community development work, though projects continue to be closely monitored and required to comply with conditions laid down by the state.

Already cynical about the Cuban state's approach to civil liberties, Castro's detractors in Miami were outraged by the announcement of the pope's visit. At the core of their apprehension was the inevitable attempt of the Cuban government to use the visit to build diplomatic legitimacy and buttress already broad international criticism of the U.S. embargo. Apprehension turned to dismay when the pope condemned the embargo as immoral and illegal under international law, a sentiment that was soon after echoed by Protestant, Jewish, and Afro-Cuban religious leaders, as well as Catholic bishops in the United States (Crahan 2006:36). But despite these political victories for the Cuban state, the pope's visit did not bring about the international relations coup that Castro had hoped for. Not only was there nothing new about Catholic condemnation of the embargo (which it has criticized repeatedly since 1968) but the Cuban state was caught off guard by unexpectedly stern public assessments of civil rights in Cuba from both the archbishop of Santiago de Cuba and the pope himself.

The mutual concessions and frustrations that the pope's visit brought the Catholic Church and the Cuban state are perhaps best described as "an example of syncretism . . . this time between Marxism and Catholicism, between the pope and Fidel" (Orozco and Bolivar 1998:539). Testament to this uneasy "syncretism" was Castro's official recognition of the church as a legitimate social actor in Cuba, even as its expanding community welfare activities were publicly portrayed as cooperative and in solidarity with the state. Ideological syncretism, in this case, was based on a curiously profane covenant: the prospect of wider public space for evangelical and civic engagement in exchange for political and material support for the state and its overburdened social service sector.

Although the church's civic capacities remain weaker than its leaders had hoped, more active community engagement since the early 1990s has allowed Christian groups to extend their influence into material and ideological terrain previously occupied by the state. The public commitments of Christian leaders to work cooperatively rather than in competition with the state to fill these spaces indicate the political sensitivity of the situation. Ultimately the ability of religious organizations to build cooperative relations with the state may be less important than their ability to build cooperative relations with one another. Horizontal linkage increases the "exchange value" of social capital at the grassroots, and therefore the legitimacy of religious organizations as representatives of civil society capable of negotiating with and influencing the state.

The official positions of the Cuban Catholic Church and the Yoruba Cultural Association of Cuba do not enhance the prospects for broad-based interreligious cooperation. While Cardinal Ortega has stated that the best hope for protecting the gains of the revolution lies in public engagement and the construction of an inclusive, spiritually conscious civil society (Crahan and Armony 2006:33), his reluctance to openly recognize Afro-Cuban religions will probably impede this goal. As for Castañeda, skeptics might identify his lack of enthusiasm for proactive engagement with the church as an indication of the Yoruba Cultural Association's affiliation with the Ministry of Culture (discussed in chapter 1). Despite this official antagonism (or perhaps because of it), interreligious dialogue will likely develop most vibrantly—as it has done historically—at the grassroots, away from public announcements and press releases.

In the remainder of the chapter I present two case studies from Santiago de Cuba that illustrate how the civic capacities of community organizations are shaped largely by their ability to accommodate spiritual and social diversity at the grassroots while maintaining internal solidarity among members. The first examines the historical evolution of an Afro-Cuban community organization whose political capacities have been shaped for nearly two centuries by its official relationship with the Catholic Church, its commitment to protecting the spiritual and material interests of its members, and its patriotic activism. The second case study considers a remarkable convergence of spirituality, homosexuality, and patriotic allegiance to the revolution in a state-operated neighborhood welfare organization.

Case Study 1: Religion and Nationalism in an Afro-Cuban Cabildo

Shortly after I arrived in Santiago de Cuba in June 2001 I was introduced to the director of the Cabildo Carabalí Isuama by the North American dance scholar Shani Shakur and later presented to its musicians by my batá drum teacher, Vicente Portuondo, who is well known in the city's musical and religious circles (not least because he is the former musical director of the Balet Folklórico Kutumba). I was honored that for the eleven months that I stayed in Santiago de Cuba the Cabildo's drummers accepted me as their student and allowed me to learn about their organization's contemporary activities through daily meetings, lessons, and rehearsals. I supplemented this experience by researching the Cabildo's history through its private collection of original documents; materials held in local libraries, museums, and bookshops; and interviews with researchers at the Casa del Caribe and with the Historian of Santiago de Cuba, Dr. Olga Portuondo Zúñiga. I debated, defended, and revised my thoughts in seminars I presented at the Casa del Caribe, the Office of the Historian, and a conference organized by the Centro Cultural Africano Fernando Ortiz (see Hearn 2002).

During the colonial era the Cabildo Carabalí Isuama possessed strong representative capacities based both on its commitment to protecting the cultural and material interests of its members and on the legal legitimacy it gained from official collaboration with the Catholic Church. The Cabildo's mutual aid functions and religious activities became less visible in the repressive environment of the republican era, and declined further after 1959, when it became formally registered and subsidized by the state as a symbol of national cultural patrimony. Over the months that I got to know the Cabildo's members, many of whom are now senior citizens, I learned how they have revived a variety of its mutual aid activities to ease the economic pressures of the Special Period. They have also become less anxious about outwardly expressing their religious heritage in public parades, and have even reestablished tentative links with the church. While these activities reflect the Cabildo's spiritual and social identity, they also exhibit its revolutionary patriotism, resulting in a striking convergence of religious and political values and symbols. It is not likely that the contemporary Cabildo will develop representative capacities comparable to those it once possessed, but its case offers insight into grassroots adaptation to political change, and suggests that the changes of the 1990s have permitted it to develop the kinds of civic prerequisites necessary for civil society action.

As early as the late sixteenth century the Catholic Church began to set up lodges called cabildos, particularly in Havana and Santiago de Cuba, to house and educate enslaved and free people of color in the ways of Christianity (Portuondo Zúñiga 2000:85). Spanish authorities tolerated cabildos because their organization along ethnic lines reduced the threat of unified slave revolts, even though they promoted the conservation of African religious identities and cultural values (Manuel 1995:20, Ortiz 1984 [1921]:24–26). While the church encouraged the veneration of Catholic saints in cabildos, Ortiz noted growing Spanish dismay that images of these saints were coming to be used as disguised representations of African deities (Ortiz 1993:61; also see James 1999).

The links that cabildos maintained with the Catholic Church in the late eighteenth and early nineteenth centuries strengthened their legal standing, empowering cabildo leaders to bring issues before civic authorities (Portuondo Zúñiga 2000:79–80). By the 1820s, cabildos in the oldest districts of Havana were even functioning as a kind of police force, rivaling the official law enforcement authorities of some neighborhoods (Bettelheim 1991:67–68). Many cabildos published and circulated newsletters addressing problems faced by black Cubans, and others successfully sponsored the professional training of their members, particularly in trades such as carpentry, masonry, and tailoring (P. Howard 1998:xv, 28). Gladys González Bueno, a historian based at the Casa del Caribe, notes that during the wars of independence (1868–1878, 1895–1898) the Carabalí Isuama and other cabildos supported the nationalist forces by carrying encrypted messages between rebel encampments in drums and flutes, while beating out specific rhythms to signal the whereabouts of Spanish troops (interview, 18 January 2002).

The colonial government of the mid-nineteenth century was extremely sensitive about organized support of independence from Spain, and saw cabildos, which were becoming at once more powerful and autonomous from the church, as a growing threat. Philip Howard notes that the Catholic feast days celebrated by the Cabildo Carabalí Isuama in this period often functioned behind the scenes as strategy meetings for independence fighters (1998:27–28). From 1877 onward cabildos were required by law to allow a state official or police officer to attend their meetings and preside over the election of cabildo leaders and the administration of funds (Brandon 1993:82). As ties between cabildos and their patron churches weakened, the government started regulating them like common social clubs, making it necessary from 1882 for cabildos to obtain a new government-issued license each year to remain officially in operation (Ortiz 1984 [1921]:22).

Unofficially the cabildos continued to be much more than social clubs, and with the legal abolition of slavery taking effect in 1886, they became less ethnically exclusive, incorporating wider circles of people into increasingly powerful networks of exchange and mutual assistance (Portuondo Zúñiga 2000:78). Although the collective funds they raised were no longer used to purchase their members' freedom from slavery, cabildos continued to finance their medical treatment, funerals, and other needs.

By 1910 a series of increasingly restrictive legal regulations under the republican government had forced most cabildos to conduct their meetings secretly and illegally, provoking Ortiz to lament their gradual transformation into "clandestine temples of witchcraft" (1984 [1921]:28). One Matanzas-based group's rare attempt at formal civic engagement in this period is noted by Jorge and Isabel Castellanos (1994:304), who identify the continuing use of a Carabalí-derived language in a public notice enjoining its readers to vote for a candidate to the senate (see facing page).

No longer able to rely on the support of the discredited Catholic Church, cabildos, writes Joseph Murphy, began to transform into autonomous devotional communities: "After independence and the end of the established church, the cabildos were reformulated specifically as cult houses called *reglas* after the regulations of cabildo life. The ethnic cabildos became semi-underground cults, each identified as a different *regla*" (1988:33). The

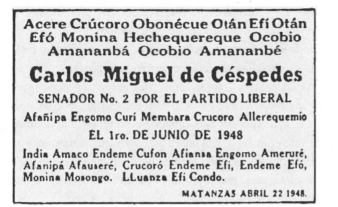

Public notice written in a Carabali-derived language. From Castellanos
and Castellanos 1994:304.

cabildos of Santiago de Cuba nevertheless maintained a strong public presence in the annual carnival, whose vibrant celebration continued in the eastern city even as its sister festival in Havana became increasingly regulated (Bettelheim 1994:70–71; Brown 2003:35, 55–61; Ortiz 1984 [1921]:18).

Today the only remaining cabildos in Santiago de Cuba are the Cabildo Carabalí Isuama and its smaller sister organization, the Cabildo Carabalí Olugo, both of which were founded in the mid-nineteenth century by enslaved Africans from the Calabar region of southwest Nigeria under the stewardship of the Catholic Church. In the 1970s the participation of both groups in the annual city carnival prompted a team of researchers at Santiago de Cuba's Universidad de Oriente to conclude that "the modern Cabildo Carabalí Isuama, despite its efforts to maintain a tradition that dates back to its foundations, is only a *comparsa* [carnival music and dance group] when it comes to its fundamental functions. . . . [I]ts characteristic trait as a mutual aid society with an ethnic basis seems to function as a very secondary factor in the contemporary structure of the Cabildo" (N. Pérez et al. 1982:35). The research report goes on to explain that in the early years of the revolution the Cabildo's economic survival and cultural preservation were secured by its conversion into a "folklore ensemble under the auspices of the National Council of Culture" (1982:29–30). According to the historian Gladys González Bueno, the Cabildo's internal mutual aid functions and characteristic political activism became less prominent at this time because of its integration into official society as a state-subsidized cultural organization (interview, 18 January 2002). This transformation publicly emphasized the Cabildo's long-term contribution to the revolutionary process, essentially turning it into a symbol of national cultural patrimony.

Interviews with its long-term members, many of whom are now in their seventies and eighties, shed light on undocumented aspects of this phase of the Cabildo's history. They reveal, for example, that in the 1960s and 1970s the Carabalí, now an official icon of national heritage, continued to conduct religious activities such as funerals and initiation ceremonies, but it did so cautiously and privately because religion at that time was widely seen as an antinationalist, destructive practice. Furthermore, explains the Cabildo's current director, tensions arose (and to some extent still do) from the membership of homosexual men:

> Men with "the problem," who were members of the Cabildo, used to dress up and dance as women in our parades. There was a time when the majority of our members were gay men, but in 1966 or 1967 the director revoked their membership because of pressure from the Council of Culture. Ever since, most of the Carabalí's members have been women.
>
> These days, very few men join the Cabildo because people might think they're homosexual. And they're right, because except for the drummers, the men who have joined typically are homosexual. Did you notice how during carnival this year quite a few "little birds" joined our parade? I don't like that because they're so fussy with their makeup and costumes; worse than women. But these days we accept them, and even some men who aren't gay like to dress up as women and dance with us. (Tula González Barba, interview, 15 October 2001)

The 1980s saw further changes in the Cabildo. Under the direction of Abelardo Larduet Luaces, a "friends of the Cabildo" group was started in partnership with the local committees for the defense of the revolution (CDRs) to encourage the participation of the community in neighborhood projects such as senior citizens support groups and recreation activities for children (Larduet Luaces, interview, 28 January 2002). The growing interest of young people in the Carabalí resulted in the inauguration of a "junior Cabildo," which conducted folkloric music and dance workshops in collaboration with local schools. Community activities continued into the early 1990s, though a lack of resources since the onset of the Special Period focused the Cabildo's attention on the well-being of its more immediate members. A rehearsal director of the contemporary Carabalí, Miguel Melgares, explained that organized mutual aid has resurfaced as a core function of the Cabildo:

With the necesidades [shortages/needs] of recent years it has become extremely difficult for the older members to get by. Many of them don't have families, and that's where the Cabildo comes in. Culture [the Ministry of Culture, which grew out of the National Council of Culture] only gives us 12 Cuban pesos each per month, so we have to ask members to contribute whatever they can to our collections.

If a member is sick then we of the Cabildo pray for them together and visit them in their house and they feel better because they know that their brothers and sisters care about them. We bring cakes we've made and gifts, and together all this helps their physical recovery. Last month, for example, we visited the Cabildo's king, who is very old and was stuck at home for some weeks. (Interview, 14 August 2001)

The rehearsals of the Carabalí Isuama, which also function as administrative meetings, similarly demonstrate a preoccupation with the well-being of its forty-seven permanent members. Collections of clothing and gifts for needy members and their families are augmented by monthly dues, used to purchase food, medicine, and other necessities. An anonymous ballot decides precisely how and when these resources are used. The Cabildo's director, Tula González Barba, spoke of her plans to construct apartments on top of the Cabildo's lodge as a dormitory for elderly members. This, she hoped, would make it easier to attend to their needs and solve the problem of transporting them to meetings.

As well as protecting the material interests of its members, the Cabildo also cares for their spiritual well-being. According to deputy director Ricardo Marimón:

For the past few years, when a member dies, we go to the official funeral to play Carabalí music. Before bringing the body to the [Santa Ifigenia] cemetery we play the tumbas [Carabalí drums] at the church, and again before the burial. There are specific rhythms to say goodbye to the person and ancient alabanzas [religious farewell songs] that we have received from our Carabalí ancestors. Two years ago we did the funeral of Tomasa Kindelan, who was one of our primary courtiers. It was such an important occasion because it was the first time in as long as I can remember that the Carabalí brought the drums to the church and had a funeral procession in the street. We had to make sure we did the ceremonies correctly because she was an hija de Oyá [devotee of the Santería deity Oyá], the patron of cemeteries. (Interview, 17 August 2001)

The alabanza songs are sung over the cadence of a Carabalí rhythm called *Obiapa*, which is played on the tumbas in between spoken Catholic prayers. But the funeral described by Marimón was somewhat unusual for its public display of spirituality, which, according to the Universidad de Oriente study mentioned earlier, would have been even less likely in the late 1970s: "From what we can discern it is very possible that in private a few of the members practice some kind of religious activity, but this is not true of the *Cabildo* as a whole. . . . [T]he group does not presently exhibit any activities that clash with the ideological line of the revolution" (N. Perez et al. 1982:31).

As I studied with the Cabildo's musicians I gradually began to appreciate the depth of its religious foundations. My musical training began not with drums or even with songs, but with a series of instructive discussions about the Cabildo's spiritual life. "The first thing to learn about," said the percussion director, "is our patron saint":

> On 16 May this year we went to the church of Trinidad to celebrate the feast of our Patron Saint, San Juan Nepomuceno. You should know that he is a miraculous saint, known for silence and tact. One honors and asks the saint with one's heart. He cleanses you of evil thoughts and feelings, and neutralizes the bad actions and intentions of other people, so that they're not effective. This is why we always pray to him before performing in the streets, so that we might prevail.
>
> This is also the function of the *quitapesar* and *prenda*,[1] but I can't tell you about those yet. If you want to know more you'll have to ask the dead people in the cemetery, because one can't give everything. As we of the Cabildo say, if I told you all the things that the old people told me, I wouldn't be anyone. And if I don't exist, then who am I? (Personal communication, 5 July 2001)

Proceeding on a need-to-know basis, the percussion director explained that the spiritual core and most ancient instrument of Carabalí music is the *chá-chá*. This is a set of two shakers, fabricated in the style of the ancient kingdom of Dahomey, woven by hand from palm leaves and filled with the "consecrated stones of Santa María." As the rhythmic foundation of the "marcha lenta" (slow march) and the "toque de ataque" (attack rhythm), the chá-chá is the gateway to the larger Carabalí orchestra, so it was here that I began.

Toward the end of my stay in Santiago de Cuba I was aware of having only scratched the surface of the profound interpenetration of music, religion, and politics in the Cabildo Carabalí Isuama. One of my final lessons concerned a small figurine, the Reina Africana [African Queen], who resides in

{ Three instruments of the Cabildo Carabalí Isuama's orchestra: redouble
{ (left), chá-chá (center), and tragalegua (right). Carnival 2001.

the Cabildo's lodge, is present at ceremonial events, and is brought out to
parade with the Cabildo on important occasions. Marimón explained, "The
Carabalí were some of the earliest enslaved Africans to enter Oriente [the
eastern part of Cuba], brought to work the cane and coffee plantations. That's
why you see a doll of a black woman in the Cabildo. We used to leave her in the
Cabildo but these days we bring her out with us, always accompanied by the
melé.[2] People call this doll African, but nobody knows who this African is.
What we do know is that she is our mother" (interview, 17 August 2001).

Concealed in her dress, the Reina Africana carries a small pocket containing magical substances that enable her to protect the Cabildo's lodge and
calm conflictive energies that may arise during disputes. Also known as Ma
Rufina, the Reina figurine is present in other important religious houses in
Santiago de Cuba, and is considered by researchers at the Casa del Caribe to
be "one of the figures that most powerfully characterizes African ancestry in
religious temple-houses" (Miyares 2002:163). For many of the city's residents, the Reina serves as a reminder of the anonymous thousands of people
whose work and culture laid the foundations not only of the Cabildo Carabalí Isuama but of the city itself. For members of the Carabalí she is testament to this legacy as well as the Cabildo's religious heritage, which despite
a history of disguise and concealment remains central to its daily functioning. Increasingly present in carnival and other public parades, the Reina
Africana indicates the Cabildo's growing confidence to publicly express its
spirituality and assert the historical fact that it has always been much more
than a folklore ensemble. While the Cabildo's religious heritage seems to be

The Reina Africana, carried by the Carabalí's principal dancer. Photo by the author.

emerging with new visibility, its patriotic political orientation has been evident for centuries. According to González Bueno:

> During the Ten Years War [1868–1878], the Carabalí hid and transported guns and ammunition inside their drums, called tragaleguas, especially on feast days. They also carried messages and medicine between the mambise [independence fighters] camps. Usually they would play "slow march," but upon encountering Spanish troops they would play "attack rhythm." During the War of Independence of 1895, the Cabildo's members provided the same service to the freedom fighters. . . . Their songs, directed at the colonial Spanish government, were satirical and insulting. (Interview, 14 August 2001)

The Carabalí recalls this history through a colonial-era song that it still sings:

Mal Cubano me ultrajabas	Bad Cuban, you insulted me
Porque soy Carabalí	Because I'm Carabalí
Te llegó tu mal momento	Your bad moment has come
Ahora te acuerdas de mí	And now you remember me
Y entonces, pariente, me dice eso así:	And so, cousin, you tell me:
Ha ha ha ha ha ha ha	Ha ha ha ha ha ha ha
Cara mala, hierba mala	Bad face, bad weeds

Hay que cortar de raíz	Must be cut out at the root
Con el machete en la mano	With the machete in the hand
Hay que cortar de raíz	Must be cut out at the root

The song, in which the weeds signify the Spanish, is typical of the late colonial era:

> The Carabalí has always shown the rebellious spirit of Antonio Maceo, because in the Cabildo were commanders and high officials of the liberation armies, like the seven Baracoa brothers, who were linked to the independence fighter Guillermón Moncada. Notice the content of their "Song of the Invasion," which chronicles the route of the liberation army from Baraguá in the east of Cuba to Mantua in the west.[3] While these songs recorded historical events, many of them were very dangerous to sing. (González Bueno, interview, 18 January 2002)

With time the songs became more direct and explicit. The following song was performed by the Carabalí during parades in the early years of the twentieth century, following the first of the two military occupations by the United States (1898–1902, 1906–1909):

| Cuba eh, Cuba Cuba o | Cuba eh, Cuba Cuba o |
| Cuba, Cuba mía, blanco la jodió | Cuba, my Cuba, white man ruined you |

Or, in another form:

| Cuba eh, Cuba Cuba o | Cuba eh, Cuba Cuba o |
| Cuba, Cuba mía, blanco la vendió | Cuba, my Cuba, white man sold you |

Studying percussion with the Carabalí I noticed that this song has a third version, which has been adapted to life after the Revolution of 1959:

| Cuba eh, Cuba Cuba o | Cuba eh, Cuba Cuba o |
| Cuba Cuba libre, Fidel la libertó | Cuba, free Cuba, Fidel liberated you |

Abelardo Larduet Luaces, the Cabildo's former director, insisted that this last version of the song is a genuine expression of the group's patriotism: "The Carabalí has always been revolutionary: for the independence of Cuba, for freedom, and when the revolution triumphed, pro-Fidel. In 1959 many of these people felt truly free for the first time ever" (interview, 28 January 2002). Since 1959 the Carabalí has created new songs, like "Un Cubano Coloso" (A Colossal Cuban), which celebrates the exploits of Fidel Castro. The Carabalí has always paraded with large flags depicting themes like

The Cabildo Carabalí Isuama (with the author), performing in Parque
Céspedes, Santiago de Cuba, January 2002.

African identity and Caribbean unity, but today one notices what must be a
recent addition: flags that celebrate the benefits of collective agriculture,
women's rights, national education campaigns, and the country's political
leadership. The juxtaposition of these themes in parades led by the Reina
Africana amounts to a remarkable convergence of ethnic, religious, and
political imagery.

Singing the praises of the revolution before a crowd of onlookers one day
and Afro-Cuban funeral songs at a Catholic cathedral the next, the Cabildo
Carabalí Isuama exhibits a blend of political and religious commitments that
has matured over close to two centuries. During the colonial era it possessed
representative and civic capacities that drew strength from its official relationship with the institutional church and its protection of members' interests through mutual aid activities and concealed religious practice. These
religious practices continued into the republican and revolutionary eras,
though their privacy was maintained into the late twentieth century as the
Cabildo filled its new public role as an official symbol of national culture.
In response to political changes and economic needs since 1990, the group's
representative capacities are reemerging, particularly through deepening
mutual aid functions and more open expression of religiosity. There are even
signs that it is reestablishing links with the church through open celebration
of feast days and funerals at the cathedral and the Santa Ifigenia cemetery.

Although the revival of the Cabildo bears directly on the daily well-being

{ Members of the Carabalí (with Shani Shakur of New York University, left)
displaying a processional flag that reads, "Somos libre y soberano; Fidel
nos libero" (We are free and sovereign; Fidel liberated us). Carnival 2001.
Photo by the author.

of its members, it does not in itself signify a resumption of its former
political activism or representative advocacy. What it does signify is the
gradual development of organizational attributes that could facilitate the
attainment of these capacities in the future. Central to this process in the
Cuban context is the consolidation of internal bonds through mutual aid
activities and cultural conservation, the tentative formation of external linkages across religious and cultural divides, and public recognition of the
state's social contributions. This combination of characteristics has surfaced in a broad range of community organizations, suggesting that the
conditions for active civic participation are emerging at the grassroots. A
final case study of a neighborhood organization in Santiago de Cuba suggests that such prerequisites for the formation of civil society have begun to
emerge not only among independent community organizations but also
within the institutions of state.

Case Study 2: The Peña Deportiva Félix Roque Pécora

As its name suggests, the Peña Deportiva Félix Roque Pécora has the official
responsibility of promoting sports and recreation, in this case for young
people in the Santiago de Cuba neighborhood of Los Hoyos. In 2002, three
years after its creation, the Peña had 156 registered members and was one

of thirty-one such organizations in the city managed by the Instituto Nacional de Deporte e Recreación (National Institute of Sports and Recreation,
INDER). During my stay in Santiago de Cuba I developed a friendship with
the Peña's director, Carmen Nuria, whose responsibilities involved not only
organizing local baseball matches and field trips to basketball tournaments
but also linking unemployed neighbors with potential employers via the
Ministry of Work, "troubled" women with the Federación de Mujeres Cubanas (Federation of Cuban Women), and "delinquent" youth with law enforcement authorities.

I was immediately struck by the strength of local enthusiasm for the Peña,
based on its ability to advocate local interests before official authorities,
secure material resources for its members, and reach out to a broad social
base, including religious believers and homosexuals. I was further struck
that the Peña achieved these results under state management. In practice it
seemed to function as an institutional intermediary between the formal state
bureaucracy and informal community life, reflecting a curious blend of local
and national loyalties and allegiances.

The Peña's multiple allegiances were proudly exhibited in its program of
energetic monthly street festivals. These gatherings adorned the already
vibrant social scenery of Los Hoyos, a neighborhood where residents usually
leave their front doors open and frequently visit neighbors to exchange pots,
pans, and ideas, while men play dominos at makeshift street corner tables.
Commencing in the invigorating cool of early evening, the Peña's street
festivals often drew crowds of over four hundred men and women, young
and old, to a barricaded local street whose location was announced by word
of mouth. Seating themselves on wooden benches, collapsible plastic chairs,
or on the floor around a raised stage, spectators enjoyed the music and
dance of aspiring local talents, educational presentations on themes like
nutritional health and beautification, stand-up comedy acts, and the proud
bestowal of sporting awards and academic diplomas. These occasions were
always held in commemoration of a historically important national event,
providing a symbolic theme for the evening. In my diary I recorded some
impressions of a school induction ceremony hosted by the Peña.

RITUAL IN THE STREET

Outside the Antonio Maceo museum stand about two hundred children
in neat rows. Half of them are entering their first year of primary school,
and the other half, now entering their sixth year, have the responsibility of
putting blue scarves around the necks of the younger children to mark the

event. Carmen tells me that this is also the anniversary of Che Guevarra's falling in battle in Bolivia, and she soon puts on a cassette of the national anthem, which everyone sings. Carmen pulls me aside to tell me, "We always use political music for political occasions." The street is filled with symbols: the Cuban flag, a table with a large picture of Che's head balanced on it and the words "diligent, loyal, honest, strong" embroidered into the tablecloth.

Each of the new students approaches the table in a procession and drops a flower into one of three large glass bowls containing water. One of the older students stands next to the table and takes a document from Carmen. She reads it clearly, deliberately, and very loudly. It's a copy of a letter that Che sent to Fidel from Bolivia. During a pause in the reading the children shout in unison "¡Seremos como el Che!" [We will be like Che!]

After the speech Carmen looks at me and frowns, but I'm not sure why. She's gesturing toward the friend I brought with me, Renato from San Pedrito, who's fallen asleep on a doorstep. I indicate my apologies to Carmen and try to discreetly wake him up, but she's still not satisfied. She's touching her head, and she hisses to me to make him take his hat off. I look at his hat and the problem strikes me as embarrassingly obvious now: it has a large United States flag on the front.

—Santiago de Cuba, October 2001

Whether an altar or a memorial shrine, the table was the symbolic focus of the induction ceremony, and it infused the occasion with a strong patriotic atmosphere. While the procession of students resembled, to my eye, something akin to the Catholic Eucharist, the table may have been intended to invoke the ceremonial practice of Espiritismo, a spiritual tradition in which deceased ancestors are commemorated (and contacted) through half-filled glasses of water. Espiritismo was introduced to Cuba in the mid-nineteenth century through the writings of the French engineer Hippolyte Rivail (alias Allan Kardec) and Amalia Soler, who had promoted its practice in Spain since the 1830s. Blending the mystical practice of ancestor consultation with Christian moral teachings and a rigorous "scientific" protocol, Espiritismo developed unique characteristics in the Cuban creole environment (Cabrera 1971:64–65). According to the Puerto Rican literary critic Arcadio Díaz Quiñones, the multilinear evolution of Espiritismo in Cuba captured the interest of Fernando Ortiz, and was "a fundamental feature in the origin of the concept of transculturation" (1999:14).

Two primary strains of Espiritismo are recognized by contemporary Cuban scholars: Espiritismo de Cordón and Espiritismo Cruzado. The former brings together a group of devotees who sit or stand in a line or circle to read Catholic prayers before seeking to communicate with Cuban aboriginal and African ancestral spirits, either through a single medium or collectively. The latter, practiced more widely in Santiago de Cuba, is characterized by the use of objects and ritual procedures adopted from Afro-Cuban religions of Yoruba and Bantu origin (Miyares 2002). Given the historic depth of popular religious practice in the district of Los Hoyos, which has been well documented by anthropologists at Santiago de Cuba's Casa del Caribe (Millet 1989, 1997; Miyares 2002), it is not unlikely that the induction ceremony was indeed intended to evoke religious sensibilities. As Ivor Miller (2000) has argued, the Cuban state has long played on the spiritual sensitivities of the masses to garner popular support by displaying quasi-religious imagery through televised ceremonies and pubic displays. According to this hypothesis, the red and black flag of Castro's revolutionary 26th of July movement was double-coded from the start to attract the loyalty not only of militant patriots but also of those who identify with the Santería deity of new beginnings and endings, Elegguá, whose colors are red and black. Miller is not the first to identify this phenomenon. Gerardo Mosquera, for instance, writes, "On occasions revolutionary publicity is organized in the wall murals of some Revolutionary Defense Committees (CDR) through compositions that resemble the canons of domestic altars" (quoted in Miller 2000:41). And according to Tony Harrison, "When you go into any office of the UJC [Young Communists League] . . . you'll find almost always the table pushed against a wall, and up there above the table, three photos, Fidel, Che, Camilo. There you are already, your altar" (quoted in Miller 2000:41).

In Los Hoyos, Carmen did not publicly advertise her personal religious beliefs, but any visitor to her house would surely notice the water-filled glasses of Espiritismo placed in front of photographs of deceased ancestors on the shelf in her hallway, and even her own Reina Africana figurine watching over the living room from on top of the bookshelf. Her Peña, on the other hand, openly celebrated the Afro-Cuban religious roots of Los Hoyos, and on one occasion was even invited to perform the folkloric dances of Ochún at a local police barracks.

Religious expression was not the only form of behavior that, while previously discouraged by the Castro government, made a proud appearance in Carmen's patriotic public gatherings. Also afforded space for open discussion and expression was homosexuality, which has a long history of repression in Cuba. Antihomosexual sentiment in Cuba reached its height in the

{ Fidel Castro and the three white that doves perched on him during his
{ inaugural speech in 1959. Doves are a Christian representation of the Holy
{ Spirit, while in Santería they symbolize the deity Obatalá, patron of clarity
{ and purity.

mid-1960s, when the newspaper El Mundo affirmed that "no homosexual
represents the Revolution, which is a matter for men, of fists and not feath-
ers, of courage and not trembling, of certainty and not intrigue, of creative
valor and not sweet surprises" (quoted in Hodge 2001:21). But as the following diary excerpt shows, public expression of homosexuality, at least in the
Peña's neighborhood gatherings, is no longer feared:

PARTY IN THE STREET

This evening's gathering is to celebrate Fidel's seventy-fifth birthday. Carmen commences the proceedings by leading the crowd of about
[three hundred] in song: "Feliz Cumpleaños a Fidel" [Happy Birthday
Fidel]. Then she reads a poem about a "Bright Star that Rose in the Sierra
Maestra," and when she's finished everyone shouts "¡Patria o Muerte,
Venceremos!" Then it's time for the show. Two men dressed as women
start things off, miming a bolero. At one point there's a technical problem
and the music cuts out, but the audience is very taken with the performance and raises its voice to sing the words and clap the time. About a
minute later, when the sound comes back, the crowd is completely in sync
with the tape.

When the song is over, one of the singers changes into jeans and a T-shirt, and chooses two female volunteers from the audience to demonstrate hairstyling techniques and how to apply makeup. Some people shout comments to him, like, "Where did you learn to do that so well?" He replies: "I went to school, unlike some people. Now pay attention!" The audience laughs at these exchanges, which in the end seem to fill more time than the beautification techniques themselves. After this come the dance performances. As usual, there's a salsa dancing demonstration followed by a group of four teenagers and a younger boy, who perform Santería dances with recorded batá drumming. They all wear the traditional costumes and dance the deities San Lázaro and Changó. The little boy can't be more than four or five years old.

After the gathering is officially over, Carmen puts on salsa music for people to dance to and takes me into her house, which the performers are using as a dressing room. She introduces me to a group of cross-dressers, who tell me about their work. Orlando says that they do the performances to educate the community about social tolerance. Until last year, he and a friend had been operating a weekly disco for homosexuals in the nearby Plaza Marte but there had been a public protest and somebody was shot. Since the disco closed down, they've been working with Carmen, which is proving more successful.

—Santiago de Cuba, August 2001

The socially diverse community of Los Hoyos was brought together at these events through a unifying patriotic bond. Carmen told me about the educational potential of this bond:

> At the activity the other night there were only thirty-eight chairs, but over three hundred people. All those people seated in an orderly way, without fights or arguments, is proof to everyone that social organization and discipline are the best characteristics that a person can have. We also try to expand people's idea of culture through the transvestite performances. Some people don't like that, but we're not the only ones doing it. Sometimes there are TV shows that feature transvestites; this is culture.
>
> We also educate people through concursos [lecture demonstrations] in the street. For example, the police force gave a presentation at one of our activities not long ago. They spoke about the importance of police work in the community. We've also had presentations by Medicos sin Fronteras [Doctors without Borders], who spoke about sexual health and gave out

free condoms. In this way, through these meetings, we instill revolutionary values in the community. We usually ask the community to join us at *tribunas abiertas* [large public marches in support of the revolution]. We don't just go for fun but to work. This is one way we can get resources for the Peña. If we work hard and *reclamar* [raise our voices] well then we get free drinks, clothes, and other prizes. (Interview, 31 August 2001)

The Peña was well rewarded for its efforts. Certificates and awards from the Municipal Communist Party, the Federation of Cuban Women, and the Ministry of the Interior were a proud memoir of the prizes the Peña had won, such as all-expense-paid, week-long holidays to sporting events around the country and subsidized trips to the Baconao amusement park for the Peña's most exemplary participants. Carmen also used the Peña's official recognition to negotiate an arrangement with the Elvira Cape city library, which lent her up to four hundred books a month for a home library. At one point she even intervened on behalf of some neighborhood adolescents, who were going to be arrested for a series of disorderliness offenses. She successfully negotiated with the police officers to discreetly withdraw the charges on the condition that she assume responsibility for their attendance to a technical education course and their participation in community work.

If the official privileges earned by the Peña resulted from its promotion of grassroots patriotism, then the effectiveness of its neighborhood projects was driven very much by Carmen's tireless dedication to her community. Although she was eager to share the details of her work with me, our conversations were usually interrupted by the constant stream of visitors seeking everything from Carmen's romantic advice to her assistance with finding a job. The little spare time she did enjoy was used to engineer prizes for children's competitions, like hula hoops out of electrical tubing and jump ropes out of plastic wires from the base of old chairs glued to discarded sewing spindles. She put these prizes in small plastic bags donated from local shops and, with a knife heated over a flame, sealed the bags and rewarded well-behaved children, who were delighted to receive what appeared to be packaged, manufactured items that would usually be sold in convertible pesos.

It is perhaps inevitable that the Peña would at some point attract the interest of a foreign development agency. In November 1998 a representative of the French Organización para Relaciones Artísticas-Culturales Latino Europeo (ORACLE) visited Carmen and, impressed with her community work, set up a project in Santiago de Cuba to collaborate with the Peña. He made initial donations in person, which Carmen faithfully passed on to locals as

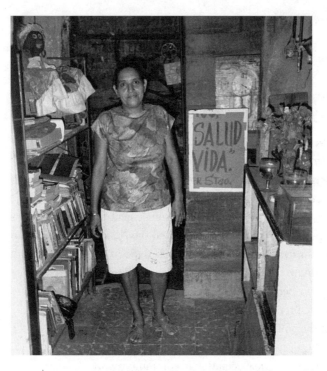

Carmen Nuria with part of her home library and her small home shrine
(including the half-filled glasses of Espiritismo), watched over by the
Reina Africana (top left). Photo by the author.

she saw fit: three large boxes of clothing were handed out at street gatherings, and an electric piano was made available to aspiring young musicians. The Peña's relationship with the NGO, however, began to collapse in
May 1999 when Carmen received a telephone call from its representative in
France, who asked her if she had received a stereo hi-fi system that he had
sent. She knew nothing of the donation so she called the customs office and
found that the object was being held in Havana because a U.S. $300 importa-
tion fee had not been paid. This puzzled Carmen because she knew that
foreign NGOs are permitted to send donations to Cuba through ICAP (Cuban Institute for Popular Friendship), MINVEC (Ministry of Foreign Investment and Economic Collaboration), and other state institutions without
incurring an importation fee. Furthermore, Carmen's collaboration with the
NGO Doctors without Borders, set up in conjunction with INDER (National
Institute of Sports and Recreation) and the Ministry of Health, had involved
duty-free donations of sexual health kits and condoms, which she distributed at her monthly gatherings.

The officials at MINVEC were surprised to learn from Carmen about the French NGO, which had apparently been operating in Cuba without an official state license. They tracked down the stereo system in the customs office and delivered it to Carmen, but warned her to avoid any further contact with the NGO, whose activities were declared criminal and liable to attract severe penalties for Cuban collaborators. The donation was nevertheless greatly appreciated and came to be used by local radio journalists in Los Hoyos to record their weekly broadcasts, adding further excitement to the communal atmosphere of Carmen's living room. Handed over in the end by MINVEC, the donation served to remind Carmen and her community that although the Peña may enjoy certain freedoms to represent and advocate local interests, these freedoms have a limit.

It is important to note that this configuration of societal power relations, which robustly maintains the government's supreme socioeconomic authority, is accepted and endorsed by many community organizations in Cuba. In Carmen's opinion, the hegemonic status quo has generally worked to her advantage because it facilitates coordinated planning and representation among Santiago's peñas:

> INDER has all the personal details like addresses and telephone numbers of all the members of all the peñas, and for this reason INDER has good control over us and our activities. Roughly once a month INDER calls the peñas' leaders to meet at its headquarters in the stadium on the Avenida de Las Américas. We always learn from each other when we share our experiences and plan our neighborhood activities as a team. (Interview, 31 August 2001)

> INDER is very short of resources, so it keeps its eyes open for foreign organizations that can help us. Individually the peñas have a problem of communication with foreign NGOs because we have no idea what ones are out there to help us, but INDER knows this and it helps us by linking us up with groups like Doctors without Borders. It also helps us to coordinate with state institutions that can help us here in Santiago de Cuba. I have known some organizations that try to work on their own, unregistered, because they don't want their personal details recorded by the government, but in the end they all try to become legalized because it helps them get what they want more easily. (Interview, 21 September 2001)

Although legal conditions limited the Peña's ability to independently develop international collaborations, in Carmen's view her organization's official standing in the bureaucratic system facilitated the establishment of locally beneficial linkages with the city library, the police, MINVEC, the Ministry of Work, and Doctors without Borders. For the expanding number of community organizations seeking official registration, adherence to sometimes restrictive legal conditions represents the paradoxical challenge of attaining greater leverage with the state while simultaneously demonstrating deference to its authority. Most organizations, like the Peña, have approached this challenge through a strategy of local empowerment based on the promotion of community interests and the gradual establishment of domestic linkages in collaboration with, rather than independently of, the state. The upshot for the state has been greater local responsibility for community welfare, shoring up the underresourced social service system and in many cases consolidating local allegiance to the revolution. Mindful of the political delicacy of the situation, many community organizations view social engagement as a nonconflictive opportunity for diversifying the ideological bases of society through evangelization, spiritual openness, and even public acceptance of homosexuality.

The mobilization and exchange of ideological and material resources resulting from this kind of activism represents a process of change and ferment currently under way within the Cuban revolution. This is evident in neighborhood welfare initiatives spanning organizations like the Peña, mutual-aid associations like the Cabildo Carabalí Isuama, and Christian welfare projects, all of which exhibit a combination of allegiances to community and state interests. This process of exchange and counterpoint is crucial for understanding the character and potentials of Cuban civil society. Indeed, a conceptual approach to civil society that integrates official legal authority with unofficial local social capital, accommodating the presence of the state and the representative capacities of community associations, reflects an intellectual trajectory spanning the most recent work of Cuban sociologists such as Rafael Hernández and Jorge Luis Acanda González back to the seminal work of Antonio Gramsci. Awareness of the "mixed" character of Cuban civil society is important for recognizing how popular needs are asserted and legitimated not only through formal channels of representation but also through informal expressions of faith, culture, and community.

CONCLUSION

DEVELOPMENT AND DIALOGUE

The preceding chapters suggest that the interaction of state legal power with local community solidarity and foreign capital sometimes reflects a zero-sum process of competition and domination, and other times a positive-sum process of collaboration and interdependence. Community associations that become legally registered often have to subordinate local commitments to centralized economic priorities and national development goals, but the official legitimacy and support they gain can serve as a platform for expanding their activities over time. Similarly, decentralized engagement with community groups requires the underresourced state to cede ideological and administrative ground at the grassroots, but this ultimately consolidates its broader political authority and administrative capacities. Initially secure in their aims, foreign development agencies are usually forced to reshape their objectives and loyalties around this complicated political terrain, but by doing so they earn the trust necessary for introducing new ideas and development models in a respectful and collaborative way.

From a zero-sum perspective government intervention tends to stifle independent local initiative, while the retrenchment of the state from the civil sphere can give rise to new forms of local voluntarism and social support (Fukuyama 1995, Schambra 1994). Conversely, from a positive-sum position a robust state can actively nurture a stable and progressive environment in which it is possible for a vibrant and independent civil society to emerge and flourish (Salamon 1995, Skocpol 1995). These analytic models have developed in contexts where the independent, nonstate character of civil society is either well established, as in the United States and Western Europe, or quickly expanding, as in Eastern Europe in the early 1990s. By contrast, political reality in Cuba does not reflect a dualistic social structure characterized by autonomous civil society groups on the one hand and robust state institutions on the other. Rather, it shows an interpenetration of state authority and independent action in a civil sphere that is more "mixed" than elsewhere. In this environment community interests do not typically develop along a "linear" path toward independent official representation, but instead have become at least partially integrated into state hegemony. Researchers, consultants, and others interested in democratization in Cuba should recognize that attempts to add or subtract "state" and "society" from each other do not on their own grasp the complexity of the Cuban political context.

Focusing on processes of interdependence, exchange, and counterpoint helps to clarify how state-society integration has deepened with the formation of networks and webs of interaction across the formal and informal sectors and the incorporation of local social capital into officially led projects. One result of this process is that organizations that were historically absent from the official projects of the revolution, such as religious groups, have augmented their public capacities, particularly in the area of social welfare services. Christian organizations, encouraged by legal authorization for greater public expression and social intervention, have shown expanding abilities to channel foreign donations and development financing. Similarly, Afro-Cuban religious communities have developed official ties with decentralized neighborhood welfare initiatives because of their concern for the interests of a historically marginalized sector of the population.

Religious groups in Cuba have not coalesced into a coherent independent movement, but they have shown more flexibility and plurality than in Eastern Europe, where pressure for a unified voice among a diverse array of oppositional sectors both limited democratic expression prior to the Soviet collapse and inhibited its emergence afterward (Linz and Stepan 1996:273). This kind of coerced conformity, or "excess of community" in Woolcock's terms (1998:171), is unlikely to develop among Cuban religious groups because their tendency toward informal practice connects them both to one another and to a wide range of popular interests. It is more likely that their lack of political consensus, underscored by openness and flexibility at the grassroots, harbors broader representative potential than a "democratic ecology of associations" constantly under pressure to fall in line with dominant interests (Armony 2004:23, Warren 2001). The test of this potential will be the extent to which religious groups continue to protect internal interests while expanding cooperative relations with the state and with one another.

Regarding the growing visibility and social influence of Afro-Cuban religious groups, Rogelio Martínez Furé observes with characteristic style that "little by little the bird makes its nest" (interview, 11 May 2002). But if official recognition and local empowerment are the raw materials of a well-built nest, then for some practitioners of Afro-Cuban religions, commercial tourism has become the golden egg. Many initiates have taken advantage of international interest in Afro-Cuban folklore by specializing in cabaret and nightclub performances, though they often view these as sacred expressions of religious culture. State organizations like the Asociación Cultural Yoruba and the Casa del Caribe have the paradoxical responsibility of promoting this kind of religious tourism while institutionally representing the spiritual interests of believers. Skeptical of their ability to do so, grassroots Santería groups such as Ilé Tun Tun and Ifá Iranlowo view community building and respect for religious orthodoxy as the genuine golden egg, which global tourism is trying to steal. This clash of market-friendly and community-oriented approaches reflects a fundamental tension between vertical modes of engagement with the state and the formation of horizontal lines of solidarity independent of it. Aware of this tension and pressed to earn a living, babalawos like Miki Alfonso have attempted to balance community loyalty with commercial ambition. Their retention of sacred information shows the hand of tradition guiding Santería's adaptation to a changing socioeconomic landscape, allowing them to work as intermediaries between their religious communities, foreign tourists, and state institutions.

The decentralized development projects in Old Havana and Atarés also attempted to reconcile the objectives of Afro-Cuban religious communities with the financial rewards of tourism, though through officially licensed projects set up by the Grupo para el Desarrollo Integral de la Capital (Group for the Integrated Development of the Capital, or GDIC) and the Office of the Historian of the City. While state and nonstate actors were both responsible for initially allowing the commercial potentials of these projects to fall out of balance with community needs, it was the collaborative efforts of both that led to the eventual implementation of neighborhood health education and antidrug campaigns. Collaboration between state and community actors proceeded mainly through informal agreements and social ties that operated in parallel to formal structures of development planning. As Nan Lin has observed, in socialist contexts informal channels have often played a crucial part in resolving local problems by facilitating the flow of information from the bottom up (2001:111). The expansion of this phenomenon in contemporary Cuba suggests that independent actors at the grassroots, often in collaboration with decentralized state institutions, are assuming greater responsibility for local welfare.

The question of responsibility for local welfare is central to understanding the character of civil society in Cuba. The activities of foreign NGOs in Cuba and the attempts of the state to mediate their interactions with community organizations open an analytic window into this problem. Cuba has attracted the attention of foreign NGOs largely because the prospect of empowering and strengthening the self-sufficiency of community organizations resonates with the interest of international donors in "building civil society." Cuban authorities are aware that this objective typically involves promoting local autonomy from the state, and in response have asserted control over the design and implementation of projects. Nevertheless, the commercialization of the permaculture magazine *Se Puede* and the gentrification of the Santa Ifigenia cemetery show how the state's urgent need to generate finances has often prioritized commercial viability over local welfare outcomes. Initiatives such as the Italian School Workshop demonstrate the potential benefits of integrating community interests with commercial productivity, but the frequent prioritization of the latter objective has weakened the state's claim of stewardship over civil society. This has resulted in the widening of political and social spaces at the grassroots that operate less directly within the state's administrative and ideological hegemony.

As these spaces expand they are being occupied by sectors of the population that were previously excluded from the official projects of the revolution. Social diversity at the grassroots, however, appears to have strengthened rather than weakened popular support for the revolution, largely because local initiatives have tended to work in collaboration, rather than in competition, with the state. Nevertheless, through this process community actors have acquired important organizational prerequisites for civil society action, such as greater capacities for protecting internal community interests and a more active approach to building external linkages with state and nonstate institutions. Christian welfare initiatives, for instance, have eased the pressure on the state to provide social services but have also raised official concerns about the emergence of interreligious partnerships and the potential consolidation of an alternative social agenda. Similarly, the Cabildo Carabalí Isuama continues to publicly advocate Cuban political sovereignty and the social accomplishments of the revolution, even as its revived mutual aid functions and increasingly public display of religious heritage strengthen its organizational autonomy and agency. Finally, the Peña Deportiva Félix Roque

Pécora in Santiago de Cuba has broadened local support for the revolution by including religious believers and homosexuals in its patriotic activities, though by doing so it has stretched the revolution's ideological limits at the grassroots.

The gradual enlargement of local initiatives into social and ideological terrain previously occupied by the state signifies a transformation currently under way within the Cuban revolution. Future studies into the nature of sociopolitical transformation in Cuba (and elsewhere) would benefit from continuing attention to forms of interaction between state institutions and community associations, incorporating both political and cultural issues into their research framework. This would facilitate an integration of top-down and bottom-up analytic approaches, an endeavor whose value has been already been demonstrated particularly well by Michael Woolcock (1998) and Michael Burawoy and Katherine Verdery (1999:2). Projects that bring together political analysis with anthropological method are well positioned to examine the "meeting grounds" between state and society and raise awareness about the mutual influences that cultural traditions, social relationships, and political structures exert on each other (Migdal 1994:23, 2001; Somers 1993:595).

Studying and writing about state-society relations in Cuba helps to establish that international engagement with the island based on capacity building and support for the institutional reforms already under way has better prospects for strengthening civic democracy than antagonistic attempts to bring about "regime change." This position is supported by the conclusion of numerous policy and research reports that over forty years of the U.S. trade embargo has strengthened rather than weakened the position of hardline elements within the Cuban administration and made peaceful reconciliation with the United States less likely. The U.S. position continues to draw international criticism, reflected in a 183-to-4 United Nations vote in November 2006 condemning the trade embargo. Unmoved, the Bush administration has recently invested U.S. $80 million in its Commission for Assistance to a Free Cuba to "influence Cubans to turn away from communism and move to democracy and a free-market economy" (Hudson 2006), though to date most of this money has been spent outside Cuba.

Contrary to the wishes of the U.S. government, in 2008 Raúl Castro succeeded his older brother and will likely confer leadership to a more reform-oriented administration. With reference to economic reform in China, William Ratliff notes that "Raúl Castro could become something of a Deng Xiaoping, a leader who would be receptive to extensive economic though not political reforms and involvement by Cubans living abroad" (2004:30). Raúl's expansion of the Cuban military's economic activities through the company Gaviota strengthens this possibility, as does his obvious interest in the Chinese model of reform, particularly with regard to opening the economy while maintaining the party's grip on political authority. China is now Cuba's second-largest trading partner after Venezuela, with bilateral trade doubling in 2006 to reach nearly U.S. $2 billion. The Chinese and Cuban governments have recently signed trade accords that expand commercial investments beyond nickel extraction and tourism into areas such as transport and the local manufacture of high-tech electronic appliances. Chinese companies such as Haier and China Putian Corporation have publicly stated that they intend to take advantage of highly skilled, cost-effective Cuban labor in order to expand their reach into the Latin American market (China Putian Corporation 2005). The significance of Sino-Cuban relations should not be underestimated and should be researched for their impact on both the reform process in Cuba and the character of Chinese engagement with Latin America.

International economic relations will impact strongly on the management of local development in Cuba. It is possible that with the passing of the Special Period and with a sustainable economic recovery, the Cuban state will come to refill the administrative spaces it was forced to vacate in the early 1990s. Legal reforms designed to allow greater social and economic freedoms ultimately have no constitutional basis and over the past decades have been implemented and retracted in response to changing political conditions and official priorities (Jatar Hausmann 1999:34). Indeed, phases of economic decentralization and opening in Cuba have typically been followed by periods of recentralization and reassertion of state authority. This pattern roughly coincides with the electoral cycle of provincial (two-and-a-half-year) and municipal (five-year) governments, which have tended to demonstrate their legal weight early in their tenures by reigning in the more progressive initiatives of their predecessors (Hearn 2006:145). Nevertheless, the emergence of community self-help organizations over the past decade, legally registered or not, suggests a gradual process of civil pluralization capable of amplifying the voices of previously silent constituencies (Kaufman 1997:2–6). The state clearly aims to maintain collaborative relations with these constituencies, and while it is impossible to determine at this time how loud their voices will become, they will in all likelihood remain audible. As Max Azicri writes, changing practices and expectations at the micro level can sometimes have an enduring influence on decision making at the macro level:

It is in the details more than at the macro level that the nature of things is defined. How will the reforms be implemented, and what kinds of social relationships will develop between the population and the government and among the citizens themselves? Will the nature of these and other interactions define the emerging system better than grandiose reforms? Sometime official policy has confirmed what was done at the grassroots level, where informal practices originated. New expectations created by such practices and the official decisions confirming them, even if temporary, should carry some weight in the ultimate character of the emerging system. (2000:305)

Other analysts are less optimistic that Cuba under its current government has a future at all. Irving Louis Horowitz and Jaime Suchlicki, for example, argue that global moves toward free market economies, combined with political stagnation in Cuba, have increasingly isolated the Castro government, rendering it incapable of building international dialogue:

By the middle of 1998 there was and is a widespread consensus that Communist Cuba is an isolated regime, drifting somewhere between limbo and the backwater. From left to right, liberal and conservative opinion alike now accepts the premise that the regime has little if any potential for establishing open markets, competitive and multiple political parties, or free popular elections. . . . [T]here has now evolved a deep "thick" consensus that the system as such, Cuban Communism as such, is an antidemocratic blight on the deep undercurrents of change that now characterize the hemisphere as a whole. . . . There has been no indication that Castro intends to truly open up the island's political or economic system or promote a peaceful solution to Cuba's deepening crisis. (1998:xv–xvi)

As the Cuban economy recovers, the extent to which local priorities will figure into official development actions remains to be seen. For projects to retain the collaborative character they have assumed over the past decade will require the continuing commitment of the state to engage rather than isolate community actors by drawing them into publicly beneficial strategies of development and governance. It will also challenge community groups to constantly innovative strategies for negotiating local interests with official institutions while maintaining high levels of internal cohesion and solidarity. Case studies from Peru (Carlessi 1989), Mexico (Rodríguez Velázquez 1989), Brazil (Gregório Baierle 1998, Rocha 1989), and Venezuela (Corrales

2001) have shown that internal solidarity may indeed be the most valuable asset that unregistered community groups possess in their attempts to secure concessions from state institutions and development agencies. Such examples show the centrality of community cohesion to enduring political influence, but they also show that even minor economic gains and material concessions, like improved access to water and electricity, can erode the local resolve necessary for larger civic engagement.

In the context of intensifying global economic integration, how community groups will continue to protect local interests, and how the Cuban state will continue to protect national sovereignty, are questions that deserve continuing scrutiny. I raised the issue in a letter to the Historian of Havana, Eusebio Leal, whose response expressed characteristic revolutionary optimism:

In this day and age, when global influences condition all processes, and where nowhere is free from the threat of danger, Havana offers a spirit of hope. In the face of globalized foreign models, Cuba raises the flag of self-determination as a symbol of identity. Today we proudly revive our most ancient traditions and exhibit our model for preserving patrimony as a goal of social and community development, not only in theory but with tangible results.

We endeavor to look at the past as a point of departure, but with our eyes on the future, which is the only way to conserve one's patrimony while confronting the dynamic challenge of sustainability. Using tourism as a mechanism for development, we advocate a world without boundaries, with culture and mutual respect as our guide to fruitful and enriching relationships between our peoples. (Personal communication, 25 April 2002)

Integrating local tradition with global economics, Leal locates cultural integrity at the core of sustainable development. By framing commercial goals in terms of social values, he expresses the resolve and commitment of one small country to defend its identity in a system of global interaction. It is a position that resonates with John Tomlinson's observation that "the cultural terms of modernity are not fixed, but open to challenge and, however difficult it may prove, to change" (1991:169). This does not suggest an outright rejection of global capitalism so much as an attempt to protect a range of spiritual, social, and material interests through a process that Roland Robertson (1995) has called "glocalization." Ortiz's theory of transculturation signaled essentially the same process at work in the formation of Cuban nationhood, and it has been one of the goals of this book to show it at work in contemporary welfare initiatives.

Celebrating the vitality of Cuban cultural dynamics in the twentieth century, Gustavo Pérez Firmat concludes that "transculturation, a coinage that denotes transition, passage, process, is the best name for the Cuban condition" (1989:23). At the start of the twenty-first century this observation is borne out in emerging international and domestic collaborations, though whether or not processes of dialogue and exchange continue to shape the Cuban condition remains to be seen. The merchandise in a small state-managed convenience store at Havana's José Martí International Airport suggests that one way or another they will: among an array of glossy magazines on sale to departing visitors, I noticed one targeting potential investors, depicting on the front cover a seashell full of U.S. dollar bills. This represents profitable financial returns, the magazine explained in Spanish and English, because it is the symbol of Ajé Chaluga, the oricha of commerce.

NOTES

Introduction

1 In 1993 the Cuban government legalized domestic trade in U.S. dollars, valued at roughly twenty-five Cuban national pesos per dollar in 2000. In November 2004 the U.S. dollar was replaced by the Cuban convertible peso (CUC), which maintains a comparable exchange rate. In addition to the symbolic benefit of removing U.S. dollars from domestic circulation, their replacement with convertible pesos augments Cuba's import capacity by concentrating hard currency earned from international trade and remittances in the hands of the state. Both convertible and national pesos can be legally held by Cubans, but the higher value of products sold in convertibles makes them difficult to attain for Cubans with lower incomes.

2 The notion that active civil society tends to entrench rather than overcome systemic inequalities was foreshadowed by Pierre Bourdieu, who argued that dominant groups have the most to gain from investing their support and trust in the institutions of a sociopolitical system that favors them (Bourdieu and Passeron 1977). Bourdieu argued that elites systematically invest resources in indoctrination programs that teach subordinate sectors to accept their place in the social hierarchy, to play by established societal rules, and to "misrecognize" this process as education.

3 This is not to say that the Cuban Catholic establishment and the state worked in total isolation from each other prior to 1990. Tentative moves toward church-state cooperation emerged in the early 1970s as leaders on both sides found common ground in a progressive social agenda. Church-state rapprochement deepened in the ensuing decades, but it was only after the mid-1990s that specific collaborative projects began to emerge on a broad scale (see chapter 4).

4 This is not to say that collaboration with the state is the only way for independent associations to attract international support. The Zapatistas in Chiapas, Mexico, for instance, and outlawed dissident movements throughout the world (including Cuba) draw in varying degrees on overseas sources of technical and financial support.

5 The Helms-Burton Act, signed in December 1996, strengthens key aspects of the 1992 Cuban Democracy Act by prohibiting international corporations and governments that trade with Cuba from trading with the United States. Specifically, it "urges the President to take steps to apply sanctions described by [the Cuban Democracy] Act against countries assisting Cuba" (quoted in Cisneros 1996:50). Nevertheless, two of the act's most important components have not been systematically enforced. These are Title III, which would allow Cuban exiles to press claims in U.S. courts for properties expropriated from them by the revolutionary government in the 1960s, and Title IV, which would impose sanctions against foreign investors whose activities involve properties expropriated from North American nationals.

6 All translations from Spanish are by the author unless otherwise stated.

1. Spirits in Motion

1 In a similar vein, recent research on social capital and reciprocal trust (*guanxi*) in China has shown that when interpersonal relationships become characterized by purely bureaucratic or instrumental objectives, larger structures of long-term cooperative trust tend to erode (Gold et al. 2002, Smart 1993:402).

2 A strikingly comparable situation is reported by Philip Taylor (2001:138–158) in Vietnam, where fortune tellers, musicians, and other performers have taken creative advantage of widening market opportunities in the 1990s, and been widely perceived as a "threat" to traditional culture as a result.

3 Rumor has it that when Spiro trains students in San Francisco to play batá drums, he ensures the simultaneous development of their character and musicianship by making them clean his house and garden!

2. Decentralization and the Collaborative Spirit

1 Systems of social welfare provision in Cuba have undergone phases of decentralization and recentralization at least since the 1800s. Largely in response to a lack of central government capacity in much of the country, religious and secular community associations developed mechanisms for welfare delivery well into the 1900s and again during the Great Depression into the 1950s. For a historic analysis of religious associationalism in Cuba, see Crahan 2003; for an analysis of state centralization and decentralization after 1959, see Fagen 1969 and Dilla Alfonso et al. 1993.

2 Woolcock (1998:175) argues that if a given community's stock of social capital is to provide a sustainable basis for launching development initiatives, it must be complemented over time by the construction of new, externally oriented horizontal linkages and vertical synergies.

3 The popular council is the administrative office of locally elected government officials that manages neighborhood actions and disputes (República de Cuba 2000:3).

Created in 1990, Havana's 105 popular councils share previously centralized municipal responsibilities, particularly in the area of urban planning. Most municipalities comprise 5 to 7 popular councils, and the term is employed in daily usage interchangeably with "suburb" or "district."

4 Increasingly, foreign agents of social and commercial development share this responsibility. However, at present the Cuban Ministry of Foreign Investment and Economic Collaboration (MINVEC) meticulously regulates how foreign organizations operate in Cuba, particularly with regard to grassroots initiatives like those discussed here. For a discussion of international NGOs and their relationships with Cuban authorities, including MINVEC, see chapter 3.

5 One of the most vivid, complete, and widely referenced chronicles of the sacred parables of Santería is Natalia Bolívar's Los Orishas en Cuba (1990).

6 The Spanish word regla literally means "rule." In the title of Bolívar Aróstegui and González Díaz de Villegas's book, though, the "Reglas de Palo Monte" can be interpreted as the "Orders" or "Ways" of Palo Monte, just as Santería is often called "La Regla de Ocha" or "The Way of the Orichas." According to several of my informants, "Palo Monte" refers to the sacred poles or sticks (palos in Spanish) brought from the countryside (monte) for use in religious ceremonies.

7 Three state institutions have since been modeled on the Office of the Historian of Havana to manage the economic development of much smaller historic centers in the cities of Santiago de Cuba, Camagüey, and Trinidad.

8 The CDRs are organized at a street-by-street level, each square block of four streets forming a larger administrative unit or manzana. A CDR's primary responsibility is to ensure compliance with the law at the neighborhood scale, ideally resolving problems without involving higher authorities or the police. CDR representatives are elected in their neighborhoods and manzana presidents usually maintain communication with the delegates of their popular council and other locally relevant organizations, like the Federation of Cuban Women (Federación de Mujeres Cubanas, or FMC) and, in this case, the Office of the Historian.

4. Patriotic Spirits

1 The quitapesar (literally "take away worry") is the largest drum of the Carabalí orchestra, accompanied by the tragalegua and redoble (smallest drum). According to N. Pérez et al. (1982:22n1), the quitapesar is brought out only in heated musical competition with rival ensembles because of its "certain special power." The prenda is an Afro-Cuban religious cauldron-like object historically used by the Cabildo. For a discussion of Cuban prendas, see Thompson 1983:121–124.

2 The melé is the end of a soil-tilling hoe that recalls the agricultural tool once used by enslaved Africans and their descendents. It is struck with an iron bolt to provide the rhythmic pulse of the Carabalí orchestra, and is used in a similar fashion in Santería bembé celebrations.

3 For a partial transcription of "Song of the Invasion" see Fernández 1995:176.

REFERENCES

Acanda Gonález, Jorge Luis. 2003. Introduction to Rafael Hernández, *Looking at Cuba: Essays on Culture and Civil Society*, 1–9. Gainesville: University Press of Florida.

Adams, Kathleen M. 1984. "Come to Tana Toraja, 'Land of the Heavenly Kings': Travel Agents as Brokers in Ethnicity." *Annals of Tourism Research* 11:469–85.

Agüero, Felipe, and Jeffrey Stark. 1998. *Fault Lines of Democracy in Post-Transition Latin America*. Miami: North-South Center Press.

Aguilar, Luis E. 1972. *Cuba 1933: Prologue to Revolution*. New York: Cornell University Press.

Albacete, Lorenzo. 1998. "The Poet and the Revolutionary." *New Yorker* 73 (44): 35–41.

Alexander, Jeffrey, Bernhard Giesen, Richard Munch, and Neil Smelser. 1987. *The Micro-Macro Link*. Berkeley: University of California Press.

Alfonso, Pablo. 1985. *Cuba, Castro y los Católicos: Del Humanismo Revolucionario al Marxismo Totalitario*. Miami: Hispanoamerican Books.

Alonso Tejada, Aurelio. 1995. "Catolicismo, Polítca y Cambio en la Realidad Cubana Actual." *Temas* 4:23–32.

Alvarez, Sonia. 1997. "Reweaving the Fabric of Collective Action: Social Movements and Challenges to 'Actually Existing Democracy' in Brazil." In *Between Resistance and Revolution: Cultural Politics and Social Protest*, edited by Richard G. Fox and Orin Starn, 83–110. Rutgers: Rutgers University Press.

Amira, John, and Steve Cornelius. 1992. *The Music of Santería: Traditional Rhythms of the Batá Drums*. Crown Point, Ind.: White Cliffs Media Company.

Armony, Ariel. 2003. "Civil Society in Cuba: A Conceptual Approach." In *Religion, Culture, and Society: The Case of Cuba*, edited by Margaret E. Crahan, 17–35. Washington, D.C.: Woodrow Wilson International Center for Scholars.

———. 2004 *The Dubious Link: Civic Engagement and Democratization*. Stanford: Stanford University Press.

Asociación Cultural Yoruba de Cuba (ACYC). 2002. *Letra del Año de 2002*. La Habana: ACYC.

Australia Cuba Friendship Society (ACFS). 2000. *Report from the Melbourne Australia Cuba Friendship Society: National Consultation—Albury*. Melbourne: ACFS.

Australian Agency for International Development (AusAID). 2003. *Annual Report 2002–2003*. http://www.ausaid.gov.au/anrep/rep03/default.cfm (accessed 13 January 2004).

Australian Conservation Foundation (ACF). 1998. *AusAID NGO Environmental Initiative: Annual Project Report, Year 1, July 1996–December 1997*. Melbourne: ACF.

———. 2000. *AusAID NGO Cooperation Program: Activity Proposal Year 2*. Melbourne: ACF.

Ayorinde, Christine. 2004. *Afro-Cuban Religiosity, Revolution, and National Identity*. Gainesville: University Press of Florida.

Azcuy Henríquez, Hugo. 1995. "Estado y Sociedad Civil en Cuba." *Temas* 4:105–110.

Azicri, Max. 2000. *Cuba Today and Tomorrow: Reinventing Socialism*. Gainesville: University Press of Florida.

Baltar, José. 1998. "El Rescate y Promoción de la Cultura Popular Tradicional." In *Estudios Afro-Cubanos*, edited by Lázara Menéndez Vázquez, 357–387. La Habana: Universidad de La Habana.

Barbón Diaz, María Regla. 2000. *La Comunidad de Atarés*. La Habana: GDIC.

Barthes, Roland. 1967. *Elements of Semiology*. London: Jonathan Cape.

Bascom, William. 1969a. *Ifá Divination: Communication between Gods and Men in West Africa*. Bloomington: Indiana University Press.

———. 1969b. *The Yoruba of Southwestern Nigeria*. New York: Holt, Rinehart, and Winston.

———. 1980. *Sixteen Cowries: Yoruba Divination from Africa to the New World*. Bloomington: Indiana University Press.

Bendaña, Alejandro. 1998. "Which Way for NGOs?" *IRC Bulletin* 51. http://www.irc-online.org/content/bulletin/bu1153/index_body.html (accessed 15 June 2003).

Benítez Pérez, Maria Elena. 1999. *Panorama Sociodemográfico de la Familia Cubana*. La Habana: Editorial Ciencias Sociales.

Benítez Rojo, Antonio. 1992. *The Repeating Island: The Caribbean and the Postmodern Perspective*. Durham: Duke University Press.

Betancourt, Victor. 1995. *El Babalawo: Médico Tradicional*. La Habana: Página Regional.

Bettelheim, Judith. 1991. "Negotiations of Power in Carnaval Culture in Santiago de Cuba." *African Arts* 24 (2): 66–75.

———. 1994. "Ethnicity, Gender, and Power: Carnaval in Santiago de Cuba." In *Negotiating Performance: Gender, Sexuality, and Theatricality in Latin/o America*, edited by Diana Taylor and Juan Villegas, 176–212. Durham: Duke University Press.

Blau, Peter Michael. 1964. *Exchange and Power in Social Life*. New York: Wiley.

Bolívar Aróstegui, Natalia. 1990. *Los Orichas en Cuba*. La Habana: Ediciones Unión.

Bolívar Aróstegui, Natalia, and Carmen González Díaz de Villegas. 1998. *Ta Makuende Yaya y las Relgas de Palo Monte: Mayombe, Brillumba, Kimbisa, Shamalongo*. La Habana: Ediciones Unión.

Bolívar Aróstegui, Natalia, and Mario López Cepero. 1995. *¿Syncretismo Religioso? Santa Barbara/Chango*. La Habana: Pablo de la Torriente.

Bourdieu, Pierre, and Jean-Claude Passeron. 1977. *Reproduction in Education, Society, Culture*. Beverly Hills, Calif.: Sage.

Brandon, George. 1993. *Santeria: From Africa to the New World*. Bloomington: Indiana University Press.

Brathwaite, Edward Kamau. 1995. "Creolization in Jamaica." In *The Post-Colonial Studies Reader*, edited by Bill Ashcroft, Gareth Griffiths, and Helen Tiffin, 202–205. London: Routledge.

Brecher, Jeremy, Tim Costello, and Brendan Smith. 2000. *Globalization from Below: The Power of Solidarity*. Cambridge, Mass.: Southend Press.

Brown, David H. 2003. *Santería Enthroned: Art, Ritual, and Innovation in an Afro-Cuban Religion*. Chicago: University of Chicago Press.

Brunner, Edward M. 1989. "Of Cannibals, Tourists, and Ethnographers." *Cultural Anthropology* 4:339–349.

———. 1991. "The Transformation of Self in Tourism." *Annals of Tourism Research* 18:238–250.

Büntig, Aldo J. 1971. "The Church in Cuba: Toward a New Frontier." In *Religion in Cuba Today*, edited by Alice L Hageman and Philip E. Wheaton, 95–128. New York: Association Press.

Burawoy, Michael, and Katherine Verdery. 1999. *Uncertain Transition: Ethnographies of Change in the Postsocialist World*. Lanham, Md.: Rowman and Littlefield.

Burt, Ronald. 1992. *Structural Holes: the Social Structure of Competition*. Cambridge, Mass.: Harvard University Press.

Buscarón Ochoa, Odalys, Niurka Nuñez González, Hernán Tirado Toirac, and Marcos Marín Llanes. 1996. *La Caracterización Etnocultural de los Grupos Raciales: Un Analysis Comparativo*. La Habana: Centro de Antropología de Atarés.

Cabrera, Lydia. 1971. *El Monte*. Miami: Colección Chichereku en Exilo. Originally published 1954.

Cardenal, Ernesto. 2003. "The Catholic Church and the Revolution." In *The Cuba Reader: History, Culture, Politics*, edited by Aviva Chomsky, Barry Carr, and Pamela Maria Smorkaloff, 505–508. Durham: Duke University Press.

Cardoso, Fernando Henrique, et al. 2004. "Report of the Panel of Eminent Persons— Civil Society Relations, We the Peoples: Civil Society, the United Nations and Global Governance." United Nations Document A/58/817. http://www.un.org/reform/a87_817_english.doc (accessed 3 December 2004).

Caribbean Tourism Organization (CTO). 2002. "Tourist Arrivals by Market 2001." http://www.onecaribbean.org/information/documentview.php?rowid=178 (accessed 25 May 2005).

———. 2005. "Stay Over and Cruise Arrivals—2004 YTD." http://www.onecaribbean.org/information/categorybrowse.php?categoryid=242 (accessed 25 May 2005).

Caridad Cruz, María. 1997. *Educación Sobre Permacultura en la Ciudad de La Habana*. La Habana: Fundación de la Naturaleza y el Hombre.

Carlessi, Carolina. 1989. "Lima: The Reconquest." *NACLA Report on the Americas* 23 (4): 14–21.

Castellanos, Jorge, and Isabel Castellanos. 1994. *Cultura Afrocubana: Las Religiones y las Lenguas.* 3d ed. Miami: Ediciones Universales.

Castro, Fidel. 1982. "Intervención del Comandante en Jefe Fidel Castro ante Representantes de Iglesias en Jamaica, 1977." In *Acerca de la Religión, la Iglesia y los Creyentes.* La Habana: Edición Política.

———. 1986. *Fidel and Religion: Conversations with Frei Betto.* Sydney: Pathfinder Press.

Castro Flores, María Margarita. 2001. "Religions of African Origin in Cuba: A Gender Perspective." In *Nation Dance,* edited by Patrick Taylor, 54–62. Bloomington: Indiana University Press.

Centro de Investigaciones de la Economía Mundial (CIEM). 2000. *Investigación Sobre el Desarrollo Humano y Equidad en Cuba, 1999.* La Habana: Cacuayo, S.A.

Centro de Investigaciones Psicológicas y Sociológicas (CIPS). 1998. *Panorama de la Religión en Cuba.* La Habana: Editorial Politíca.

Chauvin, Lucien. 1997. "Cuba Opens Its Doors to Greater Church Life and Charity Services." *National Catholic Reporter* 33 (18): 10.

China Putian Corporation. 2005. Public announcement at the Havana Trade Fair, 4 November 2005.

Cisneros, Milagros. 1996. *Respectful Engagement: Cuban NGO Cooperation with Latin America, Europe, and Canada.* Philadelphia: American Friends Service Committee International Division.

Clemente, Rafael Cepeda, Elizabeth García, Rhode Zorilla, and Carlos Stanard. 1995. "Causas y Desafíos del Crecimiento de las Iglesias Protestantes en Cuba." *Temas* 4:52–61.

Cohen, Jean L. 1999. "American Civil Society Talk." In *Civil Society, Democracy, and Civic Renewal,* edited by Robert K. Fullinwider, 55–85. Lanham, Md.: Rowman and Littlefield.

Cohen, Jean L., and Andrew Arato. 1992. *Civil Society and Political Theory.* Cambridge, Mass.: MIT Press.

Cohen, Jean L., and Joel Rogers. 1995. "Secondary Associations and Democratic Governance." In *Association and Democracy,* edited by Erik Olin Wright, 7–98. London: Verso.

Coleman, James S. 1988a. "Social Capital in the Creation of Human Capital." *American Journal of Sociology* 94:95–120.

———. 1988b. "The Creation and Destruction of Social Capital: Implications for the Law." *Notre Dame Journal of Law, Ethics, and Public Policy* 3:375–404.

———. 1993. "The Rational Reconstruction of Society." *American Sociological Review* 58:1–15.

Collins, Randall. 1981. "On the Microfoundations of Macrosociology." *American Journal of Sociology* 86:984–1014.

Comisión Organizadora de la Letra del Año Havana (COLAH). 2006a. *Letra del Año 2006.* La Habana: COLAH.

———. 2006b. Mensaje para la UNESCO sobre el "Evento Letra del Año" en Cuba, photocopy of communiqué of the Ifá Iranlowo temple of Cuba to UNESCO. Ifá Iranlowo temple private archives, Havana.

Comité Estatal de Estadísticas (CEE). 1999. *Anuario Estadístico de Cuba, 1988*. La Habana: CEE.

Communist Party of Cuba. 1976. *Tésis y Resoluciones del Primer Congreso del Partido Comunista de Cuba*. La Habana: República de Cuba.

Corbea Calzado, Julio. 1996. "La Virgen de la Caridad del Cobre: Construcción Simbólica y Cultura Popular." *Del Caribe* 25:4–11.

Coronil, Fernando. 1995. Introduction to Fernando Ortiz, *Cuban Counterpoint: Tobacco and Sugar*, ix–lvi. Durham: Duke University Press.

Corrales, Javier. 2001. "Strong Societies, Weak Parties: Regime Change in Cuba and Venezuela in the 1950s and Today." *Latin American Politics and Society* 43 (2): 81–113.

Coyula, Mario, Miguel Coyula, and Rosa Oliveras. 1999. *Los TTIB: Hacia un Nuevo Tipo de Comunidad en La Habana*. La Habana: GDIC.

——. 2001. *Towards a New Kind of Community in Havana: The Workshops for Integrated Neighborhood Transformation*, translated by Adrian H. Hearn. La Habana: Grupo para el Desarrollo Integral de la Capital.

Coyula, Mario, and Mayda Pérez. 1996. *The GDIC: Advanced Ideas for a Sustainable and Participatory Urban Development in Havana*. La Habana: Grupo para el Desarrollo Integral de la Capital.

Crahan, Margaret E. 1979. "Salvation through Christ or Marx: Religion in Revolutionary Cuba." *Journal of Inter-American Studies and World Affairs* 21 (1): 156–184.

——. 1982. *The Church and Revolution: Cuba and Nicaragua*. Melbourne: La Trobe University Institute of Latin American Studies.

——. 2000. "Cuba: Politics and Society." In *U.S. Policy toward Cuba*, edited by Dick Clark, 25–29. Washington, D.C.: Aspen Institute.

——. 2003. *Religion, Culture and Society: The Case of Cuba*. Woodrow Wilson Center Reports on the Americas 9. Washington D.C.: Woodrow Wilson International Center for Scholars.

——. 2005. "Civil Society and Religion in Cuba: Past, Present, and Future." In *Changes in Cuban Society since the Nineties*, edited by Joseph S. Tulchin, Lilian Bobea, Mayra P. Espina Prieto, and Rafael Hernández, 231–242. Woodrow Wilson Center Report on the Americas 15. Washington, D.C.: Woodrow Wilson International Center for Scholars.

Crahan, Margaret E., and Ariel C. Armony. 2006. "Rethinking Civil Society and Religion in Cuba." Paper presented at the 26th International Congress of the Latin American Studies Association, 15–18 March, San Juan, Puerto Rico.

Crook, Larry N. 1993. "Black Consciousness, Samba Reggae, and the Re-Africanization of Bahian Carnival Music in Brazil." *The World of Music* 35 (2): 90–108.

Cros Sandoval, Mercedes. 1979. "Santería as a Mental Health System: An Historical Overview." *Social Science and Medicine* 13b:137–151.

Cuban Council of Bishops. 1995. *La Voz de la Iglesia en Cuba*. Mexico: Buena Prensa, A.C.

Daniel, Yvonne. 1995. *Rumba: Dance and Social Change in Contemporary Cuba*. Bloomington: Indiana University Press.

de La Fuente, Alejandro. 2001. "Recreating Racism: Race and Discrimination in Cuba's 'Special Period.'" *Socialism and Democracy* 15 (1): 65–91.

de Céspedes, Carlos Manuel. 1995. "¿Puede Afirmarse que el Pueblo Cubano es Católico o No?" *Temas* 4:13–22.

de Lahaye Guerra, Rosa María, and Rubén Zardoya Loureda. 1999. "Las Letras del Año: Entre el Azar y el Destino." *Catauro* 1:118–138.

de Tocqueville, Alexis. 1964. *Democracy in America*. New York: Washington Square Press. Originally published 1835.

del Rey Roa, Annet, and Yalexy Castañeda Mache. 2002. "El Reavivamiento Religioso en Cuba." *Temas* 31:93–100.

Diamond, Larry. 1999. *Developing Democracy: Toward Consolidation*. Baltimore: Johns Hopkins University Press.

Díaz Quiñones, Arcadio. 1999. "Fernando Ortiz y Allan Kardec: Espiritismo y Transculturación." *Catauro* 1 (0): 14–31.

Dilla Alfonso, Haroldo. 1993. "Cuba: La Crisis y Rearticulación del Consenso Político (Notas Para un Debate Socialista)." *Cuaderno de Nuestra América* 20:20–45.

———. 1999. "The Virtues and Misfortunes of Civil Society." *NACLA Report on the Americas* 32 (5): 30–36.

Dilla Alfonso, Haroldo, Armando Fernández Soriano, and Margarita Castro Flores. 1999. "Movimientos Comunitarios en Cuba: Un Análisis Comparativo." *Cuban Studies* 28:100–124.

Dilla Alfonso, Haroldo, Gerardo González, and Ana Teresa Vincentelli. 1993. *Participación Popular y Desarrollo en los Municipios Cubanos*. La Habana: Centro de Estudios sobre América (CEA).

Domínguez, Jorge I. 1999. "International and National Aspects of the Catholic Church in Cuba." *Cuban Studies* 19:43–60.

Doyle, Timothy, and Doug McEachern. 1998. *Environment and Politics*. London: Routledge.

Duharte Jiménez, Rafael. 2001. *Santiago de Cuba y Africa: Un Diálogo en el Tiempo*. Santiago de Cuba: Instituto Cubano del Libro (Ediciones Santiago).

Durkheim, Emile. 1993. *The Division of Labor in Society*. New York: Macmillan. Originally published 1893.

Eckstein, Susan Eva. 1994. *Back from the Future: Cuba under Castro*. Princeton: Princeton University Press.

Economist. 2000. "NGOs: Sins of the Secular Missionaries." Editorial. *Economist* 354:25–27.

Edwards, Michael. 2004. *Civil Society*. Cambridge: Polity Press.

Encuentro Nacional Eclesial Cubano (ENEC). 1986. *Documento Final del Encuentro Nacional Eclesial Cubano*. Rome: Don Bosco.

Evans, Peter. 1995. *Embedded Autonomy: States and Industrial Transformation*. Princeton: Princeton University Press.

———. 1996. "Government Action, Social Capital and Development: Reviewing the Evidence on Synergy." *World Development* 24 (6): 1119–1132.

Fagen, Richard R. 1969. *The Transformation of Political Culture in Cuba*. Stanford: Stanford University Press.

Federke, Johannes, Raphael de Kadt, and John Luiz. 1999. "Economic Growth and Social Capital: A Critical Reflection." *Theory and Society* 28 (5): 709–745.

Fernández, Olga. 1995. *Strings and Hide*. La Habana: Editorial José Martí.

Fernández Robaina, Tomás. 1993. "The 20th Century Black Question." In *Afro-Cuba: An Anthology of Cuban Writings on Race, Politics, and Culture*, edited by Pedro Pérez Sarduy and Jean Stubbs, 92–105. London: Latin America Bureau.

———. 1997. *Hablen Paleros y Santeros*. La Habana: Editorial Ciencias Sociales.

Fernández Soriano, Armando. 1999. "Realidades, Retos y Posibilidades de los Municipios Cubanos en el Fin de Siglo." In *Gobiernos de Izquierda en América Latina*, edited by Beatriz Stolowicz, 165–182. Mexico City: Paza y Valdés, Universidad Autónoma Metropolitana.

Fiorina, Morris P. 1999. "Extreme Voices: A Dark Side of Civil Engagment." In *Civic Engagement in American Democracy*, edited by Theda Skocpol and Morris P. Fiorina, 395–425. Washington, D.C.: Brookings Institution Press.

Foley, Michael W., and Bob Edwards. 1996. "The Paradox of Civil Society." *Journal of Democracy* 7 (3): 38–52.

———. 1999. "Is It Time to Disinvest in Social Capital?" *Journal of Public Policy* 19 (2): 141–173.

Friedman, John. 1989. "The Dialectic of Reason." *International Journal of Urban and Regional Research* 13 (2): 217–236.

Fukuyama, Francis. 1995. *Trust: The Social Virtues and the Creation of Prosperity*. New York: Free Press.

Fundación de la Naturaleza y el Hombre (FNH). 1997. "Crecimiento Económico y del Consumo con Criterios Sustentables." *Medio Ambiente y Consumo* 2 (9): 1–2.

García Franco, Raimundo. 2000. *La Participación de los Religiosos Cubanos en la Vida Social del País*. Transcript of La Mesa Redonda, 25 December 2000. Havana: Juventud Rebelde.

Geertz, Clifford. 1973. *The Interpretation of Cultures*. New York: Basic Books.

Giddens, Anthony. 1977. *Studies in Social and Political Theory*. New York: Basic Books.

———. 1990. *The Consequences of Modernity*. Stanford: Stanford University Press.

Girardi, Giulio. 1994. *Cuba después del Derrumbe del Comunismo: ¿Residuo del pasado o germen de un futuro nuevo?* Madrid: Editorial Nueva Utopía.

Goffman, Erving. 1969. *The Presentation of Self in Everyday Life*. London: Penguin.

Gold, S. J. 1995. "Gender and Social Capital among Israeli Immigrants in Los Angeles." *Diaspora* 4:267–301.

Gold, Thomas, Doug Guthrie, and David Wank. 2002. "An Introduction to the Study of Guanxi." In *Social Connections in China: Institutions, Culture and the Changing Nature of Guanxi*, edited by Thomas Gold, Doug Guthrie, and David Wank, 3–20. Cambridge: Cambridge University Press.

González, Edward. 1996. *Cuba: Clearing Perilous Waters?* Special report for the Secretary of Defense. Santa Monica: RAND.

González, Edward, and Richard A. Nuccio. 1999. *Conference Proceedings: The RAND Forum on Cuba*. Washington, D.C.: RAND.

González, Reynaldo. 1998. "A Pope in the Land of Orishas." *Cuba Update* 18 (4/5): 27–35.

González-Wippler, Migene. 1992. *The Santeria Experience: A Journey into the Miraculous.* St. Paul, Minn.: Llewellyn Publications.

Gramsci, Antonio. 1971. *Selections from the Prison Notebooks of Antonio Gramsci.* Edited and translated by Quintin Hoare and Geoffrey Nowell Smith. London: Lawrence and Wishart.

Granma. 1987. "Cubatour International Folklore Workshop." Editorial. *Granma Weekly Review,* 10 May: 10.

Granovetter, Mark. 1973. "The Strength of Weak Ties." *American Journal of Sociology* 78:1360–1380.

Gregório Baierle, Sérgio. 1998. "The Explosion of Experience: The Emergence of a New Ethical-Political Principle in Popular Movements in Porto Alegre, Brazil." In *Cultures of Politics, Politics of Cultures: Re-envisioning Latin American Social Movements,* edited by Sonia E. Alvarez, Evelina Dagnino, and Arturo Escobar, 118–138. Boulder, Colo.: Westview Press.

Grupo para el Desarrollo Integral de la Capital (GDIC). 2001. *La Maqueta de La Habana.* La Habana: GDIC.

Gunn, Gillian. 1995. *Cuba's NGOs: Government Puppets or Seeds of Civil Society?* Washington, D.C.: Center for Latin American Studies, Georgetown University.

Gupta, Akhil. 1995. "Blurred Boundaries: The Discourse of Corruption, the Culture of Politics, and the Imagined State." *American Ethnologist* 22 (2): 375–402.

Hagan, J., R. MacMillan, and B. Wheaton. 1996. "New Kid in Town: Social Capital and the Life Course Effects of Family Migration in Children." *American Sociological Review* 61:368–385.

Hagedorn, Katherine J. 2001. *Divine Utterances: The Performance of Santería.* Washington, D.C.: Smithsonian Institution Press.

Hagopian, Frances. 1998. "Democracy and Political Representation in Latin America in the 1990s: Pause, Reorganization, or Decline?" In *Fault Lines of Democracy in Post-Transition Latin America,* edited by Felipe Agüero and Jeffrey Stark, 99–143. Miami: North-South Center Press.

Hammond, Jack. 1999. "The High Cost of Dollars." *NACLA Report on the Americas* 32 (5): 24–25.

Harnecker, Marta. 1999. "Democracia y Socialismo." *Temas* 16/17:120–135.

Hearn, Adrian H. 2002. "Viven Los Cabildos: El Caso de la Carabalí Isuama." In *ACTAS: Cultura Africana y Afroamericana,* 107–111. Santiago de Cuba: Centro Cultural Africano Fernando Ortiz.

———. 2004a. "Afro-Cuban Religions and Social Welfare: Consequences of Commercial Development in Havana." *Human Organization* 63 (1): 79–88.

———. 2004b. "Guardians of Culture: The Controversial Heritage of Senegalese Griots." *Australian Journal of Anthropology* 15 (2): 129–142.

———. 2006. "Economic Reform in Cuba and China." In *Cuba in Transition? Pathways to Renewal, Long-Term Development, and Global Reintegration,* edited by Mauricio Font and

Scott Larson, 143–158. New York: CUNY Graduate Center. http://web.gc.cuny.edu/bildnercenter/cuba/documents/CITBookFMpdfbychapter_000.pdf (accessed 23 July 2006).

Hearn, Adrian H., and Michael Spiro. 2004. "Sacred Allegiances: Decentralized Development and the Rhythm of Community Religion in Cuba." Research seminar at the University of California-Berkeley Center for Latin American Studies. See http://www.clas.berkeley.edu:7001/Events/spring2004/index.html.

Helg, Aline. 1995. *Our Rightful Share: The Afro-Cuban Struggle for Equality, 1886–1912.* Chapel Hill: University of North Carolina Press.

Heller, Patrick. 2001. "Moving the State: The Politics of Democratic Decentralization in Kerala, South Africa, and Porto Alegre." *Politics and Society* 29 (1): 131–163.

Henken, Theodore. 2006. "A Taste of Capitalism: Entrepreneurship, Informality, and the Second Economy in the Rise and Fall of the Cuban *Paladar*, 1990–2005." Paper presented at the "Cuba In Transition" Symposium, The Graduate Center, City University of New York—Bildner Center for Western Hemisphere Studies, March 30–31.

Henthorne, Tony L., and Mark M. Miller. 2003. "Cuban Tourism in the Caribbean Context: A Regional Impact Assessment." *Journal of Travel Research* 42:84–93.

Hernández, Rafael. 2003. *Looking at Cuba: Essays on Culture and Civil Society.* Gainesville: University Press of Florida.

Herskovits, Melville. 1967. *Dahomey, an Ancient West African Kingdom.* Evanston: Northwestern University Press.

Hill, Matthew J. 2007. "Reimagining Old Havana: World Heritage and the Production of Scale in Late Socialist Cuba." In *Deciphering the Global: Its Scales, Spaces, and Subjects,* edited by Saski Sassen, 59–76. New York: Routledge.

Hodge, Derrick G. 2001. "Colonization of the Cuban Body: The Growth of Male Sex Work in Havana." *NACLA Report on the Americas* 34 (5): 20–28.

Horowitz, Irving Louis, and Jaime Suchlicki. 1998, *Cuban Communism.* New Brunswick: Transaction Publishers.

Howard, Marc M. 2002. "The Weakness of Postcommunist Civil Society." *Journal of Democracy* 13 (1): 157–169.

Howard, Philip A. 1998. *Changing History: Afro-Cuban Cabildos and Societies of Color in the Nineteenth Century.* Baton Rouge: Louisiana University Press.

Hudson, Saul. 2006. "Report to Advise Bush on Post-Castro Cuba." *Boston Globe,* May 23. http://www.boston.com/news/world/latinamerica/articles/2006/05/23/report_to_advise_bush_on_post_castro_cuba/?rss_id=boston.com+%2F+News (accessed 1 August 2006).

Huber, Joan. 1991. *Macro-Micro Linkages in Sociology.* Newbury Park, Calif.: Sage Publications.

Inglehart, Ronald. 1999. "Trust, Well-being and Democracy." In *Democracy and Trust,* edited by Mark E. Warren, 88–120. Cambridge: Cambridge University Press.

Ireland, Rowan. 1991. *Kingdoms Come: Religion and Politics in Brazil.* Pittsburgh: University of Pittsburgh Press.

——. 1999. "Popular Religions and the Building of Democracy in Latin America: Saving the Toquevillian Parallel." *Journal of Interamerican Studies and World Affairs* 41 (4): 111–136.

——. 2000. "The Dancing Spirits of World Capitalism: Globalisation, Popular Culture and Citizenship in Salvador, Bahia." *Journal of Iberian and Latin American Studies* 6 (2): 109–128.

Ishkanian, Armine. 2001. *Women"s NGOs in Armenia: The Challenge of Working at the Global-Local Nexus*. Paper presented at the American Anthropological Association annual meeting, 30 November, 2001, Washington, D.C.

James, Joel. 1999. *Los Sistemas Mágico-religiosos Cubanos*. Caracas: UNESCO.

Jarvis, Darryl. 2004. *Changing Economic Environment in Southeast Asia: ASEAN, China and the Prospects for Enhanced Cooperation*. Sydney: Research Institute for Asia and the Pacific (RIAP).

Jatar Hausmann, Ana Julia. 1999. *The Cuban Way*. West Hartford: Kumarian Press.

John Paul II. 2003. "Pope John Paul II Speaks in Cuba." In *The Cuba Reader: History, Culture, Politics*, edited by Aviva Chomsky, Barry Carr, and Pamela Maria Smorkaloff, 635–636. Durham: Duke University Press.

Kahn, Joel. 1997. "Culturalizing Malaysia." In *Tourism, Ethnicity, and the State in Asian and Pacific Societies*, edited by Michel Picard and Robert E. Wood, 99–127. Honolulu: University of Hawai'i Press.

——. 2001. "Anthropology and Modernity." *Current Anthropology* 42 (5): 651–680.

Karade, Ifa. 1994. *The Handbook of Yoruba Religious Concepts*. York Beach, Me.: S. Weiser.

Kaufman, Michael. 1997. Introduction to *Community Power, Grassroots Democracy, and the Transformation of Social Life*, edited by Michael Kaufman and Haroldo Dilla Alfonso, 1–24. London: Zed Books.

Kirk, John M. 1989. *Between God and the Party*. Tampa: University of South Florida Press.

Knight, Franklin. 1990. *The Caribbean: The Genesis of a Fragmented Nationalism*. New York: Oxford University Press.

Kuper, Adam. 1999. *Culture: The Anthropologists' Account*. Cambridge, Mass.: Harvard University Press.

Latin American Regional Report (LARR). 2003. "Rocky Relations with E.U." *Caribbean and Central America*, special issue of *Latin American Regional Report* 3 (8): 6.

Levine, Daniel H. 1992. *Popular Voices in Latin American Catholicism*. Princeton: Princeton University Press.

Light, Ivan, and Stavros Karageorgis. 1994. "The Ethnic Economic." In *The Handbook of Economic Sociology*, edited by Neil J. Smelser and Richard Swedberg, 646–671. Princeton: Princeton University Press.

Lin, Nan. 2001. *Social Capital: A Theory of Social Structure and Action*. Cambridge: Cambridge University Press.

Linz, Juan J., and Alfred Stepan. 1996. *Problems of Democratic Transition and Consolidation*. Baltimore: Johns Hopkins University Press.

MacDonald, Laura. 1995. "A Mixed Blessing: The NGO Boom in Latin America." *NACLA Report on the Americas* 28 (5): 30–35.

Manuel, Peter. 1995. *Caribbean Currents: Caribbean Music from Rumba to Reggae*. Philadelphia: Temple University Press.

March-Poquet, José M. 2000. "What Type of Transition Is Cuba Undergoing?" *Post-Communist Economies* 12 (1): 91–117.

Martínez Furé, Rogelio. 2001. "Cubanía." *Bohemia* 10:10–12.

Marx, Karl. 1981. *Capital*. Harmondsworth: Penguin Books. Originally published in 1867.

Matibag, Eugenio. 1996. *Afro-Cuban Religious Experience*. Gainesville: University Press of Florida.

Mauleón, Rebeca. 1993. *The Salsa Guidebook: For Piano and Ensemble*. Petaluma, Calif.: Sher Music Company.

Maza Miguel, Manuel P. 1999. *Esclavos, Patriotas y Poetas a la Sombra de la Cruz: Cinco Ensayos sobre Catolicismo e Historia Cubana*. Santo Domingo: Centro de Estudios Sociales Padre Juan Montalvo.

McDavid, Hilton, and Diaram Ramajeesingh. 2003, "The State and Tourism: A Caribbean Perspective." *International Journal of Contemporary Hospitality Management* 15 (3): 180–183.

Menéndez Vázquez, Lázara. 1995. "Un *Cake* para Obatalá?!" *Temas* 4:38–51.

———. 2002. *Rodar el Coco: Proceso de Cambio en la Santería*. La Habana: Editorial de Ciencias Sociales.

Mesa-Lago, Carmelo. 2000. *Market, Socialist, and Mixed Economies—Comparative Policy and Performance: Chile, Cuba, and Costa Rica*. Baltimore: Johns Hopkins University Press.

Migdal, Joel S. 1994. "The State in Society: An Approach to Struggles for Domination." In *State Power and Social Forces: Domination and Transformation in the Third World*, edited by Joel S. Migdal, Atul Kohli, and Vivienne Shue, 7–34. Cambridge: Cambridge University Press.

———. 2001. *State in Society: Studying How States and Societies Transform and Constitute One Another*. Cambridge: Cambridge University Press.

Miller, Ivor L. 2000. "Religious Symbolism in Cuban Political Performance." *Drama Review* 44 (2): 30–55.

Millet, José. 1989. *Grupos Folklóricos de Santiago de Cuba*. Santiago de Cuba: Editorial Oriente.

———. 1997. *Carnaval, Barrio y Tradicion Santiaguera*. Santo Domingo: Universidad Autonoma.

———. 2000. "El Foco de la Santería Santiaguera." *Del Caribe* 32:110–119.

Miyares, Raúl Ruiz. 2002. "Elementos Africanos en el Espiritismo Cruzado Santiaguero." In *ACTAS: Cultura Africana y Afrocubana*, 162–167. Santiago de Cuba: Centro Cultural Africano Fernando Ortiz.

Moore, Carlos. 1970. "Cuba: The Untold Story." *Soulbook* 3 (2): 54–73.

———. 1988a. *Castro, the Blacks, and Africa*. Los Angeles: University of California Press.

———. 1988b. "Race Relations in Socialist Cuba." In *Socialist Cuba: Past Interpretations and Future Challenges*, edited by Sergio G. Roca, 175–206. Boulder: Westview Press.

Moore, Michael P. 1989. "The Fruits and Fallacies of Neoliberalism: The Case of Irrigation." *World Development* 17 (11): 1733–1750.

Moore, Robin. 1997. *Nationalizing Blackness: Afrocubanismo and Artistic Revolution in Havana, 1920–1940*. Pittsburgh: University of Pittsburgh Press.

——. 2001. "Revolución con Pachanga? Dance Music in Socialist Cuba." *Canadian Journal of Latin American and Caribbean Studies* 26 (52): 151–177.

Moreno Vega, Marta. 2000. *The Altar of My Soul: The Living Traditions of Santería*. New York: One World.

Moreno Vega, Marta, and Robert Shepard, dirs. 2002. *Cuando los Espíritus Bailan Mambo*. Documentary film. New York: Caribbean Cultural Center.

Morris-Suzuki, Tessa. 2000. "For and Against NGOs." *New Left Review* 2:63–84.

Murphy, Joseph M. 1988. *Santería: An African Religion in America*. Boston: Beacon Press.

Newton, Kenneth. 1997. "Social Capital and Democracy." *American Behavioral Scientist* 40 (5): 575–586.

Nuñez González, Niurka. 1997. *Creación de un Complejo Turístico-Cultural en el Barrio de Atarés*. La Habana: Centro de Antropología de Atarés.

Obeyesekere, Gananath. 1997. *The Apotheosis of Captain Cook: European Mythmaking in the Pacific*. Princeton: Princeton University Press. Originally published 1992.

Organization for Economic Cooperation and Development (OECD). 1995. *Participatory Development and Good Governance*. Paris: OECD.

Olshan, Marc A. 1997. "Return of the Repressed." *Commonwealth* 124 (18): 10–11.

Oppenheimer, Andres. 1992. *Castro's Final Hour: An Eyewitness Account of the Disintegration of Castro's Cuba*. New York: Touchstone.

Orozco, Román. 1993. *Cuba Roja*. Madrid: Cambio 16.

Orozco, Román, and Natalia Bolívar. 1998. *Cuba Santa: Comunistas, Santeros y Cristianos en la Isla de Fidel Castro*. Madrid: El País.

Ortiz, Fernando. 1913. "Los Comedores de Niños." *Revista Gráfico* (La Habana) 2 (17): 5–6.

——. 1929. "La Semulina de la Virgen de la Caridad del Cobre." *Archivos del Folklore Cubano* 4 (2): 161–163.

——. 1943. "Por la Integración Cubana de Blancos y Negros." *Ultra: Mensuario de Cultura Contemporánea* (La Habana) 77: 69–74.

——. 1950. *La Africanía de la Música Folklórica de Cuba*. La Habana: Ministerio de Educación, Dirección de Cultura.

——. 1973. *Los Negros Brujos: Apuntes para un Estudio de Etnología Criminal*. Miami: Ediciones Universal. Originally published 1906.

——. 1984. "Los Cabildos Afrocubanos." In *Ensayos Etnográficos*, edited by Miguel Barnet and Angel L. Fernández. La Habana: Editorial de Ciencias Sociales. Originally published in *Revista Bimestre Cubana* 16, no. 1 (1921).

——. 1985. *Los Bailes y el Teatro de los Negros en el Folklór de Cuba*. La Habana: Letras Cubanas. Originally published 1951.

——. 1987. *Los Negros Esclavos*. La Habana: Editorial Ciencias Sociales. Originally published 1916.

——. 1993. *Etnia y Sociedad*. La Habana: Editorial Ciencias Sociales.

——. 1995. *Cuban Counterpoint: Tobacco and Sugar*. Durham: Duke University Press. Originally published in 1940.

Osa, Maryjane. 1996. "Pastoral Mobilization and Contention: The Religious Foundations of the Solidarity Movement in Poland." In *Disruptive Religion: The Force of Faith in Social Movement Activism*, edited by Christian Smith, 67–85. New York: Routledge.

Otero, Gerardo, and Janice O'Bryan. 2002. "Cuba in Transition? The Civil Sphere's Challenge to the Castro Regime." *Latin American Politics and Society* 44 (4): 29–57.

Palmer, Catherine A. 1994. "Tourism and Colonialism: The Experience of the Bahamas." *Annals of Tourism Research* 4:792–811.

Palmié, Stephen. 1995. "Against Syncretism: 'Africanizing' and 'Cubanizing' Discourses in North American Orisa Worship." In *Counterworks*, edited by Richard Fardon, 73–104. London: Routledge.

———. 2002. *Wizards and Scientists: Explorations in Afro-Cuban Modernity and Tradition*. Durham: Duke University Press.

Pearce, Jenny. 2000. "Development, NGOs, and Civil Society: The Debate and Its Future." In *Development, NGOs, and Civil Society*, edited by Deborah Eade, 15–43. Oxford: Oxfam.

Pedraza, Teresita. 1998. "This Too Shall Pass: The Resistance and Endurance of Religion in Cuba." *Cuban Studies* 28:16–39.

Pérez, Louis A. 1986. "Politics, Peasants, and People of Color" *Hispanic American Historical Review* 63 (3): 509–539.

———. 1992. "Protestant Missionaries in Cuba: Archival Records, Manuscript Collections, and Research Prospects." *Latin American Research Review* 27 (1): 105–120.

Pérez, Nancy, Clara Domínguez, Rosa Rodríguez, Orlando Silva, and Danubia Terry. 1982. *El Cabildo Carabalí Isuama*. Santiago de Cuba: Editorial Oriente.

Pérez Alvarez, Mayda. 1996. *Hacia una Política Local de Mejoramiento Ambiental con Participación Comunitaria*. La Habana: GDIC.

———. 1998. *El Diseño Participativo Comunitario*. La Habana: GDIC.

Pérez Firmat, Gustavo. 1989. *The Cuban Condition: Translation and Identity in Modern Cuban Literature*. Cambridge: Cambridge University Press.

Pérez Sarduy, Pedro. 1998. "And Where Did the Blacks Go?" *Cuba Update* 18 (4/5): 36–41.

Pérez Sarduy, Pedro, and Jean Stubbs. 1993. *Afro-Cuba: An Anthology of Cuban Writings on Race, Politics, and Culture*. London: Latin America Bureau.

Petras, James. 1999. "NGOs: In the Service of Imperialism." *Journal of Contemporary Asia* 29 (4): 429–440.

Portes, Alejandro. 1998. "Social Capital: Its Origins and Applications in Modern Sociology." *Annual Review of Sociology* 24:1–24.

Portes, Alejandro, and Julia Sensenbrenner. 1993. "Embeddedness and Immigration: Notes on the Social Determinants of Economic Action." *American Journal of Sociology* 98 (6): 1320–1350.

Portuondo Zúñiga, Olga. 1985. "Viajeros en el Cobre." *Santiago* 60:150–162.

———. 1995. *La Virgen de la Caridad del Cobre: Símbolo de Cubanía*. Santiago de Cuba: Editorial Oriente.

———. 2000. "Cabildos Negros Santiagueros." *Del Caribe* 32:78–85.

Pritchard, Bill, and Adrian H. Hearn. 2005. "Regulating Foreign Direct Investment: Southeast Asia at the Crossroads." In *Regulation and Competitiveness: Explaining Foreign Direct Investment Flows in Southeast Asia*, 1–22. Singapore: Institute of Southeast Asian Studies (ISEAS).

Proyecto Comunitario de Conservación de Alimentos (PCCA). 2000. *Condimentos y Plantas Medicinales*. La Habana: PCCA.

Putnam, Robert D. 1993. *Making Democracy Work: Civic Traditions in Modern Italy*. Princeton: Princeton University Press.

———. 2000. *Bowling Alone: The Collapse and Revival of American Community*. New York: Simon and Schuster.

Quiroz, Alfonso. 2003. "The Evolution of Laws Regulating Associations and Civil Society in Cuba." In *Religion, Culture, and Society: The Case of Cuba*, edited by Margaret E. Crahan, 55–68. Washington, D.C.: Woodrow Wilson International Center for Scholars.

Ramos, Miguel. 1998. "Ashé in Flux: the Transformation of Lukumí Religion in the United States." Paper presented at the 47th annual conference of the Center of Latin American Studies, University of Florida, Gainesville.

Ramos Bravo, Liudmila. 1999. "El Problema de la Formación de Valores en la Regla de Ocha o Santería." B.A. honors thesis, Universidad de Oriente, Santiago de Cuba.

Ramírez Calzadilla, Jorge. 2000. *Religión y Relaciones Sociales: Significación Sociopolítica de la Religión en la Sociedad Cubana*. La Habana: Centro de Investigaciones Psicológicas y Sociológicas (CIPS).

———. 2001. "La Religión en la Obra de Fernando Ortiz." Computer printout. La Habana: Centro de Investigaciones Psicológicas y Sociológicas (CIPS).

Ratliff, William. 2004. "China's 'Lessons' for Cuba's Transition?" Cuba Transition Project, the Institute for Cuban and Cuban American Studies, University of Miami. http://ctp.iccas.miami.edu/Research_Studies/WRatliff.pdf (accessed 20 February 2006).

Reció, Milena, et al. 1999. "Sociedad Civil en los 90: El Debate Cubano." *Temas* 16/17:155–175.

Redfield, Robert, et al. 1936. "Memorandum for the Study of Acculturation." *American Ethnologist* 38:149–152.

República de Cuba, Asamblea Nacional del Poder Popular. 2000. *Ley No. 91 de los Consejos Populares, Capítulo III, Artículo 21*. La Habana: Gaceta Oficial de la República, edición extraordinaria.

Ritter, Archibald. 1998. "Entrepreneurship, Micro-enterprise and Public Policy in Cuba: Promotion, Containment or Asphyxiation." *Journal of Interamerican and World Affairs* 40 (2): 63–94.

Robertson, Roland. 1995. "Glocalization: Time-Space and Homogeneity-Heterogeneity." In *Global Modernities*, edited by Mike Featherstone, Scott Lash, and Roland Robertson, 25–44. London: Sage.

Rocha, Jan. 1989. "Sao Paulo: Acting on Faith." *NACLA Report on the Americas* 23 (4): 36–40.

Rodríguez Velázquez, Daniel. 1989. "Mexico: From Neighborhood to Nation." *NACLA Report on the Americas* 23 (4): 22–28.

Rosaldo, Renato. 1989. *Culture and Truth: The Remaking of Social Analysis.* Boston: Beacon Press.

Rosenblum, Nancy L., and Robert C. Post. 2002. *Civil Society and Government.* Princeton: Princeton University Press.

Rotberg, Robert I. 2001. *Patterns of Social Capital: Stability and Change in Historical Perspective.* Cambridge: Cambridge University Press.

Rushing, Fannie Theresa. 1992. "Cabildos de Nación y Sociedades de la Raza de Color: Afro-Cuban Participation in Slave Emancipation and Cuban Independence, 1865–1895." Ph.D. dissertation, University of Chicago.

Sahlins, Marshall. 1981. *Historical Metaphors and Mythic Realities.* Ann Arbor: University of Michigan Press.

——. 1999. "Two or Three Things That I Know about Culture." *Journal of the Royal-Anthropological Institute* 5 (3): 399–422.

Salamon, Lester. 1995. *Partners in Public Service: Government-Nonprofit Relations in the Modern Welfare State.* Baltimore: Johns Hopkins University Press.

Salskov Iversen, Dorte, Hans Krause Hansen, and Sven Bislev. 2000. "Governmentality, Globalization, and Local Practice: Transformations of a Hegemonic Discourse." *Alternatives* 25 (2): 183–222.

Sansone, Livio. 1996. "The Local and the Global in Today's Afro-Bahia." In *The Legacy of the Disinherited: Popular Culture in Latin America: Modernity, Globalization, Hybridity and Authenticity,* edited by Tom Salman, 197–219. Amsterdam: Inter-university Center for Latin American Researhc and Documentation (CEDLA).

Scarpaci, Joseph L., Roberto Segre, and Mario Coyula. 2002. *Havana: Two Faces of the Antillean Metropolis.* Chapel Hill: University of North Carolina Press.

Schambra, William. 1994. "By the People: The Old Values of the New Citizenship." *Policy Review* (Summer): 32–38.

Sergiat, Pedro. 1993. "Solutions to the Black Problem." In *Afro-Cuba: An Anthology of Cuban Writings on Race, Politics, and Culture,* edited by Pedro Pérez Sarduy and Jean Stubbs, 77–90. London: Latin America Bureau.

Sinclair, Minor. 2000. *NGOs in Cuba: Principles for Cooperation.* Boston: Oxfam America.

Silver, Ira. 1993. "Marketing Authenticity in Third World Countries." *Annals of Tourism Research* 20:302–318.

Skocpol, Theda. 1995. *Social Policy in the United States: Future Possibilities in Historical Perspective.* Princeton: Princeton University Press.

Slater, David, ed. 1985. *New Social Movements and the State in Latin America.* Dordrecht, Holland: Inter-university Center for Latin American Researhc and Documentation (CEDLA), distributed by Foris Publications.

Smart, Alan. 1993. "Gifts, Bribes, and *Guanxi*: A Reconsideration of Bourdieu's Social Capital." *Cultural Anthropology* 8 (3): 388–408.

Smith, Christian. 1996. *Disruptive Religion: The Force of Faith in Social Movement Activism.* New York: Routledge.

Somers, Margaret R. 1993. "Citizenship and the Place of the Public Sphere: Law, Community, and Political Culture in the Transition to Democracy." *American Sociological Review* 58 (5): 587–620.

Stubbs, Jean. 1989. *Cuba: The Test of Time.* London: Latin American Bureau, Taller para la Revitalización Integral del Barrio San Isidro (TRIBSI).

———. 2001a. *Caracterización Social del Consejo Popular San isidro.* La Habana: Oficina del Historiador de la Ciudad.

———. 2001b. *Proyecto Sociocultural Comunitario "Okan Oddara."* La Habana: Oficina del Historiador de la Ciudad.

Tamayo, Juan O. 1998. "In Cuba, a Clash between Religions: Afro-Cuban Creeds, Catholics at Odds." Editorial. *Miami Herald,* 12 January, 1A.

Taylor, Philip. 2001 *Fragments of the Present: Searching for Modernity in Vietnam's South.* Crows Nest, N.S.W., Australia: Allen and Unwin.

Tester, Keith. 1992. *Civil Society.* London: Routledge.

Thomas, Hugh. 1971. *Cuba; Or, The Pursuit of Freedom.* New York: Harper and Row.

Thompson, Robert Farris. 1983. *Flash of the Spirit.* New York: Random House.

Tomlinson, John. 1991. *Cultural Imperialism: A Critical Introduction.* Baltimore: Johns Hopkins University Press.

United Nations. 2000. *Contribución de las ONGs Cubanas e Internacionales Radicadas en Cuba Para el Forum del Milenio.* La Habana: United Nations (ONU).

United Nations Educational Scientific and Cultural Organization (UNESCO). 2005. "Proclaimed Masterpieces 2005." http://www.unesco.org/culture/intangible-heritage/index.htm (accessed 10 January 2006).

United Nations Office for Project Services (Oficina de las Naciones Unidas para los Servicios a los Proyectos, UNOPS). 2001. *El Programa de Desarollo Humano Local: Líneas Directrices, Fase 3.* La Habana: Programa de Las Naciones Unidad Para el Desarrollo (PNUD).

———. 2003. *El Programa de Desarrollo Humano Local en Cuba (PDHL).* La Habana: Programa de Las Naciones Unidad Para el Desarrollo (PNUD). http://www.onu.org.cu/pdhl/Documentacion/ResultadosEnero-Dic2003_ESPANOL.pdf (accessed 2 February 2007).

United States Government Accountability Office (USGAO). 2006. *U.S. Democracy Assistance for Cuba Needs Better Management and Oversight.* http://www.gao.gov/new.items/d07147.pdf (accessed 2 February 2007).

Uriarte, Miren. 2001. *Social Development, Community Development: After Economic Crisis, Cuba Looks Forward.* Boston: College of Public and Community Service.

Uslaner, Eric M. 1999. "Democracy and Social Capital." In *Democracy and Trust,* edited by Mark E. Warren, 121–150. Cambridge: Cambridge University Press.

Vallier, Ivan. 1970. *Catholicism, Social Control, and Modernization in Latin America.* Englewood Cliffs, N.J.: Prentice-Hall.

Varela, Father Félix. 1973. "Statement Showing the Need to Abolish the Slavery of Blacks in the Island of Cuba, with Just Compensation for Their Owners." In *Documentos para la Historia de Cuba*, vol. 1, edited by Hortensia Pichardo, 269–275. La Habana: Instituto Cuban del Libro/Editorial de Ciencias Sociales.

Wall, James M. 1997. "Diplomatic Dance: Cuba's Religion Factor." *The Christian Century*, June 18, 1997, 114

Wallace, J. 1973. "Christians in Cuba." *Cuba Resource Center Newletter* 3 (1): 3–11.

Warren, Mark E., ed. 1999. *Democracy and Trust.* Cambridge: Cambridge University Press.

——. 2001. *Democracy and Association.* Princeton: Princeton University Press.

Weber, Max. 1968. *Max Weber on Law in Economy and Society*, edited by Max Rheinstein. New York: Simon and Schuster. Originally published 1921.

——. 1930. *The Protestant Ethic and the Spirit of Capitalism.* New York: Charles Scribner's Sons. Originally published 1904.

Wilson, William J. 1987. *The Truly Disadvantaged.* Chicago: University of Chicago Press.

Wood, Richard L. 1999. "Religious Culture and Political Action." *Sociological Theory* 17 (3): 307–331.

Woolcock, Michael. 1998. "Social Capital and Economic Development: Toward a Theoretical Synthesis and Policy Framework." *Theory and Society* 27:151–208.

World Bank. 1993. *Governance and Development.* Washington, D.C.: World Bank.

——. 1997. *World Development Report: The State in a Changing World.* Washington, D.C.: World Bank.

Yamagishi, Toshio, and Midori Yamagishi. 1994. "Trust and Commitment in the United States and Japan." *Motivation and Emotion* 18 (2): 129–166.

Yaremko, Jason. 2000. *U.S. Protestant Missions in Cuba: From Independence to Castro.* Gainesville: University Press of Florida.

INDEX

Dr. Adrian H. Hearn is a research fellow at the
Institute for International Studies at the University
of Technology, Sydney, Australia. He has conducted
research in Cuba and Senegal, and currently resides in
Beijing, studying Chinese engagement with Cuba and
Latin America.

Library of Congress Cataloging-in-Publication Data
Hearn, Adrian H., 1975–
Cuba : religion, social capital, and development /
Adrian H. Hearn.
p. cm.
Includes bibliographical references and index.
ISBN 978-0-8223-4180-2 (cloth : alk. paper)
ISBN 978-0-8223-4196-3 (pbk.: alk. paper)
1. Religion and civil society—Cuba.   2. Civil society—
Cuba.   3. Social capital (Sociology)—Cuba.   I. Title.
HN203.5.H43 2008
307.1'4097291—dc22   2008012950